Dear T

Thank you for being
such a kind, welcoming and
generous person. You are
~~our~~ an incredibly inspiring
New Yorker. Hope you
enjoy this book . . .

Mark

January 2021

Please Open in the Event of My Death

BOOKS

www.dearkidsbooks.com

Please Open in the Event of My Death

About the Author photo provided by Adam Masry.

For more information, please contact:
Amplify Publishing
620 Herndon Parkway, Suite 320
Herndon, VA 20170
info@amplifypublishing.com

Library of Congress Control Number: 2020903408

CPSIA Code: PRFRE0320A
ISBN-13: 978-1-64543-297-5

Printed in Canada

To those who persist

Please Open
in the
Event of
My Death

A FATHER'S ADVICE TO
HIS DAUGHTERS IN CASE
SOMETHING HORRIBLE HAPPENS
(WHICH HOPEFULLY IT WON'T BUT JUST IN CASE...)

Mark Hsu

CONTENTS

YOU REALLY HAVE TO READ THIS FOREWORD

I suppose I should recognize the terrorists.

There was a time when I would stroll into an airport, flash the boarding pass without breaking stride, reach my seat, and start chain-sawing logs before the plane took off, only to awake when I felt the clipped screech of the wheels upon landing. That was my 29-year-old, pre-September 11 self.

The day resulting in the massive loss of life, the infliction of national trauma, the reprioritization of U.S. security interests, the two wars fought abroad, and the march toward a stricter surveillance state also had the effect of transforming me into a very, very nervous air traveler, the official diagnosis being *Morbus Rabidus Batshitus*. The Chihuahua sitting in the next seat chugging extra-large coffees while hooked up to a Red Bull I.V. drip had nothing on my anxiety.

Man, sometimes it wasn't even about the terrorism anymore. A little rattle in the bulkhead would cause my head to spasm toward that sound. During flights, I mentally rewound airline crashes, thinking that I could emerge tougher if I remembered all of the horrific and mysterious details and cool-ly set them aside...only to discover that I had now convinced myself that the plane would incinerate at any second. Whenever I actually was able to catnap, I dreamt that the plane was flying right into the city, corkscrewing its way so that its wings wouldn't smash into buildings. Any in-flight movie with a smidge of emotion, well-earned or not, had me crying—not the kind where you start tilting your head upward so the tears won't spill, not the "trying to seem cool by rubbing your eye to subtly wipe away the tear" one either, but the one where I turned into a blubbering snot machine.

On every one of these flights, I would imagine my demise in gruesome detail. The tire blowing out, causing us to skid toward another taxiing plane and resulting in a perfectly symmetrical fireball to be seen from miles around. The airplane wing ripping off and casting us into a barrel roll that would easily be the coolest CGI effect in a summer blockbuster. Or two planes meeting at the exact same point of cruising altitude and causing an explosion so spectacular that at least one angel would whisper, "I know I shouldn't say this, but that was fucking awesome."

These images already dominated my thoughts even before I met my wife and had two girls, 16 months apart. Having kids changes everything, of course, and when people say that, they obviously mean that when one has completely overblown fears about dying in a silver pill 40,000 feet above sea level, he starts thinking about his two daughters first and foremost.

In a perverse way, I wish I could tell you that there was

one flight sparking all that follows, a near-death experience that reprioritized my life. Perhaps when I had to overcome the haunting memories of war and my drinking problem to take the controls of a Trans American 707 after the flight crew and Kareem Abdul-Jabbar got ill eating the fish? Nothing of the sort. Unfortunately, the truth was much more banal, but only slightly less terrifying.

Sitting by myself on yet another flight for my work as a litigation attorney, I would inevitably think about my four- and three-year-old daughters. And there was always one fact that consumed me, which was hard to believe and impossible to ignore.

My girls had seen me almost every day of their lives. We quite literally spent hours looking into each other's eyes, trying to find each other's soul. I fed them. I changed their diapers. I dressed them, many times so awkwardly that they started crying. I coaxed them to sleep. I taught them, disciplined them. They knew me as their "dada," a reliable source of unending love and comfort.

And yet, at these ages, they would not remember anything about me had I left their world on a plane.

With the same fervor that manufactured all those crashes, my imagination envisioned a future where my daughters grew up without me. There would be no lack of love. Our family and friends would form a cocoon, summoning everything they could to make sure the cataclysm would not touch the girls. They would paper over my faults, even lionize me, and I would nod in approval from heaven as my wife unveiled a 12-

foot bronze of me in a Tom Ford tuxedo, holding an astronaut's helmet, digging my heel into the face of Satan, and pointing into the distance. Yes, with this support system, my daughters would survive and emerge from the tragedy stronger than ever.

Nonetheless, the idea that I would fade away until I became just an abstract concept even to my own two daughters was nothing short of heart-wrenching. After the umpteenth time that I was convinced all was lost because the folding tray table started to shake, I decided that I needed to leave something for my girls. More meaningful than a material possession. More detailed and thought-provoking than a video. Mankind's greatest, most influential, most powerful creation, the written word. I would write a book for them.

What would I want my girls to know?

It began as advice, jotted down on pocket-sized notebooks or tapped out on my phone. When I pictured those four- and three-year-old faces, their innocence and helplessness drove me to try to barf up as much knowledge as possible. As I was finishing the manuscript, I looked back at my early notes and was mortified to discover that I had written "how to clap properly" as one of my pearls of wisdom. "Oh, so tragic what happened to Mr. Hsu...but have you seen his girls applaud?" More concerning, I became aware that much of what I wrote had already been disseminated throughout the globe on a system of interconnected computer networks called "the Internet," and that one could actually pull up advice on "how to pick out a dinner wine" within mere hours if a state-of-the-art modem from RadioShack was involved.

With the girls at such impressionable ages, I had begun by visualizing a book that urged them to lead completely upright and moral lives. An indisputable point of view, but this kind of advice isn't very grounded in real-world problems—as a New Yorker, I knew that type of advice would get them eaten alive on these mean streets. Also, kind of boring, because it would hit the same notes over and over again. And worst of all, it's the New Testament. Plagiarizing Jesus just didn't feel like the right thing to do, you know?

No, I wanted to write for my girls a Manual for Life, consisting of practical advice, the unwritten rules, the type of hard-bitten, hard-earned lessons one has accumulated by a certain age. What are the things—some obvious and others less so—that could save my daughters anxiety and pain? How could I prepare them for life without being didactic or a killjoy?

I plotted out chapters with the ruthless efficiency of a German Black & Decker instruction manual and soon realized that none of these lessons would be impactful without the first-person stories leading to them. Assuming that I would indeed perish before my time, the girls would benefit to hear about the night their mother and I met, what my memories of them were, or stories that I had never even told their mother. And there were many worth recounting. I spent much of my childhood in Tokyo and Rome as the unwitting child of a deep-cover CIA spy. That's interesting, right? And then after a great many obstacles, I became a big-firm attorney working in New York City. Who wouldn't want to know more about that exceedingly scarce breed, hardly represented in movie and TV, filled with virtue and admired by the rest of the American populace?

In search of a unified theory, I began to organize chapters by importance and also reflecting a life span. Three unnegotiable core qualities and the importance of friends would appear earlier in the book, when the girls were still young and would be finding themselves; overcoming fear and their first setbacks and developing their social skills would be later, when they would begin to interact with the external world; and finding a significant other and raising kids would arrive toward the end. All the while, I wanted to weave in as many relevant pop culture, sports, and movie references as I could, anything that inspired and entertained me. Every name-check and turn of phrase would be special and intentional. The book would leave my girls with no doubt as to who their father was—what I believed, what I remembered, what I loved.

But would this be enough?

In 2011, not long after the births of our two daughters, *The Wall Street Journal* ran an article titled "Why Chinese Mothers Are Superior," which generated more than 5,700 comments on the WSJ website, the most in its history. The article was an excerpt from *The Battle Hymn of the Tiger Mother*, written by a Yale law professor named Amy Chua, outlining the old-school Asian style of parenting, which could have been described as somewhere between strict and psychotic. There was considerable backlash against her, driven by anecdotes in the book: when she called her eight-year-old kid "garbage," repeating a cycle from when her father called her that years ago; when she demanded a better birthday card from her four-year-old daughter; when she recounted with a perverse sense of pride how she made her daughter stand out in the cold as punishment for not playing the piano correctly, her three-year-old. Within five minutes of reading the article, anyone would have had a compulsion to punch a Yale grad in the face (or perhaps more of one). I felt a discomfiting unease.

The similarities between her and me were numerous. I am also a law school grad, a second-generation immigrant born to a Chinese/Taiwanese father and a Japanese mother. I'm in the same ballpark of age as Ms. Chua and with two daughters as well. None of what she did to her girls was shocking to me. In fact, it hit a little too close to home; I could imagine my own father, long deceased, sending me a link to this article and writing, "She is right!" Yet I also agreed with her that multi-generational American kids have become soft and coddled. And in detailing all of these unflattering stories and being unapologetic about them, she certainly did not succumb to the stereotype of the Asian: meek and undisruptive.

What further propelled interest in the article and Ms. Chua's book were her impeccable credentials: Harvard undergrad, Harvard Law, *Harvard Law Review*, Yale Law professor. With Ms. Chua, parents were drawn to the sliver of a possibility that she held the secrets to "the path of success," i.e., money, power, and social status, which felt authenticated by the development of her daughters. Both went to Harvard, one graduating from Yale Law and clerking for Supreme Court Justice Brett Kavanaugh, and the other enrolling in Harvard Law.

After looking at Ms. Chua's bio and seeing that at Yale Law, she specializes in international business transactions, law and development, ethnic conflict, and globalization, I had to remind myself that I too am worthy, because over the years I have owned multiple Yale locks. After managing to avoid it for a while, I read her book as I was writing mine. By the time I finished hers, it felt no longer adequate to have children who were happy. They needed to be successful, goddammit. And after vowing many times that I would not succumb to this peer pressure and ask the most unoriginal of questions, one morning I was on the bus to school with my elder daughter Sofia when I blurted out, "What do you want to be when you grow up?"

My daughter tilted her eyes upward, as though literally envisioning her older self perched on the mountain of success. Ah yes, I thought.

"I want...to be a bird."

Oh fuck.

"No, come on, seriously."

"Okay, okay. I want to be..."

And then her eyes really lit up.

"...a mermaid!"

Decisively defeated, I could not help but marvel at my daughter's troll game. There was still hope.

We live in a time where it is difficult to filter voices, when it appears that the louder you are or the more followers you have, the more right you are. As I wrote this book and reflected upon my own shortcomings and failures, I became racked with doubt. Who was I to say what would lead to personal and professional fulfillment? Was my advice foolishly anachronistic? In spite of my best intentions, was I in fact setting up my children to be noble failures?

And then I remember this moment.

Long, long ago, when I was a senior-level associate, I was staring at my computer. The stars were out, Manhattan-style—thousands of office lights framed by the nighttime sky. A call from Frank three offices down.

"Drink?"

We went to this whiskey bar near Central Park South. It was early in the week, so it was a contemplative evening, not a rowdy one. And we jumped from one topic to another until we settled on one of our firm's newer clients, a businessman who loved the spotlight and flaunting of all his symbols of success—the wealth, the arm candy, the friendships with the high and mighty. Our firm was giddy just to have the privilege of representing him.

The thing was, we both knew this businessman was a charlatan, more filled with bluster than substance. Windbag, scumbag, douchebag—take your pick of 'bag. Even his huge wealth seemed to be a façade. In fact, that was why our firm was being retained: he was suing a journalist who had questioned the extent of his wealth, which seemed grotesquely pointless to me. We both knew that he wasn't a generous person. For all of his headline-grabbing antics, we couldn't think of a single charity with which he was associated, even one of those sham ones. Compared to the run-of-the-mill titan of industry, he still managed to outdo others as a giant prick.

And yet, my friend rued, this businessman reigned supreme over humps like us—guys who worked hard, played by the rules, and tried to live like decent human beings with proper moral compasses. No matter. In the game of life, this businessman could always point to the scoreboard.

"No."

No, I said. Sure, there would be many people who were easily impressed by the guy's trappings of fame and fortune, but were they your target audience? Are those the people you hang out with and consider your friends? Wouldn't you rather be well-regarded by people whom you respected and admired in return?

Rolling the whiskey around in his mouth, my friend thought about it for a bit and finally concluded, "Yeah, you're right." Then we moved on to the next topic. I'm 95 percent sure it had to do with girls or whether the NYC real estate market would crash.

I flash back to that conversation and ask myself whether I truly believe in what I had said back then. Approximately 12 years later—after the explosion of reality shows, the dominance of likes and RTs and hot takes, extremism run amok, a coarser level of discourse, the seeming flexibility of truth and the apparent triumph of style over substance—would I still say the same thing?

Yes. An unequivocal, emphatic yes. Yes.

All things considered, that means something, because in 2016, that businessman became the 45th President of the United States of America.

This book is addressed to my daughters. Maybe the advice

doesn't work if you want to be president of this country. But it is for everyone else in between. I hope you enjoy it.

Mark

1

HOW YOU ARE

Dear Sofia and Alessandra,

I'm guessing that if you sit down with a typical middle-aged man with the usual accompanying responsibilities—spouse, kids, house, car—and ask him to reminisce about his life as a single guy, he would gently lay down his stack of bills, lean backward in a chair ergonomically ill-equipped to handle his weight, and stare out the window until tears course down his face.

"Your life is over."

You hear this, mostly from guys, when you say that you're about to have a kid. They think back to the unfettered life of a single dude—getting plastered at McSorley's on a Wednesday night, swearing up a storm without heed to whether your kids are around, going through an entire day without absorbing the ear-curdling whine of your child, sleeping alone in your own bed or in a strange one. Indulging in that non-stop, self-perpetuating egoism.

I did that too. But I wasn't the Casanova dashing from dinners to dates to social events; instead, I was drinking to excess, golfing poorly, and watching every below-average movie on cable released between 1999 and 2006, leading Kessler to christen me the Clown About Town.

Every once in a while, when the solitude descended and New York City was poised to extinguish me, I still held out hope that I would become a parent one day. It's not just women who feel that biological urge, you know. If my life resembled a critically reviled movie starring Ashton Kutcher, one morning I would have stumbled out of Apartment 24P to find a swaddled newborn in the hallway with a tear-stained note from the mother stating that she couldn't take care of it and that as the father, I was this baby's only hope. What would have made this scenario instantly unrealistic was that during this time, Tibetan monks got more action than I did. I resolved that if I turned 40 and was still single—a mere eight years away—I would adopt a child, a frightfully naïve ambition and easily the inspiration for another horrendous movie starring Ashton Kutcher.

Approximately five years later, your mother and I got news that we were pregnant with you, Sofia. At our advanced ages of 35 and almost 41, the looming, constant thought in our heads (well, at least mine) was the possibility that if something went wrong, that might have been our one and only shot at having a child. Every appointment to the doctor—the genetic test, the ultrasounds, the fetal heart monitor sessions—generated tension akin to the last five minutes of the *Sopranos* series finale. And for your mother and me, it was not as though we were walking out into the safe, welcoming streets of New York afterward. In our slightly over-blown and irrational mentality, the city was even harsher than usual—every automotive vehicle, every ranting lunatic on the sidewalk, and every aggressive commuter on the subway platform personally became a threat to your very existence.

Thus, the date of your birth was not "the happiest day of my life," as many parents are contractually obligated to say. It was by far the most exhausting, as I finally exhaled after holding my breath for many, many months, and every cell in my being released the tension and let the energy drain out. And that night around 11:30 p.m. on my way home from Mount Sinai Hospital on 5th Avenue and 101st Street, I thought:

"I've just joined the human race."

Eight months later, with the clock ticking yet again and against long odds, your mother became pregnant again with you, Alessandra. This time, having lived through a previous pregnancy and birth, we could now relax and really enjoy the experience. That was a mistake.

The first sign that something wasn't quite right was your mother's size. She was getting really big, which might sound like the sign of a big and healthy baby, but instead it signaled a problem: your mother was suffering from edema and retaining too much water. One particularly disappointing date night ended with us at St. Vincent's Hospital in the Village. Your mother was given medication that could have caused heart complications in you. If there had been a tear in your tiny heart, Alessandra, the doctors would have had to perform heart surgery while you were still in utero. Just imagine that.

From all those days we spent in the hospital, I'll always remember the colorful blobs. The color Doppler ultrasound would trace the direction and amount of blood flow into your tiny heart; the shapes morphed into red and yellow and orange, depending on the doctor's positioning of the wand. And your mother and I stared and squinted into them, not having the faintest clue as to what we were looking at or looking for, hoping that the blobs would somehow spell out: SHE GONNA BE OK. And when you came into this world, we melted in relief yet again.

By the time you leave for college, either your mother or I probably will have taken a photo of you every couple of days. All of them together would make a nifty flipbook of your lives.

Let me tell you about the things that won't show up in the flipbook, the extended scenes. Some are worthy of the family album and others are most assuredly not. But if I hadn't forced myself to revisit them and recall everything I could and why they held importance to me, the details would have dimmed over time until just the glow of the memory remained. You.

•..................•..................•

Anyone who grew up with a true love of comedy in the 80s and 90s idolized David Letterman. When he switched over to CBS to host *The Late Show*, I would often catch the opening intro montage, which included a brief shot of a restaurant with a row of colorful iron jockeys standing guard outside its windows. Each of them had an outstretched arm, which appeared to welcome, but in reality seemed to beckon a challenge. I had no idea that this place was called the 21 Club, or where in Manhattan it was, because I was far, far away, in St. Louis and then Las Vegas.

About 12 years later, I was now a guest there for the first time, invited by a firm to a Christmas lunch that would inevitably turn into a boozy afternoon. Once I saw the red-checkered tablecloths and the hundreds of miniature deal toys, stuffed animals, and sports memorabilia hanging from the ceiling, I immediately recognized it as the spot where Michael Douglas hands over a million-dollar check to Charlie Sheen in *Wall Street* and tells him to buy a decent suit because he "can't come here looking like this." True to its history as a speakeasy, the place had darkened pockets where men in suits convened for power lunches. It also didn't take long for me to recognize that I was one of the youngest there and definitely the only person of color. Yes, this was undoubtedly the place where old white men talked shit about minorities.

It didn't matter. I could pass. I settled in for a martini and mingled and threw back my head when I laughed. And then I peeked at my watch.

"I gotta leave for a moment. Can you order for me?"

Moments later, I was asking a cab driver to take me 50 blocks to the preschool both of you attended, 3rd Street Music School. Before long, your mother and I were sitting in chairs more suited for two-year-olds while Miss Brenda said, "Alessandra is very independent."

Ah yes, that made sense. Alessandra, you always had that strong will, forged through your mother's tough pregnancy.

With the shadow of an older sister hovering over you, you wanted to be your own person.

"She's incredibly generous and shares her toys very well."

No, you must be speaking about the wrong child.

Another 10 minutes later, we had graduated to the upper floor, where we sat in chairs more suited for four-year-olds, leaning into Miss Cathy and Miss Eileen's comments.

"She's the conscience of the class. She'll correct others—get angry, even—when they do something bad."

"There's a bit of a clique forming in this class among the girls, but she's managed to stay away from the drama."

"Sofia is ready for kindergarten."

We managed not to overreact to these assessments; they were just preschool parent-teacher conferences, after all. Your mother and I went back to work. In the cab once again, I scrolled through texts asking where I was, when I was planning to get back, and that the entrée was getting cold. I floated through the doors and past the maître d'. I ate the 21 Club's iconic chicken hash while others whispered and laughed and drank. I beamed. All I could think about was you.

• •

We were on the early evening Jitney bus to Long Island on our way to a friend's place for the weekend. Sofia, you were less than a year old. You had been fed and were sleeping in my lap; my arms and legs were in uncomfortable and unnatural positions, but I knew I needed to dig deep and hold that pose until you fell into a deeper slumber. As I looked at your cherubic face, a thought flashed across my mind: I was blessed. Not for having a child. That was a given. No, I was blessed because you had never vomited a copious amount. Your spit-ups were small and cute and dainty, easily wiped away with a burp cloth, and it was a mira—

"BLAAAAAHHHHHGGGGGGGGGHHH."

There was milky throw up all over my green pants with hunks of cheese—chunky-style vomit. And it didn't stop. Just one heave after another as we tried to staunch the rancid flow. About 15 seconds later, I was less concerned by my drenched pants and underwear and the smell starting to waft throughout the bus full of New Yorkers who were itching to go party in the Hamptons. I was more in awe of this extra-sensory communication between us. I emitted this thought. You felt it, you sensed it. And dammit, you wanted to issue a counterpoint.

On the other hand, Alessandra, you could always barf in any mode of transportation: car/taxi, bus, airplane, train/subway. About the only way you wouldn't have barfed was if we'd used a vehicle that gave an illusion that you were sitting perfectly still, synced to the rotation of the earth. Dealing with it on a repeated basis made me a barf connoisseur. We learned not to give you any milk or cheese on the mornings of some long car rides, because that stuff coming back up was the most horrid substance ever. On the other hand, the morning you ate IKEA cookies, my thought while cleaning the car seat was, "This actually is not unpleasant."

After a while, even getting you into a car or a subway turned into a chore with attendant whining and crying. But you hadn't learned yet how to use "not," which is quite underrated in the language development of a child. As a result, there were lots of puzzled New Yorkers in subway cars who were subjected to a crying girl in a stroller screaming, "LIKE IT! LIKE IT!"

•·················•·················•

"WHAT DID YOU DO?!?"

This a question normally demanded from a parent to a child. I cast my eyes downward.

When you were born, Sofia, my obsession with eradicating all mosquitos in the apartment went up a notch. Once there's one buzzing in my ear, usually all my plans for the next couple of hours go on hold until there are three independent sources that I've definitively killed it. The idea that this mosquito could suck out blood from our precious newborn was too much to bear. Safe to say that those little bastards were so in my head, they were building real estate there.

On this night, a mosquito had me walking throughout the living room, our bedroom and your bedroom, looking at the ceilings like a deranged astronomer. Finally, I spotted one right above your crib, which was in the corner of the bedroom. After moving you, just over a year old, into the next room, I took a small ladder and set it next to the crib. Why I didn't simply move the crib so I could have a more unimpeded path to the mosquito will remain one of the great mysteries of life.

Once I ascended to the top of the ladder with my rolled-up magazine, I realized that the ceilings were actually much higher than I thought, and the mosquito continued to be tantalizingly out of reach. And at that moment, in an effort to see whether it was indeed out of my reach, I stuck a foot out and half-rested it on one edge of the crib and half against the wall. In remembering this episode, the thought of, "Was I really this stupid?" occurred to me several times—the only smart thing I had done up to this moment was move you to another room.

The damn mosquito was still out of range, unaware that it was going to meet its demise via a *Time* magazine with "The Tragedy of Detroit" on the cover. I had to go next-level and wring every ounce of my potential. I put my other foot—the one that had been firmly planted on the top step of a ladder—on the other edge of the crib, the edge not nestled up against a wall.

It is only when you're standing on a top of a crib with one foot on each edge—Van Damme-style, we may call it—that a moment of clarity will emerge, i.e., "This may not be safe." Which the crib confirmed by buckling. And which I conceded by resting one of my feet on the floor of the crib. And when I mean "resting," I mean, "crashing my foot through the floor of the crib."

If your spouse is yelling at you, "WHAT DID YOU DO?!?" and the only thought that comes to mind is, "I tried to stand upright on the edges of our infant's crib in order to kill a mosquito," it's really better not to say anything. But I had to try to defend my idiocy, which led to more screaming, and I bet that after hearing this throughout the night, the mosquito would have preferred that I ended its life right then.

● ···················● ···················●

During your first couple of years, often the only time I could see both of you girls awake was just before bedtime. That time was without price, but I knew that I couldn't just show up right before you were about to go to bed, because I knew that my mere arrival would cause you guys to be all jacked up, and it would be another 30 minutes of cajoling you back to sleep.

Every night that I was home, just before my bedtime, I would sneak into your room to make sure that you were breathing. Parents know how fraught with risk this is: needlessly waking a blissfully asleep infant is about the most asinine thing in the world. With both of you being in the same bedroom, waking up one of you inadvertently would likely lead to the catastrophic consequence of two screaming toddlers. Going into your room in the dead of night required the care of a bomb squad expert.

I would go in and listen for your breathing. Your shallow breaths were inaudible. Then I would peer into the crib and try to stare at your chest and see whether it rose and fell. Sometimes that would be the end of the inquiry and I would collapse into bed. But if I couldn't make a determination, then the "Oh my God, it's sudden infant death syndrome" thought drummed louder and louder in my head. So then I would REACH INTO THE CRIB and ever-so-gently lay my hand against your chest until I could detect the slightest crest and fall. Sofia, you would rarely notice my touch, but Alessandra, you would often spasm like I just tased you.

As you grew older, I would stand next to your cribs, and then your beds, and listen for your breathing, which became easier to detect. Sometimes during the summer, I would feel your heads to make sure that you weren't too hot. At times, before heading off on a work trip, I would linger a bit longer just to stare. That obsessive-compulsive instinct to check on you, at first driven by fear, gradually grew into something that provided me with comfort.

• · · · · · · · · · · · · · · · · · • · · · · · · · · · · · · · · · · · •

"Tellon tellon. Tellon tellon," one of you would say.

Later, one of you would respond: "Pee-son. Pee-son."

Then both of you would howl in laughter, as though a Dave Chappelle routine had been distilled to these two words.

"Why is that so funny?" we would ask. You never gave it up and maybe it was better that way, as Red had mused in *The Shawshank Redemption*: "I have no idea to this day what those two Italian ladies were singing about. Truth is, I don't want to know. Some things are best left unsaid."

Sofia, from the time you were a baby, your mother and I would catalog your grunts and cries and we would speculate what your voice would sound like. And when those first words came, we started to revel in the babble.

"That's why."

I am convinced no one in the history of the English language could say it in the manner you did when you were two years old. It wasn't exactly used as a declarative phrase. And not an interrogative either, even though it became kind of high-pitched at the end of "why," which trailed off and demanded a follow-up sentence that never arrived at its destination. Best yet, it was almost always a non sequitur. So, we would hear, "That ball is red. That's why..." leaving a wake of question marks and quizzical looks behind.

"You know what?"

I caught myself saying this at the office about a million times when you were about three-and-a-half and two years old. "I'm not sure about filing that motion. You know what? Screw it, let's take a chance." "He's difficult to deal with, but you know what, so are most lawyers." "You know what? I can't believe it's already Thursday."

Eventually I realized that I kept on saying this because when I said this at home, you two would actually interject.

"You know what?"

Your heads would snap toward me. "What?"

"I feel thirsty. I'll get a glass of water."

In your innocence, you didn't recognize that the "You know what" was simply a rhetorical question. And I loved your response so much that subconsciously I would say it all the time, regardless of where or when. It made no sense for me to explain that it was technically a question that did not need a response. You would learn in time. I was content to simply be immersed in your innocence.

●••••••••••••••••••●••••••••••••••••●

A parent's experience is not complete without trips to the hospital. When the parent is more angry than alarmed—as when you, Alessandra, had to defy us and stick a plastic bead up your nose, which led to me cursing under my breath for the next hour until you sneezed it out—then we can all laugh about it later.

When the parent has to google the child's diagnosis ("Henoch-Schonlein purpura is a rare inflammatory disease of the small blood vessels…some people may develop severe kidney disease, including IgG nephropathy, nephritis and/or nephrotic syndrome leading to kidney failure"), then it's akin to saying, "The nuclear missiles have been launched."

Sofia, your abdominal pains had been first diagnosed as indigestion. Then it was something flu-related. Then on the first full night of the new year, you woke up screaming in the middle of the night and your mother took you to the E.R. You were so strong, just over three years old, having needles stuck in you, the blood seeping through the gauze. You fixated on your Wonder Woman Barbie instead. All it took was a two-day stay at the NYU hospital and you were on the way back to your usual self.

Alessandra, you were just shy of two years old. It must have been all a mystery to you—to hear your sister crying in a markedly different tone; to see your mother, your caregiver, your grandmother, and me doting over your listless sister; to see just one of us for stretches of time in an effort to keep your routine as undisturbed as possible. Your vocabulary was solid. But something went haywire inside that little head of yours when your older sister came home after a mysterious absence of several days.

Instead of saying something, or even simply "Sofia," all you could do was make loud, unintelligible grunting noises; your brain simply could not convert your emotions sufficiently into words, and all that came out were these grunts of joy, accompanied by little hops. (It didn't matter that true to form as the older sister, Sofia acted nonplussed.) It was quite frankly, one of the reasons why your mother and I, who grew up as only children, wanted more than one child, to experience the moment when a sisterhood was cemented. Please, for the love of God, remember this moment the next time you're bickering over stupid shit like who borrowed clothing without permission.

• ⋯⋯⋯⋯⋯ • ⋯⋯⋯⋯⋯ •

"Be careful."

How many times does a parent say that when a child is beginning to walk? When you, Sofia, started walking at 13 months, you would hold out your arms straight ahead for balance, and with your herky-jerky gait, you looked like Mini Frankenstein. While you stared straight ahead, fixated on your destination, a semi-circle of arms shadowed you.

Two and a half years later, when we lived at our apartment on 34th Street, throwing away the trash in the garbage chute down the hall regularly became a five-minute ordeal. You two would tear down the narrow corridor. Invariably, the arms and legs got ahead or behind where they were supposed to be, and you, Sofia, would splat on that carpet. You would slowly get on your hands and knees, do a system check. In time, that process somehow became something to enjoy, so you would start running down the hallway and deliberately fall every 10 feet. And because, Alessandra, you always needed to emulate your sister, you would do the same. Alberto Gilardino, Fabio Grosso, Marco Materazzi...these national team soccer players could have learned something about simulating fouls and wasting time from our two little Italian divers.

When your minds were set, your mother and I were generally powerless. When we began to potty train you, Alessandra, you were able to pee in the toilet, but had a mental block for pooping there. It was like the finality of having your feces flushed down the pipes was just too much for you. Despite our best efforts to have you conform to the rest of society and take a dump in the toilet, you steadfastly stuck to this routine for a good couple of months: whenever the pooping urge struck (which was often, because you ate like a truck driver), you would ask for your diaper. You would remove your underwear, we put on the diaper, and then you would tell us to leave. "Go away! Go away."

And then you would go into the corner of your bedroom. Usually you parked yourself before the blackboard easel and doodled with chalk, your legs spread apart like before Ronaldo is about to take a free kick (as a 100 percent Messi guy, I enjoy associating Ronaldo's free kicks with you pooping).

Five minutes later: "I'M FINISHED!"

The physical milestones, as trite and unexceptional as they were, always caused me to rejoice. The times you began to smile, which led me to try to make you do more of that, which led to more smiles, a rolling snowball of happiness. Or the simplest of gestures, the wave. As adults, it's such an unremarkable movement, but when a baby learns it, you want to practically build a monument to this landmark achievement, the bridge from one human being to another. A dumbass wave. I would give anything to celebrate these milestones again for the first time.

· ● · · · · · · · · · · · · · · · · · · ●

Another watershed event for me was taking you to see your first sporting event in person. I only took Sofia, as taking two children under three years old by myself to a game would be galactically stupid. As you already know, sports mean so much to me—but which event would be your first game, Sofia? I agonized over this decision the way students choose their colleges.

You hadn't yet shown a proclivity for basketball yet. Hockey...eh. What if a fight broke out and I'd have to explain all that? Football? I'd definitely have to explain why that Giants or Jets fan was urinating from the upper deck. The default would end up being a baseball game, but then again, Yankees fans are such high-and-mighty assholes, and the Mets...that's an introduction to a lifetime of disappointment. Tennis's U.S. Open it was. Was it overkill to be thinking this much about your inaugural sporting event when you weren't even three years old? Maybe. Is it relevant that I pretended you were under two to get around the inane policy that any children over 24 months had to have a full-price adult ticket? Possibly.

At this point, it was rare for me to even have an outing with one of you alone. Because your mother didn't trust me and thought I had the intelligence of a bag of shrimp, she insisted that I put my business card into your cute little purse. I hand-wrote all sorts of important information on that card: my cell phone number, your mother's cell phone number, our social security numbers, ATM pin codes, etc. And then I sat down and explained to this 34-month-old face that if for any reason she couldn't find Daddy or got lost—not that it was going to ever, ever, ever, ever happen—she was to hand this card to an adult who could help. Because really, what could possibly go wrong with handing a card to a stranger in Queens?

And on a scorcher in late August, we took the 7 train to the Mets-Willets Point station, with me snapping photos every couple of seconds.

We entered the security line. And when this lady saw us, she smiled and went through an exaggerated show of checking every crevice of your woven purse, the one with the rooster on it. And then she gave this bag back to you.

That's when you loosened the drawstring of your purse, opened it up, and then slowly drew out my business card and handed it to her. And then my heart liquefied and I wanted to sweep you up in my arms and tearfully beg you to never, never, never, never age another day.

We bounced around from court to practice court to food court. To this day, you remember the Ben & Jerry's mango sorbet you ate. I remember when you pointed at the U.S. Open-logoed tennis ball in the gift shop and thinking to myself, man, those jerks really gouge us on everything. Were we allowed to breathe the air in Flushing, or was that free? I still bought the ball for you.

We wandered over to the smaller courts, where spectators sit on bleachers and can move around more freely. An unattended practice court was about twenty feet away. And strewn about this court were lots of U.S. Open-logoed balls.

You know those tennis ball hoppers made of wire that people use to collect balls without bending over? Well, I had my own, in adorable human form. So I lifted you up, up, and over the chest-level chain-link fence and deposited you on the empty practice court. And then I whispered, "Want to pick up some tennis balls?"

You then scurried over to pick up a couple, which looked like grapefruits in your tiny palms, and after you came to me I picked you up, up, and over the chain link fence again, so that you could hand them over and I could discreetly slip them into my bag. And then I repeated the process again because I felt like I needed to make a point to the U.S. Tennis Association. I didn't do it a third time because I thought it would be unbecoming if your inaugural sports event ended with me in handcuffs.

Over the four or five hours we were there, we may have watched less than 30 minutes of play. I could not have been more content with that.

● ⋯⋯⋯⋯⋯⋯⋯● ⋯⋯⋯⋯⋯⋯●

In time, Sofia and Alessandra, it became difficult to imagine a life before you both joined us. I struggled to remember how exactly I spent my free time as the Clown About Town. And then I went to Tulum for the second time.

The town of Tulum used to be a sleepy spot on the eastern coast of Mexico, about two hours south of Cancun. The pueblo was a fairly nondescript assortment of local stores and tourist spots, but when you took that 90-degree road to the beach and got through the thick vegetation, you arrived at a magical place. I'm not just talking about the bright white sand and the clear waters and the unbroken horizontal line of sea in the distance, but the vibe of the place, which was undeveloped but yet had some really beautiful lodging and fantastic restaurants. I say this all in the past tense because the secret is out, and the place has fallen prey to the temptations of overdevelopment.

The first time I went to Tulum was to get married. Your mother and I got engaged in July and wanted a wedding soon after, which precluded anything within the New York City area. We wanted something fun in January, which meant somewhere with palm trees. And so we stayed in Tulum for 14 days over New Year's and into the second week of January.

It was epically fun. Sixty-two friends and family members, from as far away as Japan, Italy, and Zimbabwe, spent anywhere from three days to 10 days in Tulum. It wasn't exactly bacchanalian, but we woke up when we pleased, ate whenever and whatever we felt like, drank liberally, played sports and challenged the waves, and generally had the type of unencumbered vacation that you remember from your single days. Our wedding began at 4 p.m. on a Saturday, and 62 people—three of whom were pregnant and some others who didn't drink—consumed 30 bottles of tequila.

When your mother and I retired to our honeymoon suite, around eight hours after the ceremony, I tried to stave off the spins while lying on the bed. Once I could focus, I looked up and thought, "This was the most mind-blowingly fun day ever. And this glass ceiling is beautiful—you can see all of the stars. Come to think of it, why don't more rooms have glass ceilings?"

When I woke up, I realized that it was a plain white ceiling. No glass.

The second time I went to Tulum was during Thanksgiving break, when you were just over two years and nine months old. With our families being overseas at the time, your mother and I saw an opportunity to get away for several days, and I was eager to revisit Tulum's magic.

We visited the spot where we had our wedding dinner and party—it had been less than three years, and we were surprised that even that short of a time seemed to have taken its toll. Everything seemed a bit haggard and overused. There were multiple construction spots as well, a harbinger of the future.

We had a room in this beautiful hotel on the beach and our own miniature pool in the backyard. Pre-kids, I could not have imagined a more luxurious indulgence. Post-two-kids-two-years-old-and-under, I could not have imagined a more alluring death trap. Even you two looking in the direction of the pool made me nervous.

The beach was no different. It was a constant battle to protect you: slather sunblock, block your path into an oncoming wave, make sure you weren't eating sand, etc. The only relief we got was when you were both napping at the same time, which over the course of four days, totaled about three minutes. Alessandra, you were still waking up periodically in the middle of the night, so seven hours of uninterrupted sleep in retrospect was wishing for a lottery win. And sure enough, at around three in the morning, you started screaming your head off, which set off you, Sofia, which eventually led to me tracing circles in our backyard and along the edge of our pool, screaming.

"I'M GOING OUT OF MY FUCKING MIND."

In that three minutes of peace I had on that vacation, I was kind of bummed out. I had brought all these magazines to read, and they went untouched. Every waking moment was spent entertaining you, or tending to your needs, or watching over you, and even asking for a little relief from your mother seemed like a gross imposition.

"Your life is over."

But then there were these other moments. When I watched you two, sitting on a blanket in the grass, playing with your toys together, and interacting with each other like loving siblings. When you looked out into the sea and I was wondering what exactly was going through those heads of yours, and if this trip would make any impact on your personality down the line. When a new word, a sentence, or a question marked an incremental step in your development. When we ate at a table together as a family, and you, Sofia, fed yourself, which is a monumental step for the overworked parent. And to be completely truthful—and not because I needed to provide some justification—these moments provided me with the type of happiness I had not experienced before as a single guy.

If I had to graph the two vacations, it would have gone something like this:

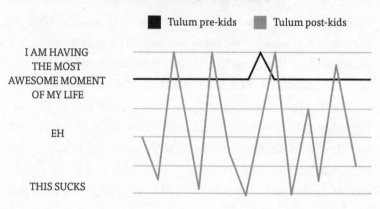

Always remember that by the time I met your mother, we welcomed the end of our previous lives. We wanted a new one, with you.

All of these non-flipbook moments that I've just described—ranging from the monotonous to the disgusting to the infuriating to the terrifying—they made me feel so much more alive. I have experienced moments of such exquisite beauty and happiness that I would instinctively want to term them as "indescribable." They are the type of moments where you desperately wish that the brain cells in charge of memories are firing at their best, for your senses to be heightened so that you can absorb every detail—the hues of your clothes, the ambient sounds, the reflected sunlight, the touch of the wind. You want the earth to spin a little slower so that the moment lasts a bit longer. Whatever you feel, you know it is fleeting, because the real world beckons, but at that moment, you feel peace. That's the feeling for which I am forever indebted to you.

2

HOW I MET SARAH

In the summer of 2006, your Uncle Dave and I went to Germany for the World Cup, traveling from Hamburg to Berlin to Frankfurt to Munich, culminating in our attendance at the France-Portugal semifinal. It was an awesome trip because, well, we had more beers than any human being could possibly count. But it was also a rite of passage that I wish you girls will experience—the road trip, usually in your carefree early 20s, when life is full of potential and there are many tantalizing paths ahead. In contrast, Uncle Dave and I were both in our mid-30s and burnt-out, jaded lawyers who needed to get away from the fucking cesspool that is New York City.

We rented a car and on a clear blue day, got on that Autobahn, renowned for having no speed limit. We were cruising along and keeping pace with everyone else, with the trees and the forests zipping by pretty quickly. Every once in a while we snuck a peek at the speedometer and that fluorescent red needle steadily moving clockwise in kilometers an hour until our curiosity overcame our ignorance, which led to us speculating about the exact kilometer/mile conversion (pre-smartphone, remember), which led to me flipping through my DK Eyewitness Guide to find the citation of a distance in both miles and kilometers, which led to me pulling out a scrap piece of paper and doing an algebraic equation by hand, which eventually led to me saying out loud, "Dude, I think you're going 116 miles an hour."

(Our top speed ended up being 210 km/hr, or 136 mph. Lest this be an endorsement of driving at ridiculously high speeds, I'm compelled to point out that there are few Autobahn accidents because drivers in Germany follow the rules and know their limitations.)

In any event, because we were driving so fast, the borders of Germany could not contain us, and we drove all the way down to Basel, the site of Switzerland's oldest university and more important, the birthplace of Roger Federer.

In the hour before sunset, when everything turned shades of gold and red, we stood on the banks of the Rhine and watched the Baselites strip down to bathing suits, putting their clothes in inflatable bags. Then they waded into the river, holding onto their bags as flotation devices. They bobbed their way downstream, past the Wettsteinbrücke bridge, until they veered ashore. Then they opened those bags and dried themselves with towels. And they put their clothes back on. It was the most peaceful, brilliantly efficient, surreal vision.

Later that evening, after gigantic plates of sausage and schnitzel and fries and many beers that had a minimum of 10 letters in each name and a maximum of three vowels, we sat down on the stone stoop of a house. We had finished talking about the NYC real estate market and moved onto girls and then I found myself saying out loud:

"This feels impossible and futile."

The statement seemed incongruous given the din of the crowds socializing near the river. But that night I expressed out loud a certain hopelessness in being able to find a compatible partner to fall in love with. There was no guarantee whether it was ever going to happen. And maybe that was okay. I hope that you don't ever have that feeling, but it's natural, especially in New York City.

There are thousands of reasons why this city provides the backdrop for virtually every movie and TV depiction of two people falling in love. But if you've lived here for a while and haven't found someone, everything that makes the city great can coagulate into this awful stew of cynicism and jealousy and desperation. When you sink to this level, you look at anyone who fulfills a certain bare minimum of attractiveness—an acquaintance, a co-worker, a waitress, a passerby, ANYONE—and wonder, you know, what are the chances of a girl like her and a guy like me getting together and making it work? And by the time that you come to a conclusion (um, more like one out of a million), she's already halfway across town.

Barry Schwartz writes in *The Paradox of Choice* that with the possibility of more options and theoretically more freedom, people's happiness doesn't increase as it logically should. Instead, there's more indecision and anxiety and stress involved precisely because there are so many choices. And this principle extends to a mate. You just can't be entirely sure that you're matching up with the best possible person when there are so many others in the city. If I met someone at a party, I generally got the sense that she was looking over my shoulder to see if there was someone else who was more attractive and charismatic and accomplished, which was incredibly rude and deflating and something I should have been outraged about, except I was doing the exact same thing.

Almost four months to the day after that night in Basel, on October 30, 2006, I went to a wine tasting charity event to raise funds for Emergency, an Italian relief aid organization that provides medical support to war-torn areas. This sounds like the type of social function that Bruce Wayne would attend, except the Clown About Town's only other option was going to a dive bar and watching Monday Night Football.

During the cocktail hour, there was this magician who was mingling and doing all sorts of infuriating magician things that make you think for a split-second that witchcraft may be involved. And that's when I made eye contact with your mother.

When I was single, whenever I met someone remotely attractive, my instinct was to look at her hands for an engagement or wedding ring. If there was one, then I kind of slowed down—it was now a preseason match, an exhibition, a friendly for which I would not be pulling out my A-game. I had zero interest in honing my pickup lines, getting in my flirting reps, and contributing to the breakup of a relationship. Instead I would be going at half- or three-quarters speed, being somewhat entertaining but not too much. I had been burned too many times finding out that a woman I was making eye contact with, chatting with, having a moment with, thinking about asking out, contemplating marrying...well, was not in fact single. That's quite a ledge to fall from, you know?

Your mother was wearing a number of rings. And clustered on her right hand were a series of silver rings—one that was a regular band, sandwiched between two others that resembled Enoki mushrooms. The rings were so pleasing to look at that I temporarily forgot that I was supposed to determine whether this woman was engaged or married. Staring at her hand until I burned another hole in these rings didn't seem like the debonair thing to do.

She caught me looking at her and said, "He's very good," referring to the magician. It was a moment built for a response with effortless suavity.

I said, "Why was the magician so good at taking tests? Because he was good at trick questions."

Nah, I have no idea what I said. Fairly sure it was some variation of "DUUUUUUUUUURRRRRRRR...me like magic."

Then she talked to her friend, Aunt Elena, in her native Italian. And that, my girls, was when a tuning fork went off in my brain.

I lived in Rome when I was 11 to 14 years old. Those four years were the most influential in my life. Living in Italy leads to a deeper appreciation for art, for eating, for history, for life. I never took another Italian class, but 30 years later, my Italian is stronger than my Japanese—living there while I was young meant that I was able to capture the native dialect, to the point where others have said that I have a strong Roman accent (which is like saying, "You have a lovely Brooklyn accent"). I am fanatical about the AS Roma and Italian national soccer teams, and to this day I still wonder whether I should have shelled out an insane amount of money to remain in Germany and go to Berlin to watch Italy win that 2006 World Cup final. And I happened to be in Italy right about when I started transitioning away from my *Boys Life* and *Sports Illustrated* magazines and started noticing these heretofore ignored creatures called "girls."

When single guys are on the prowl, they are in perpetual search for that thing that will impress the cynical, seen-it-all New York woman right there and then. In *There's Something About Mary*, Cameron Diaz muses that her ideal man would be an architect who golfs and can go to Nepal at the drop of a hat, which leads to Matt Dillon contriving a situation where he bumps into her at a golfing range, architect plans spilling out of his car trunk, and him lamenting, "All I got are these damn Nepalese coins." That is pretty much what every guy dreams of—a situation where you're pretending not to show off, but really, you're balling so, so, oh so very hard. Without a solitary doubt, this was the one time where the Japanese-Chinese guy needed to go for broke, take out the A-game and talk in Roman-accented Italian.

Her reaction was what just what I wanted, like Cameron Diaz's—the widening of the eyes, mouth slightly agape—and we proceeded to go through our personal histories and how we ended up in New York and how she was a shoe designer for brands like Benetton and Banana Republic and Juicy Couture and a bunch of other chit-chat that I couldn't possibly retain because I was determined to mentally record every cubic millimeter of her face.

I have never understood when someone is said to have "olive skin." Skin does not regularly look like the color of olives. Isn't it just a lazy shorthand for tan? Anyway, your mother had olive skin. She had these wonderfully high cheekbones and full lips, like you, Sofia. Dark, flowy hair and sharp, charcoal eyebrows, just like you, Alessandra. The classic nose that could have been taken right from a Greek bust. And her brown eyes had that kindness and little mischievous glint, just like both of you. Her looks were, as they say, right in my wheelhouse.

I feel like a small fortune could be made setting up charity events/wine tastings for single people in New York. One could raise a bunch of money for a worthwhile cause and in the process, attract men and women who are civic-minded and generous of heart, or at least people who are smart enough to pretend that they are civic-minded and generous of heart. And at these charity events/wine tastings, the organizer should make sure that the cocktails/mingling last at least two hours, because then you would be completely bombed and lose all inhibitions by the time the real wine tasting rolled around. This is what happened at this Emergency event.

A couple of hours later, we were sitting in the back of the room, and the moderator of the wine tasting started extolling the virtues of a certain regional wine. Then he summoned as much pretension as he could and asked, "Can there possibly be a grape so luscious, so exquisite?" and your mother and I both burst out laughing like a couple of third graders hearing a squeaky fart.

When the people in front of us turned around—blitzed, just like us—we began chatting with them, and one of them asked:

"Are you two married?"

This is the kind of detail that women LOOOOOOOVE and remember until their very last breaths as the very essence of kismet, when the cherubs pointed their arrows of love toward two people and aimed true. As to the type of detail that guys recall more easily, I didn't even have to go online to remember that on this Monday night, the New England Patriots handily beat the Minnesota Vikings at the Metrodome. But it wasn't lost on me that in my previous 35 years on this planet, no one had ever asked me this while I was with a woman or a girlfriend, but within 120 minutes of us meeting, a couple of strangers looked at an Asian guy and an Italian woman and asked that very question.

At the end of the night, I walked her back home and kissed her at the main entrance of her apartment building, which is definitely the kind of thing that guys remember. I then went to the bar in Midtown East where my friends were finishing up their Bud Light tasting in the dying moments of the game. And on the night that I met my future wife, I burst through the doors and uttered the prelude of every great love story.

"Yo, I just hooked up at a wine tasting!"

The relationship, having blasted through that awkward

and torturous "will she/he or won't she/he call/email" phase in record time, headed toward its next looming, logical barrier.

Kids.

I needed to know whether she wanted them. At our ages, fertility wasn't a foregone conclusion. But in that case, would she be amenable to adopting? Did she feel the overpowering need to be a parent, as I did, to take care of a human life, to teach it, to love it beyond words? If the answer was a no, then as well as it was going, it had to end.

You don't start talking about kids within weeks of meeting each other, unless you're a psychopath or 16 years old. But the question and her answer consumed me. The idea that something so beautiful could disintegrate so quickly—even just the idea of it—was physically making me sick. At that time, my guy friends and I were always complaining about how unfair it was that when we met other single women our age, they were desperate and slightly unhinged and immediately ready to commit to a lifelong relationship within days of meeting— and HOLY SHITBALLS OF IRONY, I WAS DOING THAT VERY EXACT THING.

Six weeks after we met, holed up in my office in the middle of the afternoon, I started to have what could charitably be described as a moment of high anxiety and uncharitably described as a mental breakdown. This had never happened to me before.

The breaths became more frequent and clipped, leading to a tingling in my fingertips, the tell-tale sign of hyperventilation. I knew what I was supposed to do to alleviate it, but I sure as hell wasn't going to risk a colleague barging into my office to find me wheezing into a paper bag. A dull roar was also starting to overwhelm my hearing, like my ear canals were narrowing. And then the nausea set in.

I dry heaved into the black non-recyclables trash bin. Nothing. I did it again. Nothing. With my eyes fully watered, I lay down, flat on my back, on the carpeted floor. Somehow, much easier to explain away if someone barged in. I stared at the white drop ceiling tiles as I tried to take more measured, deeper breaths. I thought for the 23rd time how lawyers count these tiles to calculate and compare the sizes of their offices and thanked God I was a well-adjusted and perfectly non-dysfunctional person.

Several minutes later, I didn't feel any different. I required an empathetic ear, belonging to someone who knew me and could understand. Uncle Dave, the one who had heard my plaintive wail in Basel for companionship, the admission that perhaps there would be no true love for me.

Apparently this memory wasn't as vivid in his mind, because his response basically boiled down to, "What the hell is the matter with you? Get your shit together."

The second person I called was your mother.

I can't emphasize this enough: when you're of marrying age, calling up the spousal candidate in question in the middle of the work day after six weeks of dating to ask whether he or she is interested in having children is probably the worst possible thing you can do. If you receive that call, you're well within your rights to hang up and immediately dial an attorney to draft the temporary restraining order.

It was not a very long call. This was the result of her being in the office and actually having work to do. For such a vital conversation, I recall very few details about it, probably due to my less-than-optimal frame of mind. But those three minutes on the phone basically set me on the right path. I'm not talking about the anxiety passing. I mean about the rest of my life.

In July, a little over eight months after our night of Emergency, we went on a trip to France to go visit your Nonna and Nonno Barry near Toulouse, and then your mother and I went up to Paris for several days. Apart from being the most romantic city on this planet, Paris was where my father, your grandfather, lived for about five years. It was after he went to Georgetown University and was kicked out for, in his words, "not improving his grades," but I suspect was more due to "playing prodigious amounts of poker." My father then went to Paris via Valencia, and the first couple of years there, he was basically drinking and carousing his way through the city.

When he realized that he needed to do something with his life, my father taught himself French, in part by reading *The Count of Monte Cristo* with a dictionary in hand. Then he applied to and got into the Institut d'Études Politiques de Paris, commonly known as Sciences Po. I will brag on his behalf and say that it's one of the most prestigious schools in the world and an incubator for France's political elite. Growing up, I had continually heard from my father about the grueling coursework and how stingy the grades were for oral examinations. It was quite a remarkable story: someone who was born and raised in Taiwan before World War II went through the United States and made his way to Paris to teach himself French and earn his bachelor's and master's degrees in political science from one of Europe's finest universities.

He passed away the year before I met your mother. He would have loved her so much—her worldliness, her elegance, her sense of humor. But maybe one way to connect the two was to go back to where he began to turn his life around.

Around 10 in the morning on July 3, under a light rain in the internal garden of the Sciences Po campus, I got down on a knee and proposed to your mother. We cried.

About six months later, on January 5, your mother and I were married in Tulum. We cried.

And about nine months later, on October 2, Sofia, you were born. We cried.

And about 16 months later, on February 11, Alessandra, you were born. We cried.

There are many, many virtues about your mother, of which I could go for days and days, but it will be as hackneyed and boring as shit. I'll tell you three particular qualities that I never thought I would appreciate.

First, your mother has an open mind. I tend to do a rigorous cost-benefit analysis before making decisions. The problem is that when you do that, you're often missing out on opportunity. Your mother has always thought that a job interview was worth doing no matter how much of a long-shot or ill-fitting, because you get your practice and you just never know where it could lead to—another reference, an idea in the interviewer's head, inspiration for you, anything.

When you have an open mind, life will take you in unexpected places, including the apartment where we live now. For six months, we traipsed all around Manhattan and Brooklyn because of her predilection to check out every place, no matter how unsightly it looked online. Looking for an apartment to rent or buy in New York City can be just about the most depressing search possible. Even when you find the best possible place within your meager means, there will invariably be some sort of string attached: inconsistent hot water, a neighbor who moonlights as a drummer for a heavy metal band, the site of a drug deal gone bad and resultant triple homicide, etc.

We walked into a place near Union Square with you in tow, about two years and six months old. It was essentially unchanged for 30 years. There was old-fashioned, tired carpeting, and bad parquet and nooks where there should have been no nooks. For some reason, the corners of every room and even parts of the ceiling were built out, so it actually seemed that the walls and ceiling were closing in on us and there was far less space. It was kind of a dump.

A shame, I thought. I love this neighborhood. It was time for us to go back to the drawing board and look for a better place, I decided. I just didn't have that broad-minded imagination your mother has. She saw its potential. She convinced me to give it a go. And we completely renovated it, built just the way we like it. Now you're growing up in this apartment, and later it'll be the place that you live in when you're in your 40s and changing our Depends.

Second, your mother can talk to someone until that person develops a leprous condition and his ears fall off. I had always found talking too much to be a huge negative. I think of this scene in *Cheers* where Sam Malone challenges Diane Chambers to shut up and not say a word for 30 seconds, or even 10 seconds, whereupon she fails a couple of times, gives up, and huffs that "Silence is overrated anyway."

But your mother's ability—passed down from her mother—to talk to anyone about anything is not only remarkable, it's quite a gift. She has that ability to be open and interested in what people do and think, and that's how she makes friends and connections and why people like her. This becomes most evident when we are invited to a stuffy social or work event. Ten minutes before we make our entrance, I'm practicing my fake laughs and earnest nods and slapping my arms like I'm ready to make my pro wrestling debut. She just goes in and manages to mingle effortlessly. It's not just the talking, it's the connecting.

Third, your mother is almost incapable of being offended. After her parents split up, she moved to England with her mother and bounced around one rough town after another, which probably helped develop her thick skin. She will not stew for days about slights and hold grudges, which is quite beautiful, because that's my primary job. Sure, there's an accompanying lack of shall we say, sensitivity, over which we've argued, but I'd rather have this fight than one in which both sides are being super-sensitive and whiny.

Speaking of arguments.

The culture clash in a fight between an Italian woman and a Chinese-Japanese man is quite stark. Generally, the stereotype of an Italian is getting really passionate and worked up over everything and yelling and arguing about it and having it wash over and forgetting about it—pretty true!

On the other hand, few are aware of this fact: you do not want to piss off an East Asian. There may not be an outward reaction to the offense. There might be a reassuring smile, even a laugh, so as not to heighten the confrontation or alert the offender that something untoward just happened. But you better damn believe that stuff goes into the vault, ready to be taken out many years later at the perfect time. Or maybe it just stays there, festering, a mental permanent black mark against this person.

I grew up in a household where the volume of your voice during a fight dictated who was winning. When my parents fought, it was akin to thermonuclear war: a flash, followed by widespread devastation, and for several days afterward, a deathly silence and many icy glares (which may not be what happens after a thermonuclear war). It took a while for me to understand that not every household undergoes this particular transformation if, say, someone didn't turn on her blinkers before making a lane change.

Your mother has taught me that no matter how awful our fight has been, there always must be a time afterward—preferably later that day, but could be the next—where we sit down like two rational adults, in level tones of voice, to pinpoint the sources of our disagreement and each resolve to do differently in the future. This seems so logical, because it is, but I had never learned it.

If our relationship is coming across as impossibly perfect, I can tell you why.

Because I really love the movies, in my spare time I've tried my hand at writing screenplays. I did the whole bit. I started out by reading the Syd Field and William Goldman screenwriting books, then countless classic scripts. Then I tapped out several of my own, first using Microsoft Word and painstakingly editing it to conform to screenplay format before I finally splurged on screenwriting software. And probably because I was in New York and single, I gravitated toward romantic comedies. It's an incredibly tough type to write, mainly because the genre always follows a certain structure: girl and boy meet, they fall in love, they encounter an obstacle, and then they reunite at the end. That is the structure of pretty much every worthwhile and unworthwhile romantic comedy ever, which is entirely comforting and maddening and challenging.

From that structure, usually the part that's usually the weakest and most easily glossed over is the obstacle, the thing that keeps the couple-to-be apart before the happy ending. Conflict is the foundation of any good story and completely necessary even within the romantic comedy, because who the hell wants to see the story of two people meeting and falling in love and living happily ever after?

Thus, most of the time, you need to have the temporary breakup: the two have a big fight and they part ways. The problem is that in real life, breakups are usually messy, and in the romantic comedy, it can't be ugly to the point where the audience no longer roots for the couple to stay together. The writer has to find something that appears to cause a large rift between the girl and the boy, that lays bare their flaws and vulnerabilities, but not where people are leaving the theater and muttering, "Boy, Tom Hanks and Meg Ryan sure turned into a couple of assholes whenever they got into a fight, huh?" Done well, this is manipulating the audience, a sort of stacking of the deck.

The whole point to all of this is that here, I am definitely stacking the deck. I'm completely skipping over the messy portions of the relationship between your mother and me. All of the wonderful schmoopy things I write about your mother and the romance of our relationship would be flushed down the toilet if I told you about some of the insane fights we've had and the ways that we've acted. (Before you imagine the worst, nothing that would get us arrested.) We have fought over microscopically trivial matters. We have fought over fundamental philosophies, which at times have made joint happiness impossible. On occasion these fights have played out in front of you, to my everlasting regret. But Sofia and Alessandra, it's very important for you to know that any worthwhile relationship will have these moments of pain and conflict and anguish, and they don't end simply because you get married.

Our wedding photos came up the other day. There's a reason why a wedding photographer costs so much, because in time, your memories of that day will gradually be replaced by the photos that are taken. We were lucky to get a very skilled photographer who posted a bunch of photos on the company's website.

When we were in the throes of trying to juggle work and two toddlers, your mother mentioned that she had just been on the site, and it was surprising to me because we have photo albums in our apartment and other albums on our computers and online, and basically because for someone to be looking at wedding photos five years after the ceremony may be a sign of a mental imbalance. So I asked why.

"I look at them usually when we're fighting, because the photos remind me of how happy we were on that day and how happy I am with you," she said.

Would it be great if your mother didn't exaggerate how little she sleeps (she will snore for hours, wake up, and complain that she didn't get enough rest)? Does it frustrate me that she doesn't get my exquisite pop culture references, and I feel progressively dumber the longer it takes for me to explain them? That I'm in several fantasy football leagues every year and she still doesn't know the basic concept of how it works? I can go on. But whenever I'm ticked off at your mother, I think of her comment and it completely takes the wind out of my anger.

The speed of our courtship was so fast that when it was happening, I remember feeling somewhat disappointed that your mother and I wouldn't have a history of us before kids— traveling together, making spontaneous plans, sleeping all day, enjoying peace and quiet, concentrating on each other. Ten years later, that wish seems comical. We were so blessed to have you enter our lives so soon that there's barely any delineation between your mother and me and our family unit's history. The history between your mother and me and your history are inextricably intertwined, as it well should be.

I look at photos from before your mother and I were married. The first trip we took together, a long weekend in Newport that featured probably the most misleading room description of all time. ("Water view!" Yes, technically if you mashed your face against the wall and looked through the window, you could see water.) A jaunt to Italy to unite with your mother on a work trip to meet Nonna for the first time. We look a lot younger. Hell, even in those photos after you were born, we look noticeably more youthful. Indiana Jones: "It's not the years, it's the mileage."

And it sounds kind of crazy given our obsession with age and the premium on looking as youthful as possible, but believe it or not, seeing how much we've aged is not the worst feeling in the world. It means that we've been through almost 10 years of history—planning three wedding ceremonies (the symbolic one in Tulum, the City Hall one in New York, the Catholic one in Tokyo), going through two pregnancies and births, applying to many preschools, enduring job firings and hirings, fighting and making up, coordinating multiple home moves, starting new careers, raising two girls. It would be nice if we continue to age together, striding ahead, facing one challenge after another, perhaps battered but never unbowed, and in the end, intact and dignified, like a pair of old shoes.

3

MIND OVER MATTER

"**N**othing is impossible."

My parents—your grandparents—said this to me repeatedly when I was a child.

"You can do anything you want if you set your mind to it."

I would look at them and nod, unblinking and earnest.

"Nothing is impossible."

This became my mantra.

And when my eight-year-old self parroted this to my classmates at school, one of them responded, "Try flying to the end of this cafeteria." I shut my ass up for the rest of lunch.

There are in fact many physical limitations that all of us have, and not all of them involve superhuman feats. Listen up, because you'll be the ones inheriting these genes.

When I went to the doctor as a one-year-old, he said that I would definitely need eyeglasses at some point. Eight years later, when I was sitting unnaturally close to the TV and complaining to my parents about the teachers not writing strong enough on the blackboard, it was time. It has played out in almost the same way and even earlier for you, Alessandra. But my vision issues were not limited to corrective lenses; I had to get regularly checked by retina specialists as well.

When you girls were about three and two years old, I finished putting you to bed and was reading emails and such on my iPhone. I wiped that screen several times, trying to get rid of this persistent grease spot. The next morning, on my way to work, something didn't feel right. I kept on looking around, toward the azure sky, against any solid background, just to see what might be the problem. And then it became clear, in a sense: everything I looked at with my right eye, the very thing I was looking at—say, the period at the end of a sentence—it seemed like someone had used the eraser at the end of a pencil to smudge it.

My education in retina issues, which already been about seven years and running, took a big jump that afternoon.

The retina is the light-sensitive tissue lining the back of your eyeball. Light rays come in through the cornea, the pupil, and the lens. The rays hit the retina, which then processes these rays and sends impulses via the optic nerve to the brain, which interprets these rays as images. And filling the inside of your eyeball is this vitreous gel. You know how you look at a clear blue sky and see a tiny amoeba-like thing? That's called a floater, a particle within the gel. As you get older, that gel starts to dissolve and become liquid, and it starts to sag like a beanbag, which is normal.

The problem was that as the gel inside the eyeball was sagging, it was pulling at my retina, which was causing that smudge at my focal point. The risk was that it could cause the retina to tear or detach—the warning signs would be flashes of light or a curtain over a portion of my visual field. Once that happened, I needed to have eye surgery within 48 hours or risk permanent vision damage. And no matter how successful the surgery was, merely having that invasive procedure would set me on the path for further eye surgeries.

There was nothing to do except wait this out—to let the beanbag sag. Maybe it would gently pull off, like a bandage, and the retina would stretch but not break, and that would be that. Or if it did tear, then it was time for surgery.

If you have hypochondriac tendencies and like your head getting messed with, I would recommend having a vision problem. You start second-guessing everything. Was that thing I saw as clear as before? What's the halo effect and is that what I'm experiencing? Am I seeing more floaters than usual? What are flashes anyway?

Of course, less than 24 hours later, I was before the same retina doctor again and just as he was about to boot me out of the office for imagining a problem where there was none, he said, "Well, you were right."

The good news was that there was no retina tear.

But the reason why I was at the office this time was different. Instead of some tiny floaters, I now saw a single giant one. If I looked at something 10 feet away, this floater was about one foot by one foot—and it was right in the middle of everything I was looking at. It was this giant translucent patch that blurred my vision, followed my focal point and bunched up at times, making it seem even darker and more ominous. There was a literal black cloud in my eye.

No no, the doctor insisted. This is good news. You don't need surgery, remember? We avoided the path to further eye surgeries?

Yeah, but...I can't fricking see. I could technically see, but through the worst Instagram filter ever, "Dirty Saran Wrap."

I am here to tell you that vision, like walking without foot pain, is very underrated. To be constantly looking through the Dirty Saran Wrap filter, blocking everything I was looking at—that was demoralizing as hell. In search of any encouragement and support, I went on a couple of online forums about dealing with floaters and instead found that other posters were contemplating suicide because their situations felt so hopeless.

In follow-up visits, I peppered this doctor with as many questions as I could think of: any eye exercises I could do, food or vitamins I could take, maybe a vitrectomy that would refill the eyeball with gel, maybe an eyeball transplant from a genetically engineered superman with X-ray vision. And after he shot down all of these options like an Army ranger sniper and took stock of the extremely glum expression on my face, the doctor told me that the mind is extremely powerful. The mind can process deficiencies and adapt and work around them. He brought up clothes. If we think about it, clothes are foreign items constantly touching our skin in weird ways, depending on how we move, but we don't freak out about it and accept it for what it is. It was an interesting thought that echoed in my head as I walked to work, suddenly preoccupied with how my suit was touching every square inch of my body.

The words did not take immediately. I'll always remember watching the opening scenes of *Prometheus* in the theater and thinking that I'll never be able to enjoy movies in quite the same way again. It was easy to fall into self-pitying mode, because the world sure feels a little bit smaller when you can't see as well.

After a while, I started to think about what exactly vision means. Yeah, heavy stuff, right?

I came to the conclusion that sight itself was important to literally navigate my way through life. I needed my eyes to stay out of physical danger, to not get run over by cars or trucks or bike messengers or any of the 14 million other inhabitants of New York City, or avoid the punches thrown by my adversary at the latest deposition. Well, certainly the floater was not preventing me from doing that because it wasn't completely blocking my field of vision. I also needed my eyes to do work, and while the floater was distracting and made it harder for me to concentrate, I could still manage to read. All in all, the floater was not risking my life or my livelihood, which meant that it was more in the "annoying" category.

But I really started to turn a corner when I realized that a critical function of vision is the creation of memories. When I got home and kissed you and you showed me macaroni glued to a piece of paper that your preschool called "art," and when I remembered it the following afternoon with a soft smile—the floater wasn't there when I reimagined that scene. That giant effin' floater would never reside in any of my memories when I recalled them. The only memory that was ruined by the floater was *Prometheus*, and truth be told, man, that movie did not live up to the hype.

The mind is often at odds with the body, and where this battle is most sharply delineated is in sports. When I was a boy, my parents told me about the legend of Shun Fujimoto, the Japanese gymnast who broke his kneecap during his floor routine at the 1976 Olympics. Refusing to even let his teammates know he was injured, he then competed in the pommel horse and rings events, culminating in a twisting somersault dismount that further resulted in a dislocated kneecap and torn ligaments. He stuck that landing and hobbled over to his coaches. His Olympics was over. His gymnastics career was also over. He also got a 9.7, the highest score of his career, which allowed Japan to win the team gold over the Soviet Union.

This story is soooooooo incredibly, indelibly Japanese: the silent suffering, the completion of a task in the face of excruciating pain, the sacrifice of oneself, and the belief in the primacy of human will. Broadly speaking, we East Asians believe that repetition and persistence can prevail over any obstacle, any pain.

We Italians...*ma stai scherzando*?!? *Che cazzo dici*? *VAI A CACARE*. Not exactly the same mentality.

Once we moved to Italy when I was 11 years old, I started following *calcio*, soccer, and became a hard-core fan, a *tifoso*, whose etymology is typhus, which says all you need to know about that person's passion. I can tell you, from 1986 and after, how each Italian World Cup campaign ended and the exact place I was when it did. My best sports memory ever was watching that 2006 World Cup final in my New York apartment—alone, because I was going to be insufferable watching it with anyone else—and watching Italy beat France on penalty kicks. Anyone who lived through Italy's previous penalty failures (1990, 1994, 1998) still finds it hard to believe that they actually won.

I am just as equally a diehard fan of AS Roma, a rarity among Italians, as their allegiance toward their hometown team is usually stronger than that for the national squad. When I arrived in Rome, the team had begun the path to its second title. On the very last game of that *scudetto*-winning season, a 3-1 win against Torino, I was in the Stadio Olimpico with my father. It was the type of bonding experience that I can only aspire to have with you some day. Among the fans ascending into a euphoric level of crazy, one of them gave me a homemade knit red and yellow scarf, and my allegiance was forever set in stone.

Even after leaving Europe, I continued to follow *calcio* from the U.S., and I'm always struck by the differences in sporting mentalities, between the cool pragmatism that is second nature to many Europeans and the never-say-die, fight-until-mathematically-eliminated drive of Americans. The juxtaposition was never starker when the U.S. national team coach Jurgen Klinsmann, a born-and-bred German, said just before the 2014 World Cup:

"We cannot win this World Cup, because we are not at that level yet. For us, we would have to play the game of our lives seven times to win the tournament."

The unbiased soccer expert would have agreed with the German's words about the U.S. team. They were ultimately accurate. They also caused the American public to go bananas, because that was like capitulating before a war.

My God, as I write this sentence, there are many, many, many flaws with the United States of America, but this is still the one place on this planet that most resembles a meritocracy. It doesn't mean that everyone starts the race at the same point. It doesn't mean that everyone is guaranteed to get what they deserve. But it does mean that here, by dint of hard work and perseverance, you are more likely to get to where you want to be. No other country comes close, be it because of immutable caste structures, government indifference, or government intent. "Nothing is impossible." Is that phrase thrown about so lightly in other corners of the world, the idea that you can do anything?

But as you two grow older, time and experience may start to erode this belief that you are in control of your destiny. Every person has had this moment when he couldn't overcome an obstacle. I'm not talking about a temporary setback, after which she decides to redouble her efforts and the motivational music swells and there's some sort of inspirational montage and she manages to show the world that she succeeded. I mean the quiet, wholly anticlimactic moment when one realizes that she does not have the capability to go any further.

When I met your Uncle Matt our sophomore year of high school, he had been playing chess for seven years. His stated future goal to anyone who would listen was "World Chess Champion." He always had a chess set on him, played during class (he reveled in describing how one teacher gave him a D and said it was a gift) and entered tournaments on the weekends. He dropped out of college to play in tournaments in Europe. And when he was 19, he was completely crushed by a 13-year-old, and to make things worse, the little snot managed to be completely condescending during the post-mortem of the match. The dream didn't die right there and then, but that was the first dagger of doubt, a sudden realization of the limits of physical or mental capability. Similar dreams have died on baseball fields and basketball courts everywhere.

For others who aren't in sports, it may happen in less dramatic fashion—a gradual dawning. You do well in school and you get a good job, do everything right, reach for greater things and discover at some point:

"Uh oh, I might have reached my ceiling."

Unlike Uncle Matt, this cold shower will hopefully occur after you enter college. Maybe then, you will come upon one of the oldest debates in all of psychology: nature vs. nurture.

I envision you being inspired and exhilarated by the number of budding scholars surrounding you—young adults beginning to grasp their enormous possibility and craving intellectual stimulation. Late into the night, you will argue: is man shaped by his genes, and are they by and large determinative of his destiny? Or is a person's environment more important—can you actually mold a person into a desired shape? There will be heated debates over free will, predestination, citation to studies with bell curves, and the term "empirical evidence" may be thrown around a number of times.

(If you're drinking and smoking a crazy amount while inhaling Doritos and learning about this by watching *Trading Places*... we're paying $80k a year for this? Come on dude, you're killing us.)

As you get older, this debate becomes less theoretical. You may, like Uncle Matt (who has transformed himself into the best crossword puzzle maker in this country), start to see your ceiling. Some of these limitations may be just physical genetic traits passed down—you've never been coordinated; when you get nervous, you tend to revert to a tic; you used to be a three-sport athlete, but you've turned into the same body shape as your mother. And then there are personality traits that appear to fall into that same category: you're thin-skinned, you hate the spotlight, you're not very good with numbers. Just like your parents. And as you get older, what encompasses "nature" will get even fuzzier. You may think, "It's ingrained in me," when it's really about upbringing and culture in which you've been raised. But at what point can you overcome your genetics and your environment by sheer will?

By the time these thoughts occur to you, they may coincide with a child of your own. And if you ever do find yourself blessed with child, you may hold a newborn smaller than your forearm and after all of the observations you make of the physical—this skin is so soft, this hair is so downy, these fingernails are so tiny—you may veer toward the more abstract. And you will ask yourself a question, half in curiosity and half in dread.

"I wonder whether this baby is going to turn out like me."

A mini debate between nature and nurture is now playing out in this little being: the struggle between the genes from your blood relatives against your ability to break away from them and forge a new destiny regardless of those predispositions.

One of the things you say that will make me drop everything and redirect my attention to you: "I can't do it." At your impressionable ages, I don't want you to even entertain the possibility of limits—I want you to persist, to stick with it, to know the satisfaction of overcoming. Alessandra, we notice this particular quality in you. You insist and you wear down and Lord, as much as we have suffered as a result, we cannot help but be in awe of your will.

But as you grow older, you will hear "I can't do it" more and more often, from others and yourself. There will be a million excuses as to why, that you don't have the time, that you were handicapped by factors out of your control, that it's not an inherent part of your character to be able to do this impossible thing.

It's not technically true. With discipline, an overwhelming number of things in this world can be accomplished. Think of all the things that you can do with unlimited discipline: have the concentration and determination to put in the work and get good grades; work out till you have that rock-hard body; put in the hours to crush every work assignment. The flip side to all of this overachievement is that you'd probably not be much fun either. You'd never be the one who hangs out for that extra beer after work, or do something crazy, or make spontaneous plans, because that discipline would rein you in. Part of being a fun person is losing that control once in a while.

So when you say you can't do it, it's usually a result of having made the mental calculus that the costs extracted from accomplishing something outweigh the benefits. This is a critical distinction from being physically unable to do it. It's still in your hands.

Once I saw the promo for this *Dateline* segment teasing something to the effect of, "Why are some people lucky and why are others unlucky?" I had to know. This was going to unlock one of life's secrets and catapult me into a rarified class. The report went into detail about these people's lives and the series of fortunate and unfortunate things that happened to them. And the answer?

Attitude.

There were in fact no drastic differences in the lives of the lucky and unlucky. The "fortunate" ones had actually gone through their share of misfortunes and tragedies—but they didn't stop at "woe is me." They continued to see themselves as lucky because they saw worse things that could have happened, managed to find silver linings in those clouds, or used those negative experiences to create a positive one. It starts with your attitude.

Even things that appear to be out of your hands are really within your reach. "Being happy" would seem to depend upon a number of extraneous forces that are completely out of your control, or perhaps something so fundamental to your being that it is immutable. But studies are showing that there are a number of things that you can do—being social, exercising, praying or meditating—that have been proven to increase your happiness. The facial feedback hypothesis, initially developed by Charles Darwin, says that facial movement can influence emotional experience. This turns conventional wisdom on its head. We normally think of smiling as the result of our emotion, but it may be the other way around—the smile actually makes us feel better. It stimulates the brain's reward mechanisms. Even when you don't mean it, you may actually be able to will your way to a better place. Fake it till you make it.

And really, who's to say what's possible? How do you even know what your limits are?

Spinning class. You'll be chugging along, barely keeping up with the others. The lungs are on fire and the legs are trembling. You'll look at the clock and see that you have twenty-three minutes left, which is 1,380 seconds, and count off 10 seconds at a time, and see what percentage 10 seconds was, and hopefully by the time you figure that out there's only 16 minutes left. There is no way that you can finish. You actually envision about what may happen if you start convulsing and whether this may actually cause a stoppage in the class. You are on the brink of collapse.

And then the instructor, "inspirationally exhorting" to date, takes a different tone.

"COME ON!!! LET'S GO!!! STOP FUCKING AROUND!!!"

Despite being heretofore on the verge of a full-body breakdown, you will reach another new level where you break through that wall of pain, and attain another plateau of energy that you could not have even imagined in your mind. Sometimes you need someone else to help get you beyond the limits you've circumscribed. As crazy as it sounds, you shouldn't just limit yourself to what your mind can imagine. It can be even more. You just need to be open to it.

For me to claim that you can solve all your problems simply by putting your mind to it—that willpower alone can overcome physical and mental infirmities—is simplistic and dangerous. But I know for damn sure that if you don't try to do it, then you're definitely going to fail. Of course, just having the mentality that you can do it won't automatically lead to triumph. But not having this mentality is like dealing yourself a crippling blow before you have even started.

This is the "nothing is impossible" mantra to which you must, must, must adhere. I don't care if you find out that in many situations, the contrary may be true. You need to start out with and hold onto a belief that you are in charge of your own destiny, that you will not be thrown about by the vagaries of random events. Without this belief, then you are going to play out your life subject to a very controlled and limited set of outcomes. Whatever you do, you don't succumb to your conditions. You go out there and set your sights on having the game of your lives seven times in a row, the odds be damned.

Nothing is impossible. Everything is possible.

And by the time you're 70, you'll be damn sure that you can fly across the cafeteria, because by then, everyone will be wearing jetpacks. "YOU DIDN'T SAY HOW I COULD GET FROM HERE TO THERE. I KNOW LOOPHOLES CUZ I'M A LAWYER, BITCH!"

4

YOUR GUIDING RULE

BALANCE

On a daily basis, this is the most important thing you need to keep in mind. I believe that the pursuit and attainment of balance in all aspects—your being, your thoughts, your actions—is crucial to a healthy and fulfilling existence.

Of course, balance means a lot of things in many different contexts. What it means to me first and foremost is that there are no absolutes. Being a lawyer has been integral in coming to this realization.

I've done a lot of asbestos litigation in my career. This practice niche is the legal equivalent of the Mos Eisley Cantina Bar from *Star Wars*, sneered at by the prestigious white-shoe law firms and comprised of some of the most wretched, villainous scum you will ever meet.

Asbestos is a naturally occurring mineral, a rock that is mined from the earth. Somehow, someway, man discovered that asbestos rock and its fibers were incredibly heat-resistant; there are cooking pots and utensils dating from 4,500 years ago that were strengthened with asbestos. Legend also has Charlemagne dining with an asbestos tablecloth, which was cleaned after meals by being thrown into a fireplace. (This easily earned its title of "Best Ninth-Century Trick That Will Blow Your Frickin' Mind.") As it began to be used in different industrial applications beginning in the 19th century, such as insulation and construction materials, asbestos was dubbed "the miracle rock."

The problem, as people began to find out, was that anyone who worked with or in the vicinity of asbestos products started to develop breathing problems. If I had a large piece of asbestos rock sitting on my desk, it wouldn't have any impact on my health no matter how long it stayed there. But if I sanded or ground the rock to release its dust and then breathed that dust, and then did it on a fairly consistent basis over a long period of time...well, I would probably come down with a disease many years later.

For those who come down with a bona fide asbestos-related illness, the end can come in a startlingly rapid manner. It starts with a persistent cough, some difficulty in breathing. A hospital visit may result in the discovery of fluid in the lungs. And if there's a diagnosis of mesothelioma, cancer of the lining of the lung or peritoneum, that person has likely about a year to live. There's a need to take that person's testimony as soon as possible. And often, to reduce the inconvenience to the plaintiff, the deposition will be held in that person's home. There may be as many as 20 attorneys converging at this dying man's home, ready to ask questions about what products he used, prod him about gaps in his memory, wait during breaks when the plaintiff is not feeling well enough to continue, then resume to try to steer him toward more favorable testimony and minimize the impact of his words.

I have been one of those defense attorneys.

The natural reaction is: "Hey dickhead, do you not have any conscience? How can you defend corporations that actually used hazardous substances in their products that killed these unknowing consumers? And you harass these people, with months left to live, in their own homes? How do you sleep at night, you immoral, money-grubbing, sleazy excuse of a human being?" (I'm really holding back on the language here.) It is understandable to get the outrage and the righteousness all lathered up—I felt that way upon finding out that I would be doing these cases. Sure, I needed to pay off my student loans, but at what cost?

But after working on these cases for a while, I realized that nothing was ever clear-cut.

Part of it was just maturing as a lawyer. Everyone expects that attorneys are pit bull advocates for causes that they truly believe in, but the mark of an excellent attorney is to be able to argue just as vehemently for a position completely contrary to personal convictions. (Reason #244 why being a litigation attorney can warp your soul.) I also would start to note the holes in plaintiffs' cases, e.g., the plaintiff claiming that asbestos products caused his lung cancer when he also smoked a pack a day for 50 years; the plaintiff testifying that he used my client's product but was obviously lying because he described in detail a product that was never made; the plaintiff who worked with many more carcinogenic products so my client's product could not have caused his injury; and so on. No matter how airtight the plaintiff's case initially seemed to be, there would be wriggle room for a colorable, if not strong, defense.

When I was still green, I met with a defense expert to talk about epidemiological and industrial hygiene studies. And in a moment of bluntness and sloth, I asked him what the tipping point was—generally, when was that moment where a person's use of certain asbestos products would lead to disease.

And I'll never forget his reaction: a look of incredulity and perhaps a touch of disappointment. His response, as though it should have been beyond obvious: "We're not going to find out within our lifetimes." These were biological changes that were happening on a microscopic level—not just cellular, not just genetic, but even further within, at the protein level—of which humans currently had only a rudimentary understanding. There were people who could be around asbestos-containing brake products for many years, smoke a pack a day, and not fall ill. Then again, there could be someone who simply moonlighted as a mechanic and many years later, discover that he did not have the constitution to withstand the damage done to his body.

I tell you all of this, about having and then easily overcoming initial reservations about representing asbestos defendants, because rarely is anything absolute. Even medicine—which is regarded as SCIENCE and therefore assumed to be this cut-and-dry area of absolutes—is replete with gray areas, because man simply has not evolved to the point where we can say for certain what cause leads to what effect.

Rarely is there stark black or white. (The only exception being Hitler. You cannot praise any aspect of him, no matter how innocuous. I'm serious, people will go bananas. And the proof is that the reflexive thought to the above is that it is an anti-anti-Hitler comment.) What I write may seem like immutable pronouncements, without any room for flexibility. But every piece of my advice is to be taken with a bit of caution, a grain of salt. When you end up reading something "outrageous" later, or pieces of advice that are seemingly contradictory, remember this caveat.

Because in the end, isn't everything negotiable and constrained by the boundaries of common sense? No matter how worthy a principle may be, when it's taken to an extreme, it can become counterproductive. Everyone can agree that you should be honest and that it's a virtue all of us should have. Well, what if you were completely incapable of telling a so-called white lie, shading the truth or even being able to be diplomatic?

"Are you planning my surprise birthday party?"

"Is that your best offer?"

"Do I need to lose weight?"

The steadfast adherence to a worthy character trait is admirable, but there comes a point when practicality overcomes idealism. (In this regard, my father would often say that pooping at the office was like stealing from your employer because you were wasting time. It took a while for me to realize how ridiculous this was. And the only appropriate reaction is to put on your best John McEnroe face and go, "You have GOT to be shitting me.")

What else does balance mean?

Because it's not about absolutes, it connotes moderation, and therein probably lies the truth of why no one ever emphasizes how important balance is. It's boring as hell. Where's the fun in moderation, in writing in Arial 12-point font about the virtues of driving 50 mph on the freeway or the sensibility of non-fat ice cream? Which headline makes you click on the story: "Practical Steps to End the Stalemate of the American Political System," or "The Twenty Politicians Who Should Be Drawn and Quartered to End American Political Gridlock"?

When you're young, you tend to veer toward extreme emotion. Either something is the GREATEST THING EVER or OMG THE WORST MOST HORRIBLE THING THAT'S HAPPENED IN HUMAN HISTORY and I realize that this is just part of being a teenager or a young adult. But just because it may come naturally to you, doesn't mean that you have to just succumb to this ping-ponging from one extreme to another. The more conscious you are of it, the more you can try to be in control. Be aware of yourselves. Willpower. Shun Fujimoto.

Balance means not going to extremes in search of short-term gratification. This seems like a killjoy statement. People tend to equate the pursuit of extremes with living life to the fullest. YOLO. (You see, kids, that's an acronym for You Only

Live Once, which was popularized in a rap song entitled "The Motto" by the Canadian rap artist Drake. But really, the correct acronym should be YLOO, because the truly grammatically correct expression should be "You Live Only Once," as "only" should be modifying "once." So I would point this out on the streets of the Bronx when you're quoting the rap artist Drake.)

But the problem with YLOO is that life is not about chasing every high. Life is not the continuous pursuit of wish fulfillment. Such a view lends itself to short-term thinking. And if you truly lived like this, it would be exhausting, and ultimately the law of diminishing returns would cut into the enjoyment of each successive endeavor.

One of the hallmarks of maturity is a recognition that even the most ecstatically fun things will lose their ability to please when you overdose on them. I saw it the first time you went to Disney World. The first day, the sensory overload and the excitement transformed you into primal creatures seeking the next rush of adrenaline as you darted from ride to store to candy shop to character meet (much like the first time I went to Disneyland 30 years earlier). The second day, there was a marked change in your demeanor—still excited, but a bit more subdued. And by the fourth day in Orlando, you wanted to stay at the hotel pool instead, which bummed me out to no end. That's all it takes for it to be the most exciting to the most mundane. Again, it certainly doesn't mean that you can't strive for that high—that's what life is all about. But you need to realize that not every day is going to be prom night, or spring break, or your wedding day, and that's okay. You need your share of the monotonous and even crappy days to make the other special days extra special.

With a proper sense of balance, you develop a heightened perception and appreciation of good and bad things. You cannot truly appreciate the good in life until you've gone through some real bad stuff. Every time your mother makes a meal—no matter how whipped-up and simple it is—I try to make sure to thank her afterward. Why is that?

Because I spent about 13 years of my previous existence making ramen, tuna fish sandwiches, or pasta as my dinner. Even at your young ages, you two have already noted how inept I am in the kitchen, as evidenced by the completion of a Father's Day class assignment that asked, "The best meal my dad makes is _____." I know how hard you must have combed your brain to come up with something, Sofia, and I'm pretty sure "cereal" is not an acceptable answer.

Anyway, I would make the tuna fish sandwich in about four minutes: two slices of Wonder Bread (maybe if I wanted to make it extra special, I'd toast them), crack open the can of tuna, put a dollop of mayo INSIDE the can, use a fork to mix the tuna and mayo INSIDE the can (thereby avoiding the need of having to wash an extra bowl), then spread it on the bread.

In my hands, even something as simple as the making of pasta seemed to descend a couple of levels of class. I should preface all of this with my insistence that I did not forsake my Italian background and can appreciate the hell out of an exquisite pasta and great food. It's just that, well, I was a single guy whose food at home tended to be viewed as fuel, not an experience.

So it was out of the question for me to heat up spaghetti sauce in a separate pan. I would dump the refrigerated sauce from the jar onto the finished pasta, mix it well, and the result would be a lukewarm concoction. When the jar ran low on sauce...ahh, that's when my intelligence went into overdrive. I would take the boiled pasta and deposit all of it INTO THE JAR, close the lid, and then shake it vigorously like I was Tom Cruise making a martini in *Cocktail*. Only then could I be completely satisfied that I got every last iota of spaghetti sauce from the jar. I'm turning red just typing these paragraphs out. And thank God those lonely and pathetic nights existed, because without them, I wouldn't remotely appreciate your mother's cooking.

When you have balance, you have perspective. With regard to unintentional, fortuitous life events—no matter how good something seems to be, there can be a detriment. This is a benefit of having the long-term view. You need to be able to see the bigger picture that the seemingly greatest and happiest and most gratifying event can potentially have a downside. Which sounds very doom and gloom, but the flip side is that the opposite is true as well. The most wretched event can yield a little sliver of light that can sustain you and strengthen you. There's a reason why "What does not kill me makes me stronger" is tattooed over thousands upon thousands of bodies (please do not do this).

Subconsciously, people crave balance, particularly when their expectations play an outsize part in their perceptions. Out-of-towners will often say that New Yorkers are nice. Wrong. It's only because New Yorkers have such a fearsome reputation for being the biggest assholes on the planet (the old joke being

"Can you tell me where the Empire State Building is, or should I just go fuck myself?") and they manage not to live up to the worst stereotypes. You can then use the gulf between expectation and reality to your advantage and in a variety of contexts. Color in a painting will pop when surrounded by neutral tones. A small, modest joke will seem hilarious when buried in a serious, deep scene. The rich, the good-looking, and the powerful always get inordinately too much credit for merely exhibiting shreds of human decency. Sometimes, the contrast can be just as impactful as an extreme.

Society lauds the extremist personality—the attention to minutiae of a Coco Chanel, the ruthless competitiveness of a Michael Jordan, the insane demands of a Steve Jobs—because it can act as a torch for human excellence and the capacity to overcome limits. And the human race is poorer without it. But balance means recognizing that everything has a cost.

On the list of the most underrated coaches in football history is Joe Gibbs, the former coach of the Washington Redskins. I think the world of him, as he's won three Super Bowls with three different quarterbacks, and more important, because he always conducted himself with a certain grace. But I also remember him recounting that after years and years of a 24/7 existence coaching the team, one night he went into his kid's room to kiss his sleeping boy good night and was shocked to find stubble on that face. If you see greatness due to a single-minded devotion to a goal, there's usually a sacrifice that had to be made: friends, a social life, a family, a non-dysfunctional family, a true enjoyment of life.

We often do not recognize that "success" is a balance of skills. For a really long time, I used to think that the great lawyers were the most intelligent ones. It made complete sense, no? The most intelligent ones usually were those who studied the hardest and accumulated the most knowledge and got the best grades. They ended up at the best law firms, and they continued to build upon that intelligence and worked on the most challenging cases and won the most and made partner first. Success was practically preordained. And then very late, sometime in my late 20s, I started to realize how exceedingly simplistic that was.

The best and most successful lawyers are not necessarily the most intelligent ones. Most of them have the work ethic. But they also need the charisma and confidence to attract clients. If they are leading the firm, they need financial acumen and an entrepreneurial instinct. They need to relate to and motivate not just fellow partners and associates, but also the support staff. They need that drive, to never feel satiated with success. All of these characteristics come into play when a great attorney emerges. If you think that it's only book smarts that determine success, that's way off. Sure, it's impressive to be able to recite entire Shakespeare monologues with facility. But the much rarer bird is someone who can do that and also quote *Dumb and Dumber*.

I should have known this. I've followed sports all my life. I knew that my idol Larry Bird wasn't the best athlete in the NBA, not even close. Wayne Gretzky wasn't the fastest skater and he never had the hardest slap shot. Tom Brady doesn't have the strongest arm. But they had other qualities to make up for these deficiencies: intelligence, vision, competitiveness, the ability to elevate their teammates' play, a love of the game that drove the unrelenting work ethic. This concept applies to virtually any other field. Is simply "the best food" the only determinant of "the best restaurant?" No. Presentation. Service. Ambience. They all play roles in what constitutes the best dining experience. There is rarely one metric that is indicative of success. You must have a balance of many.

You cannot have it all. What you should say in your very next breath is that having it all is nonetheless your goal. You strive for the best in each aspect of your life: fulfillment in your personal development, your relationship with friends and family, spiritual contentment, work, your significant other. A happy life is a balanced one.

5

"DESCRIBE YOURSELF
IN THREE WORDS"

Once you go on interviews for work, you may get a question like the above.

It will most probably be for an entry-level job, because this question is kind of lame. It's well-nigh impossible to describe yourself in three words. And merely saying these words doesn't make it so. The purpose of the question is not to necessarily find out about you, but rather what's important to you, what you think of yourself, and what you want others to know about you. If other people are asked what three words would best describe you, I would want them to mention a variation of the following. These are the qualities that must reside deep within you and constitute your very essence.

Humble. Honorable. Kind.

I can already sense how underwhelmed you are.

Yes, these qualities must sound incredibly trite and sappy

and easy to follow. The part about them being trite and sappy is true; the second part about them being easy to follow is absolutely false. It actually becomes more and more difficult the older you get. As a matter of fact, in trying to show you how difficult it is to be all of the above, I may end up convincing you that it's easier and more profitable to be an arrogant bastard with a complete lack of morals. Let's see how I do.

"HUMBLE"

Let's talk about history. Not just human history, but from the Big Bang. Scientists generally agree about the age of the universe, and I could give you a number that will end in a lot of zeroes, but it may be hard to truly wrap your heads around that figure, so let's condense that entire period into a manageable number, say one year. So from the Big Bang until the moment you are reading this sentence is exactly one year.

(Isn't this a positively revolutionary calculation of time? Only after spending days on it—actually doing the math and a timeline and everything—did I see that Carl Sagan and Neil deGrasse Tyson had already popularized "The Cosmic Calendar." But thank God no one's heard of them.)

Back to the one-year calendar of all history. When do you think dinosaurs were wiped out by that giant meteor or asteroid? Which month would that have been? July? Way off. Maybe September? No, that's when Earth would have been formed. October? Thanksgiving? Try December 25.

On that same scale, when did man start to walk upright?

Three hours before the end of the year, at 9 p.m. on December 31. The first civilization would have appeared about 15 to 20 seconds ago. Less than six seconds before the New Year, man began to write. The Revolutionary War? A half second ago. Our life spans are but a millisecond on this one-year scale of history.

All right, now that we've addressed the awesome breadth of time, let's take stock of how large this world is. There are over seven billion people on this planet, also a number that people can casually cite but really have no idea how big it is.

If you started counting now, one number per second, you would get to seven billion...in approximately 221 years. If every person were stacked on top of one another, you could go to the moon and back. More than 13 times. Seven billion steps along the equator? You would go around the earth 133 times. And finally, a fact you two can more properly appreciate: if you had seven billion M&Ms, you could fill up three Olympic-sized swimming pools.

Each one of these seven billion other people are just like you, whose aspirations and loves and tragedies are just as life-changing to them as they are to you.

I'm going through this prolonged exercise of trying to make you aware of the mind-boggling scope of time and the enormous number of people on this planet because as your father and as someone who loves you with every fiber of my being, I need to say this:

YOU AREN'T THAT BIG OF A DEAL.

It doesn't matter how acclaimed or revered or accomplished you become—you're the best-dressed kid at school, you're homecoming queen for four years straight, you're the valedictorian at Stanford, you are worth 10 billion dollars, you win the Pritzker Architecture Prize, you have 50 million followers, you become Senator, you win 19 majors, your film wins 12 Oscars, you cure cancer, you discover a way for humans to double their life spans, you learn how to set the clock on your VCR, you make a brilliant but incredibly outdated joke—let's make sure it's set in its proper context. In the grand scheme of things, we are inexorably finite.

Every person before and after us will age, with all of us having the same signs. Crow's feet around the eyes. Dimples in the wrong places. A hangover after a night of carousing, which never happened before. Weird splotches, after which we learn the term "age spots." Elasticity of the skin. Graying at the temples, or five o'clock shadow, or nose hairs, or *shudder* worse. The paunch that won't go away, no matter how hard we work out. The forgetfulness...we have that person's name right on the tip of our tongue—we can picture him right there, with that stupid face. Our journeys on this planet all end up in the same place. (Dead.)

But hold on! Don't pull the covers over your head just yet. It's a sign of a conscious and responsible mind to wonder and be cognizant about all of this. And when you can have the capacity to maintain the perspective to place your importance in the context of all of time and space, it's much easier to apply this to a personal level.

At this point in your lives, there are no stories of me teaching you humility. There is no need to. It's healthy for a child to have a good sense of ego. And you demonstrate humility in the way you are asking a million questions about how the world works. But at some point, these questions will start to wane, and it's probably because you think you know the answers. I am well aware that it is a necessary rite of passage for every teenager/early 20-something to be proved otherwise, but you need to always keep this in mind: you don't know as much as you think you do. You need to accept that others have more knowledge just by virtue of their age and experience. Even now, with all these years under my belt, I discover new and incredibly frustrating ways where I am completely wrong.

When you're humble, because you can readily accept that you do not have all the answers, you will not hesitate to ask the most basic, common sense questions—the ones that others are afraid to ask—because you will not be concerned about other people's perceptions. You will value a complete understanding of the facts, which is more important. In time, after you've reached a certain job or level and get a tough question, you will be tempted by guessing or blustering your way through an answer. Resist. It's better to be circumspect and verify later than to be wrong at the outset. And if it's a question to which you should have known the answer to in the first place...well, whose fault was that?

However great the job you did, there is always room to improve. Being a nitpicky perfectionist can be a prison in and of itself. But following the sense of satisfaction that you feel in a job well done, have the humility to think about evolving and becoming better. There's always some person who's outworking you and trying to get an edge. What are you doing to improve?

Humility enables you to keep a healthy sense of absurdity within the context of any accomplishment or any impending decision, no matter how momentous it seems. You have to strive to not take yourself so seriously, even if your job requires that you perform critical and life-saving tasks. In other words, this thought must occur to you: "I cannot believe that millions of years ago, man tried to walk upright instead of being on all fours, and now as President of the United States, I'm about to push a button that will commence a global war against Skynet and the Terminator X-2000."

You don't need to brag about what you did. You don't need to call attention to your awesome accomplishment. Countless others have done what you just did, and most likely, better. It's always more impressive to not broadcast your feats, especially in this day and age, and to have others discover what you've done. If you have happened to accomplish something of monumental importance that draws in universal accolades, then you let others point that out. You don't need to say a damn thing.

In fact, bragging about what one has and what one can do is a universal sign of insecurity. He does it to attempt to pump up his self-worth and increase his social standing and intimidate his rivals, and quite frankly, it is extremely effective, but only with the easily-impressed. But deep down, anyone who's completely confident about her abilities has no need to resort to convincing others. They already know.

Besides, whatever you did do, you did not do on your own. Someone had to have helped: people who mentored you, who worked alongside you, who worked below you. And that's not accounting for the emotional support you've received from those close to you, the family members, friends. If you are completely convinced that you did in fact do this all by yourself and absolutely no one contributed to your success (which I guarantee is not possible), then thank the Good Lord, or a higher being, or fate. Steve Jobs conceived and created a dazzling computer system whose technological features signaled the future. It was a commercial failure, because in 1988, NeXT was too far ahead of its time. For you not to be aware of the role of timing is foolhardy. Have the humility to recognize that.

It is wholly natural to wonder whether being humble pays off. In a world where people can readily present only the most beautiful and glamorous version of themselves and are only occasionally busted for résumé inflation, it's tempting to buy into the idea that those who are humble are completely trampled by those who are not.

In the United States, and by God for sure in New York City, the humble approach only works to a limited extent. I would love to tell you that a humble litigator is the most effective one, but that belongs on the shelf next to other statements such as "All your classmates are making fun of you because they like you" and "He's not calling me because he respects me too much." In any zero-sum game, where any mental edge can be crucial, your adversary must have a certain respect for or a fear of you, and you ain't going to get it by cracking self-deprecating jokes.

Because there is a fine line between humility and meekness, you can't lean on "humility" as an excuse for not going forward to accomplish what you want. But when you do start to climb up that ladder and still manage to maintain a healthy sense of humility, that's when you will start to reap its benefits. The gulf between people's expectation and reality: because so many people are accustomed to a person in charge who is an arrogant ass trumpet, they're positively shocked to see one who's not, or maybe just an occasional arrogant ass trumpet.

A series of *Harvard Business Review* articles concluded that when managers demonstrate humility by admitting mistakes, accepting constructive criticism, empowering others to take larger roles, and admitting that they are not omniscient, it inspires their followers and fosters teamwork. Of course, those articles also raise the possibility that when you are humble, the downside is that you may be perceived as weak. It takes courage to be humble, because you are taking a leap of faith that your acts won't be misconstrued into weaknesses. You need to rely upon an intestinal fortitude that unjust credit to others will be exposed, while your merits will rise above the noise.

Is there a way to instill humility within yourself?

We have already gone on a number of trips with you abroad, and who knows how much of an imprint these experiences—seeing the lush countryside of the Dominican Republic, floating through the canals of Amsterdam, moving in the controlled bustle of Tokyo, tasting the sumptuous food in

Rome—will have made upon you. But my fervent wish is that as you grow older, you continue to travel far and wide. It's well worth saving your money and foregoing that trip domestically so that you can go overseas the following year. You will go to other countries, a whole new frontier existing beyond the confines of your city, your neighborhood, and your office, and you will discover how little you know about other people's history and their culture. You will see, hear, and smell beauty that is so far beyond the scope of what you can merely see or read about. You will be witness to the sheer number of people who have much worse problems to overcome, people who are not trying to make it big, but who are merely struggling to survive. And gradually, or maybe even suddenly, it will dawn on you that you are one of many. Your problems will seem smaller in comparison. Humility will dose you the perspective you need to live a healthy, balanced life.

"HONORABLE"

You must lead a life of integrity. I demand it of you.

It certainly sounds great. "Alessandra and Sofia are such women of integrity." Man alive, I'm swelling with pride just reading that sentence. I know "Alessandra and Sofia are so gorgeous" probably sounds cooler to you, but believe me, you want people to be saying the first sentence.

Honor or integrity is hard to define. It certainly starts with being honest. My parents drilled this into me: without truth, you cannot have trust. We have already had that first conversation with you after we've caught you in a lie (and remember that if you ever have that talk with your child, you CANNOT break and laugh out loud when she's got pineapple candy wrappers strewn all over her bedroom while insisting that she didn't have any). Honesty is the touchstone of an upstanding person, someone with morals. In law, if someone testifies under oath and is untruthful about a material detail, the jury is entitled to disregard the entire testimony, because that person is no longer reliable. Without honesty, everything you say or do becomes suspect or comes under a qualifier. It seals the authenticity of a promise and the security of a secret.

Parents telling their child to be honest is not unusual, except that my father—the grandfather you never met—was a spy.

He was a deep-cover intelligence offer for the Central Intelligence Agency for 20 years. Just being able to say that he used to work for the Agency was significant, because not many operatives get to have an overt retirement. He was finally able to tell anyone what he used to do, with much pride. (The flip side of this overt retirement was having to go on an apology tour afterward to all of our friends and family about deceiving them as to his profession and background.)

He was a NOC, "Non-Official Cover." You know that scene in the first *Mission: Impossible* movie where Tom Cruise is dangling from those cables and trying to upload information onto a floppy disk without triggering sound, temperature, and touch meters? He was getting a list of NOCs around the world. In this preposterous scene in this completely absurd movie, YOUR GRANDFATHER WOULD HAVE BEEN ON THIS LIST.

There was no choice but to deceive when his job entailed getting information from allies and enemies alike; even to close acquaintances he was often untruthful about his motives, his profession, and even his name. Being a NOC meant that he was not affiliated with the U.S. Embassy, so if he happened to be detained by a foreign government, he was essentially on his own, with the U.S. government in all likelihood issuing some sort of a terse disavowal of any spying activity conducted by this person.

If my father told the truth or even engaged in candor at the wrong moment, everything in his life would have been compromised—his life, his freedom, his livelihood, his family. Precisely because he knew the cost of deception to a person's reputation, he insisted that I be honest, to tell "the truth, the whole truth, and nothing but the truth." By and large, I've dutifully followed this directive, even though it's probably hurt me professionally. People can tell when you don't truly believe what you're arguing or negotiating. But when you have a reputation for telling the truth, it allows you the benefit of consistency, which anyone, even an opposing attorney, can appreciate. There isn't second-guessing of what you really mean. There shouldn't be any further delving into your motives. Yes, I understand this is all incredibly hypocritical coming from a litigation attorney whose very existence depends on the parsing of words and who trades in half-truths and concealment of weaknesses (and those are the more scrupulous ones! The dirtbag attorneys just baldly lie and bank on the truth not coming to light).

This was also what my father drilled into me: the cover-up of a lie is usually worse than the lie itself. This was a lesson primarily learned during Watergate, but it resurfaces time and again. You'd be surprised at how insignificant the original sin was and how willing the public would have been to forgive it. But when you double down and insist that you were telling the truth or otherwise lie even more to cover, and *then* you're found out...you've lost all credibility. Good luck getting that back. It is not possible to lose your reputation twice.

You can't have integrity without truth, but its limits do not end there. You can be stridently honest but not necessarily have integrity. For example, if pressed by others, you may answer that yes, you believe that there is a certain social injustice occurring. That's being honest. But to have integrity? You need to go beyond, to consistently stand up for the upstanding moral principle—no matter the ridicule, the sacrifice of money, even the tide of popular opinion. By the time Muhammad Ali died, it was easy for people to laud his courage in refusing to serve in the army and being a conscientious objector. Back then, though, would they have supported him?

One area where you can gauge a person's integrity is responsibility/credit/blame. If you're going to be working with others, there may come a time when you have to take responsibility for things for which you personally did not do anything wrong. Yes, we missed the deadline to appeal because the wrong date was calendared. Technically, this was the clock-watching, Facebook-checking, meaningless-tweeting, dumbass paralegal's fault. But you, as the one supervising this person—who had ONE JOB THAT HAD TO BE DONE RIGHT, JUST ONE—this is where you will have to fall on your sword, take that bullet, and endure the beating. Apologize unreservedly and with sincerity, without resorting to bullshit weasely language. Oh, it's massively unfair how painful it will be. You will suffer (it need not be done silently, as you can continually remind the dumbass paralegal what you did to protect him). But in the opinions of those who matter, you will emerge a better person and one with more respect.

When you two girls become older, you will get a sense of how competitive this world is, where people will put their self-interest above a code of conduct, and where people will point to others' failure to adhere to the code as an excuse. I realize that insisting that you be women of integrity puts you in a position to be mocked long and loudly, probably more by your younger contemporaries. "You're a sucker" is a retort that quickly comes to mind. Contrary to nearly every TV show and movie out there, most of the unscrupulous do not get their comeuppance in the end. The older you get, you see more examples of completely amoral behavior, and you may start to correlate the lack of integrity with the ability to ascend to certain work positions. Maybe by then, it really may not mean as much to be a person of integrity, as anachronistic as five-cent Cokes.

I don't care. This has to be a fundamental part of your personality. You are not sheep. Look beyond the short term, and to your life, and be guided by a set of principles based in morality. Not all of these rewards will be readily apparent. But they will reap benefits for you. Because when you pass from this world to the next, people will not be focusing on your net worth, or how beautiful you were, or even what you accomplished. They will be primarily talking about the content of your character. Your sense of honor and how it manifested itself in the way that you treated your family, your friends, and those whom you barely remembered. Your name.

"KIND"

Being kind flows naturally from humility and integrity.

I've noticed that there's a certain distinction that seems to be drawn between "kind" and "nice." Niceness is almost seen as pejorative compared to kindness. According to these people, here are the distinctions between being nice and kind:

NICE	KIND
Nice people are externally motivated, driven by feelings of inadequacy and seeking approval and validation from others.	Kind people are internally motivated and the roots of kindness come from their nature, which is compassionate and loving.
Nice people bend over backward to placate and oblige, driven by a fear of others being upset with them.	Kind people have good self-esteem, which means they are assertive and can set limits.
Nice people, driven by their aim to please, end up being in unhealthy, co-dependent relationships with users.	Kind people are generous and altruistic but don't find themselves in user-pleaser relationships.

Nice people can never make a real connection, because any degree of approval from others is not a substitute for true acceptance.	Kind people, because they can accept constructive criticism, are always learning, which leads to evolution and improvement in their social relationships.
Nice people are looked down upon because they are weak and needy.	Kind people are admired for their authenticity and genuineness.
When nice people commit homicides, it's because of their crippling insecurities.	When kind people commit homicides, it's only as a natural expression of self-confidence.

Eh, to be honest, some of these labels seem a bit arbitrary and artificial; I'm not sure how being nice ended up as such a bad thing. I guess my plea to you is this: aspire to reach the higher plane of "Be kind" and considerably higher than the lower plane of "Don't be an asshole."

Kindness is rooted in basic manners. Say good morning or nod hello, say "please" and "thank you" and "excuse me" and most important, do all of these things with sincerity. You respond when you're spoken to and you return a text or an email or a voice message. Politeness is the hallmark of being kind. But obviously there's more than just rote manners. You are fundamentally respectful, gentle, and generous.

Random acts of kindness do not make you kind. The kindness must be rooted in sincerity and consistency, not the sugary type that makes people actually become suspicious of you and your motives. Anyone can be fake-nice or even genuinely kind to someone who's more famous, richer, or can help you in some way. Sportswriter Jeff Pearlman once wrote that he judged people by how they treated the waiter. (As an aside, you two must be better-than-average tippers. Tip extravagantly when the situation calls for it. You'll feel great, and it's healthy for your soul and your conscience.) I was a mail clerk and a messenger for Covington & Burling during my first two summers of college and I can still tell you the full names of partners (and their office numbers)—men and women who were giants in their 'field—who invariably smiled and said hello when passing me in the hallway. Two decades later, I can also remember those who were complete dickwads and used their speakerphones to yell at the staff.

The question of whether you are genuinely good begins to reveal an answer when things go badly. It is incredibly easy to be gracious and generous when things are going great. But what separates the women from the girls is when the crap hits the fan and when bullets are flying all around you and the world starts to crumble along the edges. I'm not saying it cannot affect you, but if no one sees a fundamental change in your demeanor and you don't treat people around you any worse, it is quite admirable.

Again, like humility and integrity, the difficulty of being kind will further become clearer as you get older. There will come a time where you will become jaded—your fortress of innocence will be eroded by failure, disappointment, heartbreak—and you may start to wonder why you need to be kind to others when you yourselves have undergone such pain.

There are an endless series of excuses as to why you couldn't be kind. What about the truly enormous stress I'm under, where it feels like life has it out for me? What if I'm a tortured genius whose brilliance is dimmed by the distraction of having to conform to societal norms and exhibiting decorum toward others? What if, by being a good person, I lose the edge that makes me one of the most important people to ever walk the earth? If you are asking all of these questions, you need a reality check, but assuming that you are indeed accurate, then I ask you to consider being kind to be an added burden to your tasks at hand. The world is full of professionally brilliant and good human beings who are not named Tom Hanks or Warren Buffett or Dave Grohl. Make it your mission to be one of them.

Again, like humility and integrity, the more senior you get and the more you've accomplished, the more credit you'll get for being kind. If you actually did an inventory of "accomplished" or "successful" people, it will absolutely depress the crap out of you how many of them are just awful human beings. So when you do something kind and are not completely driven by self-interest, people will notice it readily. It's like they recognize that the travails of life should naturally wear down a person and turn them into assholes, and the possibility of that happening increases exponentially if that person finds fame and/or fortune. Honestly, if you exhibit common decency—nothing saint-like, just some normal thoughtfulness and charity—you will receive way more plaudits than you deserve, and people remember it.

I realize that being kind comes more naturally to some than others.

When I finished my sophomore year of high school, my parents started to realize that I was the living epitome of a one-dimensional Asian student who had good grades and some academic extracurriculars and absolutely nothing else. Because I had played soccer while I was in Rome and stood out as relatively athletic in my class of 25 students, my dad and I thought that I would try out for the varsity soccer team of my U.S. high school.

It's a testament to the Asian mentality of sheer force of will that my father and I thought that even though I was now in a school of 1,600 students, had never played club soccer or junior varsity, and reached puberty several years after everyone else, I could somehow transform myself into Diego Maradona within 90 days.

It also didn't help that I embarked upon the worst planned soccer regimen in high school history. I remember that I ran like a little robot all summer. I remember the way I would breathe rhythmically as my lungs and legs burned like a slow fire. I never played any pickup games because I didn't have any friends who played, so I did endless ball drills by myself.

The day of the tryouts arrived. It began early in the morning. I vaguely remember that it was a lot of physical drills and that I acquitted myself well, which is pretty much a euphemism for being a little less than mediocre. There was a three-hour break in the middle of the day, my father picked me up, and I had lunch at home. I already knew by then. The three months of athletic training was about to go up in smoke unless I did something spectacular in the afternoon session.

With that directive echoing in my head, my father drove me back to the high school. We were driving up a slight incline on Massachusetts Avenue, and there was another kid from the try-outs standing on the side of the road. He was waiting for the bus, which meant it would take him at least another 15 minutes to get to school. He was an African student, my year, and he had as much of a chance of making the team as me, which was infinitesimal.

We drove past him and I said nothing.

More than 25 years later, this is what I remember the most about that day, even more than the humiliation I felt later that afternoon when I completely whiffed on an incoming ball and left no doubt that I would not make even the first-day cuts. It was my failure to be a compassionate human being and instead my choice to be a self-absorbed and utter dick. This failure to exercise compassion and understanding is a common regret that many people feel toward the end of their lives when they've reassessed and placed their accomplishments in their proper context. By God, I hope you girls have a conscience and that you act upon it right then and there instead of feeling the guilt over not having done the right thing.

If being kind and doing good works doesn't come naturally to you and is not your default mode, that means that you have to work on it. You may not like to engage in stupid chit chat, but if it makes the other person more comfortable, then you do it. You may want to go straight home to binge-watch an entire season of episodes, or maybe you could be a helpful ear for a friend who's been down lately. You're crazy busy and know it'll take time to review a law student's résumé and give your feedback, but this may help him find a job. You need to work at it, be thoughtful of others, and act upon it. Your effort will have to win out over your predisposition.

As you get older, you may start to ask yourselves whether it's worth it to be kind in the first place. Why not just be what you are and be nice only when it occurs to you? If the belief of a God and the afterlife doesn't persuade you, what reward is there for being kind? If you set aside religion, then it gets a little existential, which obviously means that I must reference the original *Superman* with Christopher Reeve, Marlon Brando, and Gene Hackman.

Moments before he dies of a heart attack, Clark Kent's earthbound father tells him, "And there's one thing I do know, son, and that is you are here for a reason. I don't know whose reason, or whatever the reason is, maybe it's because...I don't know. But I do know one thing. It's not to score touchdowns." This is the thought ringing in Superman's head afterward when he turns back time—defying his Krypton father's directive to never interfere in human history—to save the lives of Lois Lane and millions of others.

Although I'm hesitant to limit you, you girls are also not on this earth to score touchdowns. And finding your reason for being does not mean that you sacrifice your lives solely in the name of altruism. But I do want you to provide light in other people's lives, to make a room brighter when you walk in. At your ages now, you already do. Why let go of that amazing quality? And when you are fundamentally kind, you will find that over time, you will be surrounded by like-minded people.

Other kind, good people will come to you. These are the people who inspire and sustain you. They will become your friends.

• ⋯⋯⋯⋯⋯⋯ • ⋯⋯⋯⋯⋯ •

Sofia, when you were probably a year old and your mother was pregnant with you, Alessandra, your mother and I went to the Upper East Side to hear a woman talk about your future.

This woman spoke about all the primary school options for the three- and two-year-old children of the audience members, describing the various school zones, the charter schools, magnet schools, gifted and talented schools, and then the different application processes, and odds of success for each. As she droned on and on, with all of these parents hanging on her every word and taking notes, I started to envision your futures.

Suppose we decided to try to have you attend Hunter College Elementary for intellectually gifted children, one of the most competitive programs in the city. We would cut the $140 check simply for the right to apply; we would fill out these applications ourselves, of course, because your ABCs are just scrawls. Within a couple of weeks, we would receive a packet of materials so that you could arrange to take the Stanford-Binet test, which measures knowledge, quantitative reasoning, visual-spatial processing, working memory, and fluid reasoning. An approved psychologist would administer this test, which would be another $325 fee. Each.

But then both of you ace the test. You end up scoring in the 99th percentile and make the second round, which involves a play group and more interviews. We are now slaving over the wording of our responses to more questions about you, your behavior, your essence. And you are each selected as one of 50 incoming students from about 2,000 applications.

And then you guys apply to college, and your grades and test scores and extracurriculars (swimming, field hockey, yearbook, Mathletes, Bocce Club) are so sterling that it is a foregone conclusion that you could get into the school of your choice. And scholarships defray the cost of the four years totaling $400,000 at this Ivy League University.

And what if, against all odds, your grades got even better during university? And the challenges of college were actually not enough, so you decided to go to law school, again with your pick of the litter? And then, with the brightest and most ambitious 20-somethings in the country converging at this institution, you manage to rise to top of this class as well, which means, once again, you can choose...

...your law firm in the greatest city in the world, where the brightest, the toughest, the most dynamic attorneys practice. And at this white-shoe law firm, you rise from lowly associate, routinely billing 2,500 hours a year, enduring the tongue-lashings from your superiors, stressing out over deadlines to become a partner at this BigLaw firm. You manage to fuse the intellectual and the practical realities of practicing law, so that you are indeed an exceptional lawyer.

Suppose that over the course of these 30 years of schooling and work, your insatiable desire to succeed drives you to see the world as a zero-sum game where if someone else is doing well, that means that you are losing. You play the office politics game like a wizard, framing situations so you look better than others for the same work. You're great at the subtle dig, managing to denigrate without being overt. In fact, no one knows what you're really thinking, because you're not trustworthy—anything you say can't fully be taken at face value. And you're comfortable with that, because you have concluded that you are the only one who knows what you're doing, and doing it right.

Sure, you're married, because there's always someone who's seduced by power and wealth and ambition. And you do the kid thing because that is what societal pressures dictate and it's the thing to do, part of your crafted image. To you, everything is judged by the bottom line, which entails that every tactic—intimidation, cheating that's framed as gamesmanship, shortcuts at the expense of quality—is in play and justifiable as long as the outcome is good. You generally ignore anyone who does not fulfill your standards of status and utility—the support staff, an acquaintance, a passing stranger in need of help. Even your husband and children can sense that, and even if it's never expressed verbally, they resent you for it.

There are benefits, of course. You can acquire virtually any material object you desire without thinking about cost. In between the madness of work, you and your family take luxuriating vacations where you can enjoy moments. Your social prominence and wealth allow you to give to charitable causes, which are not causes that are particularly near and dear to your heart, but almost function as a tax on the work that you do. You would never, ever be described by anyone, even your friends, as "a good person." Instead, the proper euphemism would be, "Deep down, she's got a good heart." And the giving demonstrates that you are not evil incarnate and perhaps allows you to justify some of the bad things that you do. And this type of justification is prevalent in other aspects of your life: at work, your nastiness is tolerated because of your brilliance and productivity; at home, your moods are excused because you are the breadwinner; socially, your friends and family keep their distance because they know the pressures that you face as a wife and a mother, a high-ranking professional, a suit in New York City, the most competitive place of them all.

My girls, if all of the above happens to you—the accomplishments borne of hard work, the attendant riches and power and social status, but along with the personality and way you conduct yourselves—that will mean, in my eyes and in the eyes of most with a level sense of human comportment, that you are a fucking failure of a human being. Don't ever forget that.

6

WHAT TV SHOW THEME SONGS FROM *CHEERS, FRIENDS, THE GOLDEN GIRLS*, ETC., ARE TRYING TO GET AT

Many moons ago, long before your mother and you girls came into my life, I went out with your Uncle Rocky and Uncle Dave, my trusty and reliable running mates, for a quiet dinner and then drinks at a Midtown West bar. This was a fairly routine occurrence, us being three single guys in a city with no nightlife or interesting people to meet.

When you're having drinks and not fixating on the game on the TV or otherwise trying to get action, the conversation can go into some very meaningful areas. And right after we talked about women and the NYC real estate market, we took a detour and started talking about our biggest regrets: girls we should have asked out, schools we probably should have gone to instead, things in life we should have done differently.

Geez, I don't remember this conversation being as depressing as it is in print. It actually felt cathartic to vocalize these thoughts in our little group, to lay out our foibles and vulnerabilities. And it was an opportunity to do a little reset and vow that going forward, we would live our lives more mindfully, to take chances, to leave nothing on the table. Well, that was the intention, anyway.

No one likes to dwell on regrets, the what ifs, the coulda beens, because doing so would be an accounting of culpability, the mistakes that were made and opportunities that were missed. And I imagine that the biggest regrets would become intolerably painful toward the end of one's life, which was the subject of Bronnie Ware's book *Top Five Regrets of the Dying*. Ms. Ware, a nurse who attended to the needs of the people in the last weeks of their lives, wrote that one recurrent regret was not staying in touch with friends. People facing their imminent mortality wished that they had given more time and effort into these friendships instead of getting caught up in their own lives. "Everyone misses their friends when they are dying," she wrote.

The value of friendships is a cliché ("Where everybody knows your name," "I'll be there for you," "Thank you for being a friend") and everyone takes them for granted. And why not? Although this concept has been warped by social media, making friends shouldn't be an objective in and of itself. Otherwise, it seems too contrived. When you're growing up, it's assumed that as long as you're not a turd, you will make friends, somehow, someway, right?

Your very first friends will be spun out of connections completely out of your control: relatives, your parents' friendships with other parents, maybe even your nanny's friendship with other nannies. Your subsequent friendships will appear to be borne of less random, more substantive connections, but in fact are not—a shared love of a fad (by now, Shopkins will be as relevant as sundials), certain candy, things that are purple. Even as you go through your schooling, your friendships are largely from coincidences: the assigned seat in your classroom, the assigned dorm and roommate, the assigned smaller subgroups of a class.

However we come by them, friends are more than companions. I see both of you interact with other children and it's startling how easily influenced you can be. If there's another kid who gets to watch the iPad at the dinner table, or another who leaves food uneaten but then rushes to have dessert, or one who mouths off to a parent, it's virtually guaranteed that you will act similarly. You don't have to actually say out loud, "Well, Samantha does it." We see you testing those boundaries, and it's up to your mother and me to reinforce them.

We tend to think of parents and siblings and other blood relatives as being the strongest influences on who we become. It only occurred to me in my late 30s how much my friends molded my personality, my interests, and my ambitions. I can break down some of my core tendencies and then trace them back to friends whom I've known from high school and college. Or even little mannerisms—even now, 25-plus years after we roomed together at Johns Hopkins, I still sometimes ask questions in this weird Pittsburgh inflection because of Uncle Greg. The people you socialize with outside of the home will have an inordinate influence on you, every bit as big as your parents.

As I start to observe more elementary and junior high school-age kids, I can understand the impulse of parents who homeschool their children, to have that control over them and shield them from outside influences. If you subscribe to the theory that your kids are a product of their environment, and you can control every aspect of that environment, homeschooling sounds great. But at what point do you stop? As much you can try, it's impossible—and in fact, doing a disservice—to shield your kids from the realities of the real world.

There is surely a great book to be written about friendships and how their strength and complexity vary according to different countries and cultures. With the caveat that I'm generalizing in significant ways, here are observations shaped from my experiences.

Of my Asian side, I feel closer to my Japanese heritage: my mother is Japanese, I was born in Tokyo, and I feel a deep kinship with my Japanese relatives. I spent a total of three years in Japan until I was about seven years old. My Japanese is really not anything to write home about—it sounds pretty functional, because I don't think I have an accent, but my vocabulary is pretty much what a *gaijin* would learn after several years in the country. But I do feel as though I have proper insight into the Japanese mindset.

In this world where incivility increasingly rules, even at the highest levels of government and society, Japanese society stands apart. There is no other country that approaches the politeness and decorum of Japan.

Any foreigner to Japan is utterly astounded by the manners and thoughtfulness exhibited by its people. You see it starting with the airport workers who bundle your luggage into buses with white gloves and bow as the vehicles pull away. Change for a taxi fare is placed on a plate and handed to you, rather than directly in your hand. While you move about hotels and stores and restaurants, people are constantly greeting you aloud and bowing and saying goodbye and shouting thank you and bowing as you go out the door. My parents would always say that the department store ladies were the epitome of unnecessary decorum: the women stationed outside and inside elevators who were dressed in impeccable uniforms and used precise, coordinated hand movements while announcing in extremely formal language the floors and their wares and bowing as visitors came in and out.

But the gentility of the Japanese people does not necessarily translate to warmth, at least not by Western standards. Even among best of friends in Japan, there is still a reserve and distance. Again, to reiterate, I'm generalizing. But even Japanese people would concede that it is rare to see a baring of the soul or an outpouring of emotion to a person's closest friend. The bond between friends is rarely, if ever, expressed. "I love you," even among spouses, is about as rare as "I hate you."

At the diametrically opposite end is the Italian version of friendship. Welcoming. Boisterous. Revelatory. The symbol of this is the group meal, inviting all and anyone. On one of our trips to

Torino, your mother's home city, there was a dinner for her and her childhood friends. There were a couple of times where I really thought that an argument had broken out, when it was simply just plain old talking. The emotions that Italians express with ease flow to and from friends, whether physically or verbally.

Your mother has observed that it's harder to make strong and meaningful friendships in the U.S., and I've heard that from other Europeans as well. This may be due to the fact that we are at our essence, foreigners in this land; as friendly as Americans can be, we still need to break through the veneer to get to the core. And you will probably encounter a situation when you'll meet a cool person who's witty, fun, has the same interests, and within half an hour, you'll be bursting with things to tell each other because of that instant connection. When that night ends, you resolve to meet each other as soon you can, because you guys will be best friends forever. And then it doesn't happen. This actually happens more often than you think, especially the older you get, when you have so many family and work obligations. But the thing you should try to do is not be the flaker in this situation. You do what's within your control.

I know much less about the Chinese people—enough to know that they are worlds different from the Japanese—but maybe I can provide some insight through the lens of my father.

Your grandfather had a particularly Chinese awareness of social standing. He was born in Taiwan but always mentioned and took pride in pointing out that he was ethnically Chinese and that his lineage stretched back 34 generations. I remember him saying that he thought of ourselves as upper-middle class, even if we probably fell short of that financially. He wanted to project that image, because I certainly grew up with accessories (expensive haircuts, certain clothes, a watch that should have gotten me mugged at 13 years old) that were well beyond our means. At the very least, he wanted me to comport myself as though as I was from that strata, which no doubt tinges all of the advice that I give to you.

I can't help but feel that my father's keen awareness of social status made him selective in his choice of friends once he came to the United States and then Europe. He was proud of friends with wealth or influence or class. But even if they would have gladly gotten him invites to an exclusive party, I'm not sure whether they would have been the ones to have the heart-to-heart conversations you would expect of your best friends.

But then again, with whom could he have had them?

"Let's go for a walk."

I was fourteen. My father and I took the 301 bus from Piazza Stefano Jacini, down Via Flaminio and toward Piazza del Popolo, which translates to "the People's Square." An obelisk from the Ramses II era brought to Rome in 10 B.C. during Augustus's reign marks the center of the piazza. Eastward, a semicircular carriage drive leads up to the Pincio, the hill overlooking the city that's especially breathtaking at sunset. This hill also provides an entrance to the Villa Borghese, one of the largest parks of the city. This was also the park where your mother and I rented a surrey bike and huffed and puffed for two goddam hours while you both sat in the front and squealed with delight and told us to go faster.

My father and I walked deeper into the woods of the Villa Borghese before we sat down on a bench.

"I have to tell you a secret."

When my father told my mother that he was a deep-cover spy, in the milliseconds after hearing the words "I have a secret," my mother's quick-snap reaction was, "He has another family."

Approximately 17 years later, my father said to me that he needed to tell me a secret. My exact thought before he started his next sentence was, "I have a brother I don't know about." It's odd how genetics work.

By the end of the day, a lot became clearer in retrospect. Why I had been told continually to say "international business consultant" if a classmate asked me what my father did. Why we had friends affiliated with the U.S. Embassy but never set foot there ourselves. Why during the previous year when my father had a life-threatening illness, these American doctors seemed to swarm out of nowhere.

Within minutes of meeting a stranger, a deep-cover spy tells a lie: what he or she does for a living. The deception establishes a fundamental barrier to true friendship. No matter how someone may have seemed like a fun-loving friend, no matter how compatible their personalities or interests may have been, my father was forced to keep his distance. He could never unburden himself with anyone. His life hung in the balance otherwise. No wonder then, that perhaps he viewed friends as versions of his own image that he wanted to project, or otherwise chess pieces to be manipulated for the purpose of his work.

When I was a kid, all I really needed was just one friend.

I bounced around the world—seven different apartments on three continents—before I even began high school. The first time I lived in a place for more than four years, I was 32 years old. With no brothers or sisters, it also meant that any friends dissolved with the next move.

My third-grade year, we lived in Falls Church, Virginia, where I became tight with Antony Cramer, who was cheerful and generous and funny. A mere year later, we had to move to Needham, Massachusetts, just outside of Boston. You may not believe this, but in the early 80s, being the nine-year-old foreign kid with the quirky habits did not play well in the Boston suburbs.

After school, Brian, the skinny kid with the bowl cut, came up to me.

"Sean said that your skin is darker than ours because your mom gave birth to you through her butthole."

And then, upon my silence:

"What do you think about that?"

If only I had fallen into the category of 98 percent of Asians then forced on the path of being a doctor, I would have been armed with a rebuttal of, "Brian, that is physiologically impossible. You see, when a mature egg is fertilized by a sperm..." Or if only I had fallen into the category of two percent of Asians defying their parents and going into a creative field, I would have gone with, "Well, gee, Brian, I have very hazy recollections of that day when I was born, but..."

Instead, I found myself digging up my parents' sienna-colored leather address book and was searching, entry by entry, for Antony's phone number. After school one day, when I was alone, I called him. I remember crying into the receiver of that kitchen phone and him trying to console me and telling me that it would be okay. We sent each other a couple of letters, but that was the last time I talked to him. When you were nine years old and there was no social media, you just went your separate ways. And man, I got reamed out by my parents about the long-distance bill.

You need to remember that you do not operate under any of these cultural or professional restrictions.

You have a choice in your friends. Peer pressure can lead you to think that you're stuck with whomever you end up hanging out with. Well, that's not exactly true. You can choose to extricate yourself from that group. You have that control. You have to exhibit enough independent thought to decide what kind of friends with whom you would want to surround yourself. This is very practical on my part, but each of your friends should enrich your life in matters large or small. There should be a purpose for a friend, whether it's nostalgia, emotional support, personal growth, or education. If you find yourself getting continually upset over a so-called friend's actions toward you, that's wasted energy and you start to untangle yourself from him or her. Marriage and kids will accelerate this process because the older you get, your tolerance for the drama of certain friendships will wane. Life is just too damn short.

You will still gravitate toward those with whom you have commonality, but the truly good friends are generous in spirit and support and will speak with and be spoken to with an unvarnished honesty. With them, you'll feel like you're spending more time talking about yourself rather than listening to their woes, and paradoxically, they will feel exactly the same way. They are the ones who don't judge but will kick you in the pants when it's necessary. You'll remember them more not because they were there when you went on that trip to Vegas, but when they showed up during your parent's funeral.

I've found that vulnerability is a pretty good indicator of a friendship's strength. When those times are bad, when you reveal your insecurities, when you express your doubts, when you're willing to look as bad as you possibly can, all without the care of looking your worst before this person, then that's a pretty rare friend. These are the friendships forged from many hours spent together, discussing dreams and heartbreak, venting over work and family. In time, this type of friend will be like a longtime physician who knows your complete family history, your moods, your tendencies, and your wants.

The Beatles sing, "And in the end, the love you take is equal to the love you make." It's true for relationships with lovers and it's true for friends. Any vulnerability has to go the other way, too—there has to be a reciprocity between the two of you. There has to be a balance of the amount that you're giving and getting.

This really applies more to guys than girls, but is nonetheless critical. The amount of shit that you give your friend must be directly proportional to the amount of outward affection you show toward him. In other words, when you bust someone's balls, you eventually have to balance that out that with some genuine, external manifestation of your good feelings for him—paying a compliment, buying dinner, doing something unexpectedly kind, etc. You're not allowed to say, "Well, he knows that he's my friend, he knows that I'm kidding. He can take it." No. Here are the potential situations that will play out:

BUSTING YOUR FRIEND'S BALLS	+	COUNTERACTING NICE THINGS YOU SAY TO YOUR FRIEND	=	RESULT
"Your ex-girlfriend was so ugly that she looked out the window and got arrested for mooning."		"At least she had a good heart...because she went out with a fucking charity case like you."		You make five shine box jokes too many and get beaten to death like Billy Batts in *Goodfellas*.
"Your ex-girlfriend was so ugly you guys practiced birth control by leaving the lights on."		"Yo, you feeling all right? Want to grab a drink?"		You die like Neil McCauley's bank robber character in *Heat*, gripping hands with Vincent Hanna, the cop who shot him.
"Your ex-girlfriend was so ugly that her pillow cried at night."		Hi! I bought you two pairs of those limited-edition Air Jordans in different sizes because your feet tend to swell on hot days."		Your infatuation and erotic obsession with your friend results in you killing him like in *The Talented Mr. Ripley*.

I know it seems sort of cool where you're slinging witty insults at each other, but friendship is not supposed to be a Friars Club roast.

Selflessness, generosity, empathy. When you are younger, precisely because your friends come from those random connections, all of these positive attributes don't necessarily stand out as the reasons why these people should be your friends. But these qualities never go out of style. The older you become, the more appreciative you are of them. And when you do find that person who will make sacrifices for you and for whom you would do the same, without a hint of self-interest, this is the friendship worth maintaining.

I am starting to reach the age where it can no longer be deemed a shock when friends die. But I did lose one recently and unexpectedly. Joy had the same birthday as I, so we would call each other "birthday twin." She and I had known each other for about 13 years—went to each other's weddings, exchanged baby gifts, gone on ski weekends with our families. She said that there was a niche for me as the "funny lawyer," the one who could be technically strong and yet armed with a much better sense of humor than my contemporaries. Joy read what I wrote during my spare time, insisted that my stuff was better than what was published or on the screen, told me that I could be a real writer. And I don't think I've ever cried harder— not for my father's passing, nor for other deceased relatives, not even after the 11-and-a-half-minute mark of *Up*—than at Joy's funeral, when I spent the full hour heaving and trying to muffle my sobs.

On a random night a couple of weeks later, after pouring myself more drinks than I should have, I put on headphones that blocked out the rest of the world and listened to some Prince, a lot of his slow jam stuff.

When the music is transcendent and the mood is right, one can be elevated into a deeper level of contemplation. And the finality hit me. There would be no more communication—no letter, no email or text—that would reach Joy. There would be no guarantee that I would see her in the next life. I wondered whether I had been completely attuned to Joy's needs or tried my very best to help. I thought about whether she knew how much our friendship meant to me. And I wept some more.

A little over a month later, Prince was gone as well. This is the moment when I would give my left arm to brag to you that yes, Prince was also my friend.

The night that my lifelong best friend Prince died, and for several nights afterward, I listened to every song I had of his. I watched hours of him performing. How many times did we watch his Super Bowl halftime show or the guitar solo from his Rock and Roll Hall of Fame performance? I read practically every appreciation, finding out revelations: his sly sense of humor; what a music nerd he was, regardless of genre; how he was secretly philanthropic; the strength of his convictions, be it defying sexual stereotypes or advocating his religious beliefs or fighting against his record company. The music, the passion, the cool—all of it brought me to tears again. And I felt a real sense of loss, because I never saw him in concert. Seeing Prince perform at one of those famous intimate gatherings would have been something I took to my grave. And it would never happen.

If you would feel the same emotions should your friend disappear without warning—let's call this the Prince test, in honor of someone who went before his time—then you do not let this friendship wither for lack of effort. Let that person know how important he or she is to you. Eliminate that regret from your life.

7

JOHN FORD DIDN'T SUCK

When I was in college, I took a film study class. In retrospect, my love of *When Harry Met Sally...* and *Lethal Weapon* may not have been a good fit with this course. Instead of a screening of *Beverly Hills Cop* with students rolling in the aisles and high-fiving each other, the professor seemed to revel in the sport of creating intricate and increasingly tenuous interpretations of Very Serious Movies. Every theme, every character, every word was dissected, cleaned, filleted, and seasoned to perfection—after which everyone would consume it, close their eyes, and sigh with delight, with a slight French accent.

One of the movies we analyzed was the western *The Searchers*, and the concluding shot has John Wayne in the frame of this doorway. In a small study group, the teacher's assistant went on and on about what this shot meant, how the composition worked, why John Wayne was standing just so, and how this fit into the broader themes of the movie.

After all this intellectual masturbation, I couldn't contain myself any longer. It was finally time for me to expose truths that the rest of the sheep could not understand.

"Aren't we going too far in interpreting every little nuance of this scene? Overreaching and finding symbolism that doesn't exist? Isn't it possible that this was more or less a random shot that in fact did not have all of the hidden meanings that you're ascribing to it?"

Through gritted teeth, the teacher assistant's response only slightly betrayed the combination of simmering outrage and condescension, but she may as well have blurted, "You puny-brained troglodyte." Substantively, her answer was remarkably unsatisfying, maybe because by then I was so convinced of the validity of my point.

It took only about 20 years before I flashed back to this exchange and realized that I was an idiot.

In *The Searchers*, John Wayne's character is out to find his abducted niece, whose family was murdered by Comanches. He embarks on a five-year quest, not to rescue her, but to kill her, because he would rather see her dead than living with Native Americans. From her end, she has no desire to be reunited with her original family either; she would rather remain with her captors and adoptive family.

When he finally reaches her, instead of executing a mercy killing, he takes her up in the saddle and utters, "Let's go home, Debbie."

In this very last scene, he carries her back to her family's doorstep and sets her down on the front porch. She is sur-

rounded and embraced by the family members as she's escort-
ed into the lodge, and the camera pans slowly backward into
the home until gradually, there's this image of the Duke, framed
by the doorway and with the expanse of the American frontier
just behind. Darkness—the inside of the house—is all around
him, resulting in a nicely framed portrait of him standing just
so. He lingers at the door for a bit, then turns around and am-
bles his way out into the frontier, all the while framed by this
doorway. The End.

Yes, John Ford—it turns out that he's only one of the greatest
directors in the history of this medium and has the body of work
to demonstrate that he wasn't some flash-in-the-pan hack—did
construct this shot on purpose. It works as a bookend to the
opening shot of the movie, when a woman opens the door of
her lodge and appears to be looking for the man who's walking
away. The use of doorways in the movie are a consistent theme,
as they symbolize the entry into and departure from the two different worlds, white and Native American. No, this shot from
The Searchers—it turns out it's one of most iconic in the history
of film, so SON OF A BITCH, it really was unfortunate I decided
to single this one out—was not a happy accident.

Everything matters.

As with anything, the dissection of art can go to extremes.
I'm sure that with enough time and effort and a good bit of
self-loathing, you could make a case that *Encino Man* is a jewel
box of a movie about the duality of the human psyche. Quite
frankly, I still don't get a whole lot of modern art, and there has
to be some sort of scam going on with avant-garde art. There

are few things more insufferable than high-minded pretension and engaging in senseless and convoluted interpretation and "ah yes, that fart I just released symbolizes the noxious wasteland that we all live in."

But if you are an artist, what you do, you do with a purpose. You do something, it should have some sort of meaning. If you want to end the movie with a certain shot—or really, any shot in the movie—you better damn well make sure that you're composing it correctly. Any movement of the camera should ideally have a deeper intention; it better fit within the context of the scene and the movie itself. Any score or song you've selected should convey the deeper truth of the scene and try to employ some subtlety, i.e., don't use "All by Myself" after the main characters have broken up. You should have an internal explanation for the way the characters are dressed, the type of lighting, what they're holding, even what they're sitting on. Masters of movies don't stumble their way into the creation of iconic scenes.

Because in the end, everything matters. Everything. Everything matters. And what you will find out is that everything isn't as much as it seems.

One of the joys of law school is the soul-crushing dread of being called on in class by a professor. What ensues is the famed Socratic method: the professor asks questions of the student about one or two assigned cases, then asks more questions in a way that reveals the reasoning behind the cases' rulings and how this law would be applied in other hypothetical situations. To mix imagery, the questioning is part swordfight, consisting of the thrust and parry of questions and answers, and partly a lab scientist directing a rat in a maze toward different dead ends before finally arriving at the right answer. When the Socratic method is done perfectly, at the end of the hour the despondent student will slowly take out a canister of gasoline, pour it over his head, and light himself on fire, upon which the rest of the class will break into a refined golf clap.

The first semester of my first year, I had Contracts, which was taught by a docile, courteous human being who upon the beginning of the lecture, managed to transform into a giant dildo. And this would be a typical exchange:

"Mr. Isbell."

"Yes?"

"Tell us about *Hadley v. Baxendale*."

"Okay...um, this case happened in Gloucester, England, and—"

"Hold on. Why does it being in Gloucester make it relevant?"

Shifting of paper. An ever-so-perceptible clearing of the throat. The clicking of a pen.

"Uh...I guess it's not, really."

"All right then. Please proceed."

"This mill was cleaning grain, and it would grind it—"

"How is this important?"

A beat.

"Well, the crankshaft to this mill broke—"

"I understand that's the part that needed to be replaced, but does it matter what the mill actually did?"

"It provides some background to—"

"Tell me something."

113

"I think—"

"Is it relevant to the case disposition?"

"Well..."

(Entire pyramids have been constructed during this pause.)

"I'm sure describing the clothes the mill owner wore on the day the crankshaft broke provides some background, but it's not necessarily relevant."

(Polite golf clap.)

Whenever I'm writing something legal—pretty much every godforsaken day of my life— the voice of this dildo echoes in my head. But it is absolutely vital to effective legal writing. When you hear this voice, then editing becomes a lot easier. If you're trying your damndest to make an argument, even a complicated one, you'll be pretty surprised at how few facts are absolutely essential. Every argument, paragraph, sentence— every word—must have a purpose.

(While I'm at it, the reason why you can't have typos in your brief, beyond the obvious, is that you don't want the reader to spot an error and think that the writer is using similarly sloppy logic or is providing incongruous interpretations of cases. Same thing with your résumé. If you can't be bothered to scour the one page that is supposed to impress your future employer—everything from consistency in headings and sentence structure, grammar, a stray comma, or even an unneeded space—why should you be trusted to do anything remotely important?)

This rule applies outside of the legal realm. Chris Rock routinely says the wrong word can be the difference between funny and unfunny. Hell, even if one takes a breath at the wrong moment, it can deflate the punchline. Coaches and athletes watch hours of video to divine tendencies of their opponents—a twitch of the shoulder before a hard cut, the positioning of a glove before the windup, where the eyes dart before a penalty kick. When you see red carpet fashion, one variation—the width of the belt, the shade of yellow, the addition of an accessory—can make the difference between tacky and sublime.

"I don't know."

The older you get, the less of an acceptable answer this is. You're simply not looking hard enough.

Like a mystery novel whose revelation is dependent on an incredibly trivial detail—the material of this man's ascot was made of Varansai Resham silk, which meant that he was there during the monsoon season, which explains the diarrhea that resulted in the dry cleaning bill and the run-in with the victim's nephew's girlfriend's dog!—there is a general logic to this world, or at least a cause and effect. A lot in this world isn't as random as you think. And I would say that this is particularly true in human behavior.

That same summer when I trained 10 weeks for the soccer tryout that ended in six hours, I didn't have any extracurricular activities. I needed to make myself more attractive to colleges, so I came up with a project of reading about 30 to 40 books and writing a report on each. These books were mostly classics, pulled from recommended reading lists, and some of my father's favorites. And out of all the books that I read that summer, the one that sticks most in my memory was *Power!* by Michael Korda.

The subtitle is *"How to Get It, How to Use It,"* but the more appropriate and marketable one would have been, "How to Mind-Fuck Your Enemies, Who Are Everybody and Everywhere." I still recall very well the anecdotes extending Machiavellian principles for the modern age: the man who ordered unusually small visitor chairs in his corner office so that when guests sat down, he towered over them and the guests felt small and uncomfortable. The advice at a critical one-to-one dinner to gradually put your things—perhaps your wineglass, or your eyeglasses, or a lighter—on the adversary's side of the table, so that you invade his space and exert your dominance over him.

These aren't exactly the techniques to use if you're thinking about sainthood, or hell, just trying to be kind. And at 16 years of age, I distinctly remember feeling despair—that this life is essentially an interminable competition to get to the top of a mountain, where people are tearing at each other and using every underhanded trick to reach the apex. Now, though, after having lived in New York for 20 years, I can view this perception of life for the preposterous notion that it is. It's a futile mission with massive collateral damage, led by fools with a surplus of ego and a deficit of courage. If I'm ever invited into an office with tiny chairs, I'll be thinking what an insecure clown this guy is and contemplating whether I should actually point out this brutish attempt to gain a mental edge.

The more important takeaway from this book is that these aspects that we take for granted—posture, clothes, facial expressions—can have a tangible effect on another person, even subconsciously. I would not resort to belittling and abusing someone, but I am more than willing to use their own perceptions and biases and impulses against them. For a while, I always wore glasses when meeting opposing attorneys or a judge because I looked older (sadly, now unnecessary). I would wear bold-colored ties in an attempt to have my garb fill in the gaps of my self-assurance. When I'm talking to an adversary, I make a conscious effort to speak as little as possible, to use the silence to make the other guy feel uncomfortable and want to fill the air with a piece of information that I can exploit. (By the way, these tactics seem distinctly unkind, but if you're a litigation attorney, you're a fool not to use them. Are you starting to see a pattern?)

All of these details matter in human behavior.

These were the same details that my father obsessed over to survive in his job, and to survive altogether. Within minutes of meeting someone, he needed to assess whether this person would flip and be prepared to divulge secrets. My father needed to parse the layers of deception, to see whether a willingness to betray one's country would in turn lead to a betrayal of him.

And with much less at stake, I employ the same tactics every day whenever I interact with someone. I take stock and file away the little acts that are indicative of a person's character. Does he routinely ignore texts? Does he write, "No, that's wrong" instead of "I don't think I agree?" Does she often interrupt others to talk about herself? Is she always late or cancelling on people? When he's answering your question, is he making eye contact? Or does she ignore you altogether once she realizes that you're a junior person? Yes, it is dangerous to take a minute detail and use it to broadly generalize, which is only a couple of steps removed from the evils of stereotyping, and God knows that I have been subject to it for all of my life. But when you see a pattern of behavior, it's not that difficult to draw further insights into a person's personality.

Life can be seen as a poker table where everyone has a tell. And like poker, you need to be patient and simply observe. It can take time. But after you mentally note and you tally, you can start to foresee certain actions, and it can be astonishing as to how predictable people can be. It's like having the ability to look into the future. (By the way, my father would really appreciate my use of the poker analogy even though my preferred game is 25-cent video poker.)

But hold on, you may say. If you are attending to every detail, aren't you setting yourself up for complete paralysis by over-analysis? Won't you be overthinking everything, to the point where you cannot do anything without weighing the pros and cons of your decision? Isn't everything going to be seen as contrived? Can't you have the happiness from the spontaneity in just doing and not being so calculating? Out of all the possibilities in the English language, was the last word of Chapter Two the most appropriate one?

Yes, you are correct. And the answer, my girls, is:

BALANCE

8

WHEN YOU GET YOUR
ASS KNOCKED DOWN

More than 20 years later, the T-shirt remains in my closet. You two girls have both seen it on occasion. It's all black. In understated lettering, the front reads: "FEAR IS AN OBSTACLE FOR SOME PEOPLE." And on the back: "FEAR IS AN ILLUSION." And above those words, the stony, ghostly visage of Michael Jordan.

This was the shirt I wore when I began the New York Bar Examination, spanning 12 hours over two days.

Not exactly like walking into final exams at Cambridge University in full suit and tails, especially because I took mine in a convention center called The Egg in Albany. And I'm fairly sure that at Cambridge, sometime in the fourth hour of that first day, someone did not fart and cause another test taker to descend into a giggling fit so severe that I wondered whether this would end up causing me to lose my concentration, fail the bar, and humiliate my parents. But on this day, the fear was quite real. In order to overcome it, I needed every possible mental edge, including the armor of a shirt with the baddest baller on the planet, and the one person whose dominance and sheer force of will could convince millions that indeed, fear is an illusion.

Fear is seen as a negative, to be avoided. Just the physical sensations alone—the dropping of the stomach, the blood draining from your head, maybe a tingling in your extremities—are to put it mildly, not pleasant. Beyond the short-term, when you've tasted the pain or failure or humiliation, fear can become your prison. This fear can cause you to not do what you normally do. It can make you second-guess your decisions. It can paralyze you, lead to despondence and hopelessness.

But the fear can also be a positive. It heightens your senses, pumps up the adrenaline, and is a fantastic motivator. That fear of failure and of humiliation can spur you to do your best work. Football coaches love to do this, with Hall of Famer Bill Parcells immediately coming to mind. His style was to create and cultivate an atmosphere of fear—from the assistant coaches to the players to the scouts to the secretaries—so that everyone was primed to do their very best work. The problem, of course, is that it wears down everyone, including the person in charge, which may explain why Parcells was a head coach for four different teams and always wore out his welcome at each stop.

At your ages of five and four, we see you (especially you, Alessandra), and say, "That girl has no fear," and it's not just out of admiration, but also a certain wistfulness. As you get older, when you do experience fear, it will be less physical and more mental. This fear—you will need to harness it, the fear of besmirching your name, your body of work, and your reputation. It is one of the few items that will fuel the perseverance needed to overcome obstacles.

I'll tell you about the search for my first full-time job. I went to law school at Washington University in St. Louis, which wasn't my first choice, or my second, or my third...or my 11th. I was waitlisted at four other schools, but when they all fell through, I found myself going to a city and a region where I had never even visited. Looking back now, it was an atmosphere that very few places could have provided. After being at Johns Hopkins, where exam season seemed like a never-ending mass of gladiator fights, I was just glad to be somewhere where the students were chill and reflected the genteel charm of the Midwest.

The problem was that these genteel students were all much smarter and harder-working than I, so I was firmly entrenched in mediocrity. The reason why law schools are so competitive is that there is a forced bell curve on grades, which means that no matter how smart everyone was, there has to be a group comprising the bottom 25 percent of the class. I had already read about this in Scott Turow's One L, but it managed to only hit me after I got my awful first semester grades in Contracts, Torts, and Real Property.

There are three years in law school. If you're a rock star, you can find work at a firm the summer after your first year, but the summer after your second year is the really important one: that's when you should be getting substantive legal experience, which hopefully leads to a full-time job after graduation. But because you start interviewing for jobs at the beginning of your second year, these firms have only your first-year grades to review. As a result, these grades—the bad ones I just got— have a disproportional effect on your future. They determine whether you make law review (the scholarly journal comprised of by and large the brightest students) and they're most of the basis for a firm to interview you or ding you right off the bat.

HOW TO EXPEND THE MOST AMOUNT OF ENERGY TO GENERATE THE GREATEST NUMBER OF REJECTION LETTERS FROM LAW FIRMS IN THE MID-1990S

1. Be a first-year law student whose legal knowledge is slightly higher than someone regularly watching *Law & Order* and to a much lesser extent, *L.A. Law*.

2. While you attend a law school in St. Louis, apply only to reputable law firms in New York City and Washington D.C., two of the toughest legal markets in the country.

3. Finalize a résumé whose biggest brag is that you are in the top 50 percent of your first-year class.

4. Because email is in its infancy, print out hard copies of approximately 200 cover letters and résumés.

5. Don't have the mental capacity to learn a "mail merge" and instead indulge your sadomasochistic pleasure from manually typing in every law firm address and addressee.

6. Carefully fold your signed cover letters and résumés into

perfect thirds, insert into envelopes, and lick hundreds of stamps because no self-adhesive ones have been invented yet.

7. Walk to mailbox every day and open very polite rejection letters from many, many, many firms.

I scrutinized these rejection letters for any sign of hope. Was it a real signature or a stamp? Did it say that my credentials were "indeed impressive" or merely thank me for applying? They did say they would keep my résumé and cover on file, correct? Meanwhile, if these law firms had actually kept every application, there would be a guy carting them into a room that looked like the last scene of *Raiders of the Lost Ark*. The fear hadn't kicked in yet, because it wasn't expected for a first year to get summer work, and so I volunteered for the American Bar Association Commission on Homelessness and Poverty.

Because this job didn't pay and I had to make some money, I was working another part-time job, doing non-legal office temp work. First, I was temping once a week. And because I needed more money, I started temping twice a week. And when I started to realize that my work for the ABA Commission on Homelessness and Poverty didn't really involve any legal research or writing and would instead lead to the cruel irony of making me poor and homeless, I wanted to get paid three or four times a week. You kind of see where this is going, yes? And when my ABA boss told me to close the door behind me and said, "I'd like to sever this relationship," I got this horrifying chill down my spine, one that I've never forgotten.

The second year of law school began, and it was time to get down. Despite the mediocre grades, I was able to get onto the law review through the writing competition, so that gave me a little something extra over my fellow competition—not the students in my class year, but really, against every other law student in the country.

I needed to redouble my efforts. This time I sent out over 300 cover letters and résumés, now adding Chicago and Honolulu to New York and D.C. In personalizing cover letters, I was researching—I can't emphasize how much of a pain in the ass this was, pre-Google—the news section of LexisNexis, reading obscure newspaper articles to get a bead on different firms' clients, and dropping a line in my cover letter like, "I know that in the past your firm has represented Nomura and Mitsubishi, and I believe that my experience living in Tokyo and my language skills would be an asset to Paul, Weiss, Rifkind, Wharton & Garrison." And no, dammit, I just couldn't learn mail merge.

The pile of rejection letters grew, like they were breeding, and not just for me. We students used gallows humor to deal with the fear of being unemployed. For Halloween, my roommate went as a walking rejection letter, with more than a hundred sheets safety-pinned to his clothes. With my close-cropped haircut, short-sleeve baby blue shirt buttoned to the top, white pants and Nike running shoes, and holding a box of chocolates, I made an awesome Forrest Gump. It was then, at a belated 23 years of age, when I first realized that: 1) you should never drink heavily on an empty stomach, and 2) Maker's Mark Bourbon is not what you should be drinking heavily on an empty stomach. And as I lay crumpled in the country club bathroom stall, the door wide open so that everyone could see me in my glory, I saw the law review editor-in-chief come in, and the question that came to my mind was: "I wonder what this does to my chances of being editor-in-chief next year?" (Answer: It kind of fucks it up.)

But this time, now with law review on my résumé, I got interviews in Chicago, New York, D.C., and Honolulu (in the end, I completely chickened out on Hawaii). I ran endless interview questions in my head and practiced my answers and then I flew to New York and Washington on my dime and put on my best suit and made sure the dimple in my tie was centered and then bunched the creases of the shirt around my waist to the side. Then I flew home, obsessively checked my mailbox for the next couple of weeks, and then got a thin envelope, which meant that the job search had to continue.

After one of these rejections, I called up one of the associates who had interviewed me. I needed to find out what I was doing wrong, and my need to be humble won out over my fear of finding out my flaws.

It started with the very first sentence in my cover letter. I had written that I was interested in a position "in either your corporate or litigation departments." It made sense on one level, because when you just start law school, it's a bit unreasonable to be forced to choose a specialty for the rest of your legal career. But the vast overwhelming majority of law school students—the unwashed masses who aren't in Columbia Law or don't have a 4.0 GPA—don't have this luxury of choice. You determine what you like and build your coursework and experience around it, so by the time you send that cover letter, it's crystal-clear why you want that litigation attorney job and why you're qualified for it.

Also, in the course of our interview with this associate, I had mentioned that I was looking at firms in Washington, Chicago, Honolulu, etc. That's not exactly an indication to a firm that this prospective candidate is willing to set down roots in New York for the long haul—never mind that I was ready to lie down in traffic to be in the City forever. My honesty was killing me. Generally, I was acting like the extremely desperate law school student that I was, and by the end of my second year, there was good reason to be. I was at risk of having a huge blank spot just where my critical second-year summer experience was supposed to be.

I finished up exams and papers—my grades incrementally improved from the previous year—and went to my parents' home in Bethesda, Maryland. The year felt like a big waste: the fact remained that after all of the studying, the money borrowed for tuition, and the weekend nights slaving away in my apartment instead of partying, I had no job. Which, despite initial high-minded thoughts about learning "how to think like a lawyer" and mastering the nuances of the bedrock of all civilized societies, is kind of the damn point of going to law school.

Now I was really in truly desperate mode, and the only place I really wanted to be in was New York Fucking City. Where Tom Hanks and Peter Scolari were doing all those crazy single guy things in *Bosom Buddies*. Where Dustin Hoffman was an actor struggling to break out in *Tootsie*. Where Melanie Griffith got her Wall Street office with a window in *Working Girl*. Where *The Daily Planet* and Wayne Enterprises were born, and...in retrospect I had obviously been watching too many movies instead of studying, but the point was that this was the only place I wanted to be.

I took an Amtrak up to New York. The greatest city on Earth. The movie-set scenes of my future wildest fantasies. Where my dreams would culminate. And when I was standing there by myself in the middle of Penn Station, a primary urge began to swell inside me.

It grew and it grew until it overcame all other senses.

"I want to turn around and go back home."

Fear.

This New York City wasn't the hellhole that it was back in the 80s, but sure didn't feel safe to someone by himself who was only generally familiar with "uptown, midtown, and downtown." Standing in the taxi line, I nearly got scammed into getting into a black car when the woman behind me snapped at the driver that I wasn't interested and directed me back into line. There still was someone looking out for me.

Crashing at my friend Kathy's Columbia dorm room, I researched internships. To go into old-man mode again, this was three years before Google was incorporated, never mind operational. I went into these giant book repositories called libraries and looked up companies and researched their summer opportunities. And then I cold-called each one of these places. Forget about making money. All I needed was a desk and a computer and they could treat me like a piece of shit for three months and I would have been happy, because I needed experience, anything substantive to put on my résumé, to show that I did something legal. And after a week of excruciating ups and downs...

I still had nothing. I returned to Bethesda.

You may think that going back home would have at least resulted in returning to the comfort of a supportive home. "You know, son, you don't have a job yet, but just keep your head up. Your perseverance will eventually lead to dividends. Speak it into existence and believe." If you envisioned that exchange, girls, then thank God, because this means you are blissfully unaware of how old-school Asian parents operate. My dad reminded me constantly in less and less subtle ways that I needed to find a job (you really can't get less subtle than bellowing "GET A JOB!") and not embarrass our family. Just flat-out awful.

Now it was time for me to look at externships—essentially summer internships—with D.C. federal judges. They were unpaid, of course, but this seemed a bit more suited to my writing skills. More research and more telephone inquiries.

One day I was playing one on one with Kessler when I got into the lane, made a fake to my right, and then threw up a baby jump hook that in my mind was something that Kevin McHale would have done. When I came down the six inches from the apex of my jump, the toe of my right foot caught on the pavement, and I had to go to the hospital with torn ankle ligaments. A day later, I found out that the Honorable Emmet G. Sullivan, U.S. District Judge for the District of Columbia, was still accepting externs for the summer.

At this point, there are two kinds of pride. There is the pride in getting a job solely on merit, the satisfaction of knowing that I earned my position because of the accomplishments on my résumé. I didn't want to feel like I got a position through a connection or for sentimental reasons. I wanted to rise and fall on my qualifications alone.

And then there is the pride of not being a career pizza delivery guy after having spent six figures on a law school education. So you goddam better believe that in my best suit, I stumbled into Judge Sullivan's chambers on a pair of crutches with a cover letter and résumé in hand and generally acted like this was an appeal for the March of Dimes. I was told right then that I could work for the judge for the summer.

My father was sitting at the dining table when my mother and I got home (yes, to complete the pathetic picture, I was driven to court by my mom). When I told my father, he stayed seated. Then he started to cry. And in between his sniffles, he said, "I knew you could do it."

Yes, it was fairly ludicrous. Someone had decided that I could work with two other externs at a big table in a one-window room, for free, and I had to play up the fact that I was a cripple. But it was one of the few times that my father really expressed his pride. It was always there, to be sure, but in that moment it bubbled to the surface. I will never forget it.

I worked my ass off in that room and spent an entire summer writing an opinion in an administrative law case involving fish and wildlife licenses that could have doubled as a sleeping aid. But because this externship would not be leading to a full-time job, the mission was not accomplished. I had to get moving on finding a permanent job after my third year.

The good news: I didn't have to apply to as many law firms as the previous year. The bad news: it's because many law firms don't even consider résumés from third-year students, because their summer classes of second-year students are expected to comprise their slate of full-time associates. I plowed ahead. In the event that there could be some twist of fate that led to a stray opening, anything, I applied to all of these firms again. Although this time, because I had done the research, there was less work to do from scratch. And I still didn't learn mail merge.

And whaddya know, this time, amidst all those accumulating rejection letters...I know what you're thinking. This was the breakthrough, right?

Oh so sorry. That fall of my third year, I didn't even get any interviews in New York.

During my second year, I had also decided to apply for judicial clerkships. These clerkships are coveted because as the law clerk, you're the judge's right-hand person and it's a great way to get substantive experience writing legal opinions while typical first- and second-year graduates are doing mind-numbing document reviews. I applied for clerkships all around the country, not knowing that the Harvard and Yale and Stanford graduates had a stranglehold on the Hawaii, Puerto Rico, and Virgin Islands clerkships. (Let's not forget that back then applying somewhere cost money: buying the fancy premium weight Crane paper and envelopes and postage for a packet that included my transcript and writing sample.)

Sometime during that summer while I was externing for Judge Sullivan, Magistrate Judge Lawrence R. Leavitt from the District of Nevada in Las Vegas took a look at my application packet, my grades, and qualifications and...yes, finally, this was the big break, correct?

Wrong. He asked his secretary to send me a letter stating that my application would be kept on file. This was just a nice way of saying that he was not interested.

Out of the hundred or so judges to whom I sent application packages, I got only one expressing interest in interviewing me in the fall of my third year: the Honorable Mary Mullarkey of the Colorado Supreme Court. She was the reason why I was employed after graduation. I did not clerk for her.

Over time, you will meet the hustler, someone who's always working angles and thinking and scrapping and trying to survive. And you may, as I did, find this person to be beneath you, as you'll be turned off by the machinations and the unrelenting effort and the fundamental lack of truth. You may instead believe in the ultimate egalitarianism, that your strengths and weaknesses will stand on your own and that judgment will be rendered fairly without you attempting to overstate your credentials and hide your deficiencies.

And then you will find yourself in a position where you finally understand. The hustler does what he does because there is no other option. Fear drives the engine.

I looked up the other members of the Colorado Supreme Court to whom I had sent applications and called up those chambers to see whether they could possibly fit in an interview, because you know, this sterling Washington U. student is being interviewed by a fellow Supreme Court Justice and it would be a pity if you missed on this great opportunity and did I mention that there's 0 percent APR? I got two more interviews from that route. Eventually I would be rejected by all three of the justices.

When Judge Mullarkey gave me the interview opportunity, I also called the magistrate judges in Las Vegas.

"Hello. My name is Mark Hsu, and I had earlier applied for a clerkship with Judge Hunt. I know that Judge Hunt is extremely busy, but I was in the area for interviews and was wondering whether he had any time to meet with me."

"In the area" was more than 600 miles between Denver and Las Vegas, about an 11-hour car ride. Among the three additional interviews that I got, one was with Judge Leavitt, who had already sent me the rejection letter. And in the course of the hour-long interview, we bonded over baseball and Impressionism and the Chicago Museum of Art and many things that had very little to do with the law.

After printing out and sending approximately 900 applications to law firms and judges, and six months before my graduation from law school, I was informed that I had a full-time job waiting for me.

You will get your ass knocked down in life. As much as your sense of self-worth may take a hit and your pride may hurt, there is absolutely no shame in that. It is inevitable as the passage of time. The question is how you respond, because your true character is revealed then. Do you retreat further into a sanctuary, curl inward into a more comfortable place? Take fewer risks, because you didn't like the taste of your blood?

The fear should stoke your hunger. And quite frankly, you won't initially have that fire because of your circumstances. Your lives are too comfortable. You have enough to eat, you have enough to wear, and you do not lack for any material things. You certainly won't have that hunger because of the way we treat you. I'm sure that through carefully timed barbs and the withholding of love and affection, I could instill an insatiable desire in you to please us and thereby manipulate you into an overachiever, but how monstrous would that be.

Simply put, it has to come from within you.

By now, I'm the world-weary New York commuter riding the subways, but I've always remembered this EB White passage on a train ad:

> There are roughly three New Yorks. There is, first, the New York of the man or woman who was born here, who takes the city for granted and accepts its size and its turbulence as natural and inevitable. Second, there is the New York of the commuter—the city that is devoured by locusts each day and spat out each night. Third, there is the New York of the person who was born somewhere else and came to New York in quest of something. Of these three trembling cities the greatest is the last—the city of final destination, the city that is a goal. It is the third city that accounts for New York's high-strung disposition, its poetical deportment, its dedication to the arts, and its incomparable achievements. Commuters give the city its tidal restlessness; natives give it solidity and continuity; but the settlers give it passion.

You are from the first category of New Yorker, but my wish for you is that at heart, you consider yourself from the third category. When life puts you in that fight-or-flight situation and you're scared shitless, there must be a part of you that embraces the fear, that makes you clench your jaw and vow to kick some ass. And I guarantee that when you encounter a similar situation later, it'll get a little less scary.

By the way, as completely demoralized I got during the whole process, I never threw away the rejection letters from the firms and the judges. There is a humongous stack of them still in the storage unit of my parents' apartment building, where they are getting drier and drier and more and more crisp, biding its time and waiting for the moment when a spark from an electrical malfunction lights it up in flames and eventually brings down the entire building in a fiery conflagration. Law firms, man, they're the worst.

9

THE WISDOM OF
CHARLIE SHEEN

At some point, it will start to dawn on you. Maybe it'll be in high school, when you find yourself wondering how certain horrid people are more popular than you. You will seethe when others who cut corners and outright cheat get into better universities than you. Maybe it'll be in college, when instead of studying you will spend countless hours searching for a reason, any reason, why others are in better relationships than you. Or maybe it will finally strike you as you enter the work force, when you start to notice a parade of people who aren't as intelligent, kind, or socially adept start to ascend ahead of you. They make more money without working as hard. They move into the opulent house and you wonder if they won the lottery. They get the unbelievable breaks. They fail upward.

At your young ages, even though it's in a different context—when we tell you two that it's time to stop watching TV, or that you need to do Japanese or Italian homework, or that you must go to bed—you two have already started to voice a fundamental truth about life.

"This is so unfair."

Oh, it'll get worse.

The best I can do is refer to *Ferris Bueller's Day Off*.

When you watch this movie, you'll see that Ferris is the ne'er do well who uses his charm and wiles to scam and negotiate his way through every situation. "Oh, he's very popular. The sportos, the motorheads, geeks, sluts, bloods, wastoids, dweebies, dickheads—they all adore him. They think he's a righteous dude." And set aside from all of Ferris's admirers is his elder sister Jeanie, glowering, filled with resentment toward him and trying to pull the curtain back on all of his schemes. Toward the end of the movie, she finds herself at a police station, seated next to a very shady character played by a young Charlie Sheen.

(I felt a lot better about the title of this chapter before reading this long *Hollywood Reporter* article about the depraved depths Sheen sank to following his whole *Two and a Half Men* meltdown. But then again, "The Wisdom of the Character in a John Hughes Movie Played by Charlie Sheen" just doesn't have that same ring to it.)

Jeanie and the Charlie Sheen character exchange some pleasantries (she tells him to put his thumb up his butt, he says that she wears too much eye makeup and looks like a whore), and then he gets to trying to find out why she's at the police station. I'll put this exchange in screenplay format, because I'd like to live out my dream of writing a legendary movie scene.

INT. POLICE STATION, WAITING ROOM -- DAY

Jeanie sits on the end of a bench. On the
other end sits a WASTED TEENAGE BOY in a black
leather jacket, torn jeans. He shifts gears.

> BOY
>
> You want to talk about your problem?

> JEANIE
>
> With you? Are you serious?

> BOY
>
> I'm serious.

> JEANIE
>
> Blow yourself.

(Charlie Sheen then looks downward in about the most perfect way possible. A barking lunatic, but damn that dude
was funny.)

> JEANIE
>
> All right? You want to know what's wrong?

> BOY
>
> I know what's wrong. I just
> want to hear you say it.

> JEANIE
>
> In a nutshell, I hate my brother. How's that?

> BOY
>
> That's cool. Did you blow him
> away or something?

Jeanie laughs. A breakthrough.

                    JEANIE

No, not yet.

                    (beat)

I went home to confirm that the shithead
was ditching school and when I was
there, a guy broke into the house and
I called the cops and they picked me
up for making a phony phone call.

                    BOY

What do you care if your
brother ditches school?

Jeanie squints, incredulous.

                    JEANIE

Why should he get to ditch school
when everybody else has to go?

                    BOY

You could ditch.

                    JEANIE

Yeah. I'd get caught.

                    BOY

So, you're pissed off because he ditches
and doesn't get caught, is that it?

                    JEANIE

Basically.

The boy nods.

                    BOY

Then your problem is you.

                    JEANIE

Excuse me?

                    BOY

Excuse you. You oughta spend a little
more time dealing with yourself and a
little less time worrying about what your
brother does. It's just an opinion.

Jeanie glares at him, but she knows that he's right.

                    JEANIE

What are you, a psychiatrist? Why don't
you keep your opinions to yourself?

                    BOY

There's somebody you should talk to.

Jeanie turns to him again, this time with venom.

                    JEANIE

If you say Ferris Bueller,
you lose a testicle.

                    BOY

Oh you know him?

CUT TO JEANIE'S HAND

Curling into a fist.

A couple of scenes later, Jeanie and Charlie Sheen are making out, which speaks to the power of the bad boy charisma and something to which you should never, never, never, never, never, never, never, never, never, never succumb.

You two girls are better served spending time dealing with yourselves and less time worrying about what everyone else does. I tell you that all the time. When you two start bickering and one of you complains about the other to deflect blame, what do I say?

"Don't worry about her. Worry about yourself."

It's natural to focus on what you don't have, as opposed to what's right in front of your eyes. When I was about 11 years old, I used to draw picture after picture of the New York City skyline, coloring in hundreds of little rectangles for windows, and imagine living in one of those tall buildings, just another worker ant in this marvelous metropolis. Meanwhile, right outside my bedroom window lay the streets of Rome, one of the few cities in the world that could outshine the Big Apple.

Living in New York City would have been a sign that I made it, and I chased it for years, and I got that validation, along with the experiences, the energy and the smells, when I finally started work here. Until sometime five years later, when all of a sudden, The City—just that term alone was beginning to grate, as though there was only one in the whole world—began to sour on me.

It didn't matter that I was working at a good law firm and making a good living. There were so many more people who were more accomplished than me. There were so many more people who were making more money than me. There were so many more people who were better looking than me. There were so many more people who were uglier than me and were having sex with beautiful women. There were so many more people who were uglier than me and were having sex. The perceived failure was crushing.

Just about this time, my father was having some health issues. Maybe, I wondered, this signaled a new phase in my life, where I would make my return to the Washington, D.C. area and take care of my parents and benefit from the smaller, less intense fishbowl. Word got back to my father, who immediately called me up.

"Don't come back on my account. It would break my heart."

What he wanted me to do was fight. He rather would have wanted me to be in the big pond, even as a small fish, scratching and surviving, hanging in a chow line. And what that meant to me was that I needed to start worrying about myself. Not others.

It only took that phone call from my father to dispel any doubts about staying in New York City, but over the next several months, I overcame this envy and jealousy by concentrating on myself. Because a fundamental truth emerged: you're goddam right that there's always going to be someone more accomplished, richer, better looking, has-a-hotter-girlfriend than you. That's inevitable. There are seven billion fucking people on this planet. It's kind of inevitable, you know what I mean? If you're set on cataloguing who is less deserving than you are and other injustices, you better be prepared to spend a hell of a lot of time and be absolutely miserable in the process. But if you lead the life you want to, and you're happy with it, then guess what? Who gives a flying fuck about the others?

You'll run across so many people who make it look effortless: they won't prepare for a test or a presentation and they'll ace it, they hardly ever work out and stay slim, they have those five shots of tequila and emerge fresh-faced early the next morning. It's tempting to think that you can do the same thing, but it's dangerous to assume. You go on your own wavelength.

When you concentrate on yourself, you become less susceptible to negative peer pressure. Have the confidence to go at your pace and block out other people's judgments. When you think about it, your ability to remain calm at work depends not just on your sheer force of will ("I'm not going to freak out I'm not going to freak out I'm not going to freak out"), but also your ability to block out other people's neuroses ("I'm not going to let her freak me out I'm not going to let her freak me out I'm not going to let her freak me out").

Charlie Sheen was right: worry about yourself. He was wrong about doing mountains of coke and crack, having unprotected sex with hookers and porn stars, not using his enormous wealth and clout to do anything positive for society, squandering his talent and burning every possible bridge in Hollywood, but he was right about this.

And just in case you're not convinced, let me list the various reasons why you should steer away from being jealous of certain people. Let's call it:

WHY YOU SHOULDN'T BE JEALOUS OF THE FOLLOWING PEOPLE

RICH PEOPLE

First of all, people tend to vastly overestimate other people's wealth. When we're young, we think of people earning way more than they do ("Those kids who breakdance on the street for money must make at least $10,000 a weekend") and even as we get older, we don't do a great job of accurately determining what someone really makes and the deductions of that income. Let's say it's an entertainer who makes $2 million a year—sounds great, right? Well, a little less than half goes to taxes, so you have just over a million. Let's not forget the manager, the agent, girlfriend/wife and kids, maybe the alimony/palimony payments, the house, the car, the lifestyle in an attempt to create the illusion of someone making much more than $2 million, the lawyers to defend that one bogus lawsuit but also that meritorious one...so now they're making almost as much as those kids breakdancing on the street.

Usually the person who proclaims "Money isn't everything" is someone who hasn't had to go to bed hungry or looked at a menu and made food choices based on price. But there is a fundamental truth to that expression. There are a ton of studies that show that once you earn a certain level of income, additional salary doesn't necessarily make you happier. A mere one year after winning the lottery—an event that means that you no longer have to worry about something quite fundamental to modern society—those winners are generally not that much happier than before. It's not necessarily the money in and of itself that fails to make people happy. It's usually the effect the extra money has on the surrounding people. You got the jealous people, the ones who wish they had it and the others who think you're undeserving. You got your leeches. You got the people who make judgments based on what you have. It just complicates matters.

So when I say to you that money isn't everything, it is because you were fortunate enough to not ever grow up with the burden of having to scrape by for a living. But don't ever think that simply having money will solve all, or even most of your problems. Money is not your God.

ATHLETES AND ENTERTAINERS

"Rich and famous." I think that for most of society, the athlete and the entertainer are the shortest path to being rich and famous.

I remember reading a *Sports Illustrated* feature about an 18-year-old who was the baseball equivalent of a Mozart and had just been called up to The Show. He had a gorgeous swing and could hit for power. Physically, he was a can't-miss prospect; not only that, this kid was, as they say, wise beyond his years. Incredibly composed and mature, always giving the right answers, and respectful of the game and his elders. And of course, he was preternaturally handsome.

My primary reaction after reading this article was: man, I'm old. I was 22.

Flash forward about 20 years. The prodigy is now broken down, requiring one surgery after another. Maybe the body betrayed him because he no longer used steroids or human growth hormone, for which he's already tested positive a couple of times, leading to a season-plus ban. He signed the two richest contracts in professional sports, totaling $500 million, but the second one is continually cited as a colossal blunder for the New York Yankees.

The polish has also worn thin. Behind the manicured answers, unflattering stories have bobbed to the surface: the cutting quotes about Derek Jeter that caused a permanent rift, his steadfast denial of using steroids before he was uncovered, the running of a sleazy apartment complex, the painting of himself imagined as a centaur hanging in his apartment, and on and on. Some of these stories were primarily media-fueled creations, but Alex Rodriguez mostly brought it all on himself.

Now that I'm old, I can trace the lifespan of an athlete and it's distressingly short—from high school phenom to college player with lots of potential to serviceable professional to out of the sport to a faded memory that's on the tip of your tongue. This happens to pretty much every entertainer—she flashes into the public consciousness and you can't imagine how this person won't be a fixture forever, and then she'll fade away, a relic of an older time.

If genetics, circumstances, and your ethic can't immediately propel you into this stratosphere of celebrity and wealth, that's all right. Life is not a sprint. It's a marathon. Even A-Rod is entering into a third act of redemption. If someone finds the centaur painting, though, he's toast.

BEAUTIFUL PEOPLE

Irrefutable fact: gorgeous people have an advantage over the butt-ugly. Beautiful men and women get better service, they're perceived as smarter and more dynamic, they get promoted more easily. Babies have been shown photos of normal and good-looking people and the infants tended to hold their stare on the latter group. There are genetic and societal forces at work here. If you two happen to take from your mother's side and are blessed with beauty, there are a couple of things to remember.

First, you don't have to downplay or minimize your looks. It's ridiculous to act like it has had absolutely no bearing on your circumstances. It's an asset and it should be used accordingly, with good judgment and in moderation. Second, there comes a point where people will be very quick to judge you based on your looks—that you're dumb, or aloof, or don't have a personality, or you're vain. It's a stereotype, just as injurious as any other, and the response is not to be defensive or aggressive. You just need to be you, and let your true self become apparent.

(This is why guys go ballistic when a hot woman says that it's a hindrance to be beautiful because she's not taken seriously. It's not that it's false—men adhere to the slavish obsession to appearance, so we are well aware of the power of stereotypes. But it's bad form to complain about something that gives a person such an advantage over the rest of us Neanderthals. The equivalent for a guy would be complaining that he has so much money that his wallet bulging with cash makes it look like he has a huge penis, when in fact he has a normal-sized one, and it creates unfair expectations with the really hot women he ends up having sex with. Kind of hard to rally a prayer vigil, you know?)

The reason why you should be judicious in relying upon your looks, of course, is that they are impossible to maintain. Everyone gets old and wrinkly and looks worse for wear; the old ones who look "amazing" are being graded on a curve. And those who resort to drastic measures to chase their youth will appear even more desperate than most. Time will always humble the best-looking of us.

You can't go through life looking like a blob, but being skinny isn't all awesome either. When an actor takes on a superhero role and transforms into this ripped specimen, the standard question is how he achieved it. And the answer is always, invariably, 100 times out of 100: "I worked out three times a day and ate unseasoned chicken breasts and rice for lunch and dinner for six months." Really thin and fit people miss out on the joys of food, to let go and indulge in it without regard to appearance. It's the price they pay for earning millions of dollars and basking in the adoration of millions of fans. You should feel sorry for the poor bastards.

PEOPLE WITH PERFECT FAMILY AND SPOUSAL RELATIONSHIPS

You may get to a point where you wonder why your family is so damned dysfunctional, why your sister is so mean yet clingy and why your mother is so overprotective and why you have a father who just had to write a book about raising you and why you just can't have a normal family or better yet, be like the Khans on 10th Street, all close and ordered and perfect.

Social media obviously contributes to this envy. When you see a friend's posted photo, in front of an exquisite beach, surrounded by her friends, with the perfect filter, and if you don't feel the need to trash your 200-square-foot apartment with a window looking right into a brick wall, you're not human. And maybe by the time you're older, you'll be savvy enough to realize that this is just a moment in time that's not indicative of that person's real life. But in the event that you do not, here it is.

You usually don't know what's happening behind the confines of the walls of a household, and when you do, you'd be surprised with what you find out. Human relationships are fraught with obvious, latent, and subconscious pettiness, jealousies and grudges—doesn't matter if you're related or not. This also holds true with marriages. You may be envious of the couple who never fights and still engage in PDA. You may think that if a couple is so successful in navigating their respective professional waters, surely it's an indication that they can bring each exquisite half for a more perfect union in the hearth of their home?

Dude, let me tell you something: get your head out of your ass. You're severely deluding yourself if you think there's a perfect family or an ideal marriage. So yes, your parents having a mutual hissy fit in an IKEA over the layout of your bedroom is absolutely normal. You're going to have to deal with it.

PEOPLE WHO ARE YOUNGER

If you have any sense of urgency in how you live your life, at some point you may end up envying people who are younger than you. You will bemoan the fact that you haven't accomplished a damn thing, or wonder whether you embarked upon the wrong career, or gnash your teeth that you still haven't met the one you want to marry. You will get nicked here and there by the physical signs of aging. You will pine about the things you can no longer do. You may wish that you were five years younger, or hell, just a few...

Aside from the fact that it's tough shit and there's nothing that man can do to actually reverse the dimension of time, you need to embrace getting old. Every year is a layer of education you add, another tree ring of life.

Sure, there are times when I wish I were younger, just so that my body were a bit more fit, or better yet, that I had the ability to go out and reinvent myself career-wise. How awesome would it be if on a whim I went to an improv class at the Upright Citizens Brigade and then I was spotted by a scout and then became the most unlikely repertory player (my brilliance of course would allow me to bypass featured player status) of *Saturday Night Live*? THERE'S STILL TIME, YOU KNOW, BECAUSE nah I'm 40 fucking years old with two girls and the family would crumble if I spent 100-hour weeks to churn out sketches that didn't even make the final cut.

But there are real advantages to getting old. It's relative, but you shouldn't have to worry about money as much. You play your cards right, you should be enjoying the benefits of your hard work.

Forget about material things for the moment. In football, it seems like the prime years of a quarterback are getting pushed back further and further, into the early/mid-30s and even beyond. Among the many reasons, one is that after a while, these quarterbacks have seen practically every possible defense that's been thrown at them. They're not fazed by the things that a kid coming out of college sees. If life is a compilation of events that can fall into general categories and certain patterns, and if you're experiencing all that you can, then it becomes easier to recognize and anticipate where things are going.

I feel more confident than ever that I can walk into a room cold and know what the human dynamics are within 15 minutes. I can usually find the appropriate response—apologetic, pissed, diplomatic—based on my read of the person. I know I can ask someone where she grew up and whatever the answer is, anywhere in the world, I will have been there, will want to be there, or will be curious about what there is. Even in unfamiliar work situations or court appearances, I rest easier knowing I can rely upon my abilities and past experiences. You can't learn these types of things simply by reading about them—you need the real-world repetitions. That's the triumph of experience over youth.

PEOPLE WITH A HIGH IQ AND WHO ARE BOOK SMART

They were always the source of my envy, those who were incredibly intelligent and seemed to grasp concepts and remember things effortlessly. The more I've spent time with them, though, the more I realized that a lot of these people have something missing. Maybe it's because they've had their noses in books too long, or they just can't relate to the dumber segment of society, but more often than not, they don't have that ability to socialize and make others feel at ease, that charisma.

The fact is that by the time you reach a certain level of schooling and experience, it is no longer about how smart you are. If you're brilliant, fine, congratulations. But sociability and likeability become much more important the older you become. I've interviewed a ton of prospective associates and for every 10 applicants, I would say about five to seven could have done a good job at the firm. It's virtually impossible to distinguish all of those applicants solely based on the words in that one-page résumé (by the way, never do a two-page résumé before you're 40 years old, just shows that you lack the ability to be brief and you're more impressed with your own credentials than you should be).

I was still in law school when I interviewed with a partner of a white-shoe firm in D.C. who introduced me to the notion of the "airport test." Sure, there are lots of people who can do the same assignment really well. But can you enjoy the company of this person during a six-hour delay at the airport?

That comment made a huge impression on me. I realized that the Venn diagram of competent people and tolerable people has a surprisingly small intersection. After that interview, I wrote a personalized follow-up letter to that partner and ended it with, "I hope that I passed the airport test." The kind of sentence that demonstrated I was listening, that I got his philosophy, and that I could be that team player. And in spite of my mediocre grades and experience, you know what he did?

He still rejected me. What a prick. Law firm partners are the worst.

PEOPLE WHO ARE POPULAR

I know what a big deal it is. When we lived in Massachusetts, I actually used to fantasize about being one of the popular kids in my class—not simply being me and becoming popular, but actually taking over a popular kid's identity. I was eight years old. You may lack the looks, wealth, athletic ability, charisma, or just the coolness, and that may be what keeps you on the sidelines in middle school, junior high, high school, college.

Do not fret. Yes, every year you will turn a deeper shade of green during Carnation-Gram Day at school (this tradition may have died about 50 years ago), and prom and formal season may be fraught with anxiety and loneliness. But you never should try to be popular for popularity's sake. Chasing that popularity will make you less true to yourself. If you're unhappy because you're unpopular, being popular won't necessarily make you fundamentally happier—that's the kind of happiness that comes from within, not from the validation of others. I have a feeling you'll get this lesson after watching the conclusion of every sitcom or movie involving an uncool person.

Besides, being an outsider and having a distance from the "cool group" isn't a bad thing. When you observe from afar, you can readily recognize good people, those who aren't swayed by the bullshit of being popular. You'll also keep in mind those who treat you well regardless of what group you're associated with. If you stick to the fundamentals of being a good person—to be humble, have integrity, and be nice—you will become popular among those who matter.

Reading this over, I couldn't help but be reminded of my parents telling me that I needed to study because "intelligence makes you extremely attractive to women." The example they cited?

HENRY KISSINGER. Had I only had the independent thinking to dispute this. I need the irrefutable proof that Kissinger was banging hot chicks left and right during the 70s.

PEOPLE WHO ARE ACCOMPLISHED, HAVE HIGH IQ AND EMOTIONAL INTELLIGENCE, HAVE STYLE AND ARE GENUINELY GOOD PEOPLE

Cry mercy. Make sure you kiss their asses so they'll be nice to you and you can ride their coattails to the top.

● ⋯⋯⋯⋯⋯⋯ ● ⋯⋯⋯⋯⋯⋯ ●

You are each a unique being. It's inevitable that this one is way dumber than you and yet making oodles more money, that she has ascended to high society and is a complete charlatan, that he is a sloth and manages to be promoted over and over. I know, it's not fair and it's tough to do, but you've got enough on your plate without comparing yourself to every other person in your social circle, or in your town, or in the whole world. Otherwise, that jealousy will corrode you from the inside and simply make you more bitter, and then indeed there will be a reason why you're the one who's not advancing forward.

Your best frame of reference is you. Concentrate on yourselves.

10

YOUR PROJECTION

You girls may have gathered by now that I'm not a rabble rouser or a provocateur. I won't send back food even if it falls well short of my expectations. If someone expresses a misguided opinion in casual group conversation, I likely won't respond with, "Well, actually, you little fuckface..." No waving of middle fingers in the air for me. I prefer to settle disputes diplomatically, with a minimum of fuss.

Which is also why I love Charles Barkley and Paul Zimmerman.

Barkley is the basketball Hall of Famer who played his game like a bull in a china shop and was coined the Round Mound of Rebound. In the 90s, he crossed over from star to national lightning rod when he said in a Nike commercial, "I am not a role model. I am not paid to be a role model. I am paid to wreak havoc on the basketball court. Parents should be role models. Just because I can dunk a basketball doesn't mean I should raise your kids." He speaks his mind, whether it's basketball, race or politics—and it's hilarious and rarely politically correct.

Zimmerman, or Dr. Z, was a longtime writer for *Sports Illustrated* whose Hemingway-esque football pieces elevated the sport: after reading them, no longer did I see these players as stumbling helmets and pads running into each other, but rather as thinking, violently brutal chess pieces. I would read about his willingness to stand up for his opinions, to question the establishment and the status quo ("A foolish consistency is the hobgoblin of little minds" was his mantra), which led to a trail of disgruntled opponents in his wake: players, coaches, fellow journalists, fans.

Neither man backed down from his opinions. Neither was swayed by the tide of popular sentiment.

I will channel my inner Charles Barkley and Dr. Z for this chapter because it's not the most politically correct one—it's easy to imagine the backlash in this age when people get offended over the most innocuous actions or opinions. It's about the superficial things, the impressions that we give to others. I would classify this chapter as "You don't have to do these things, but you're making things waaaaaaay more difficult for yourself if you don't, and you completely forfeit any right to complain as a result of not following this advice." I would also say that everything in this chapter is particularly subject to the general rule of balance: there is serious potential to go astray if you apply too much of these principles.

You may be asking why can't people overlook the surface and instead try to get to the essence of me.

Simply, it takes too much time. To get to the essence of someone, you need to spend a good bit of time with him or her, and the overwhelming lot of us do not have that luxury. We naturally make split-second judgments of others based on details, some of which are ridiculous and some of which are not. (These are to be distinguished from those people whose split-second judgments are based on stereotypes and irreversible, commonly known as "asshats.")

With the adage that "you don't have a second chance to make a first impression" in mind, let's start. Imagine that you're about to meet a stranger.

An immediate way to look smart: close your mouth. You could be dressed in the finest threads from Italy, your hair and skin pampered by Hollywood's best, and just about to ascend several steps to receive multiple Nobel prizes in literature, physics, and medicine, but if your mouth is open, you will just look like a dumbass. When I was a kid, my father would go a step further and exhort me to not only have my mouth closed, but to have my lips pursed together, the "determined" look. It only came off as "constipated." All I ask is that you not be a mouthbreather.

The body. If you're fat, get in shape. If you're thin, look more robust. I'm not getting into a discussion of body image and how women and men are enslaved by media portrayals, etc. Just use your common sense and tie it to the anchor of good health. If you're looking in the mirror and you genuinely know that your body is not looking like a normal person's body, then you need to take steps to change it. This is within your hands, and if you believe in the primacy of the mind over matter, then this is possible.

That advice was kind of facile, right? Prepare to get your minds blown further. You have to dress well.

Dressing well is most important from your college years until you're about in your 40s. Before and during high school, someone who judges you solely by the way you dress is superficial and pretty much comprises every teenager in the world. When you get to college, though, hopefully you'll start forging an identity, and that means your own sense of style. When you get out into the real world, you'll be at the mercy of people who definitely will judge you based on the way you look.

If you decide that you will not dress sharp, then you better be inversely brilliant. When you don't comb your hair, wear mismatched socks, have perpetually crumpled clothes, and your name is Albert Einstein, it's pretty endearing. If you do all those things and your name is Alfred Einstein, you're just a filthy bum.

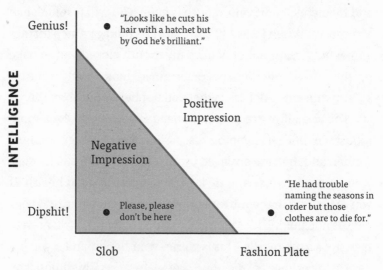

Only when you've started to establish yourself can you start to push back a little and let your preferred sense of style come out.

Doesn't have to be business attire all the time. I know that we're evolving toward a comfort society, but you still have to have the sharp power outfit. Doesn't have to be expensive. You can find something that won't completely bankrupt you. Doesn't have to be super trendy. (But if there's one thing I've learned since being with your mother, it's that when there's a clothing trend, you jump on it before it hits the mainstream and ride that sucker before it's played out and everyone realizes how stupid it is.) This doesn't apply as much to women than guys, but what's just as important as wearing nice clothes is wearing them well, meaning neatly. Nothing can completely neutralize expensive clothes like wearing them like a slob.

Without saying a word, that's the image you project. Now it's time to interact with this stranger.

You want a strong introduction. When you don't know the other person, or maybe you're only kind of familiar with her, you should be the first one to introduce yourself. The general rule is: Act like you give a shit.

Well, how can you do that? Eye contact is a must. Any strong initial connection between two human beings involves locking eyes, and there is something perturbing about someone who is unwilling to make steady eye contact. You give a genuine smile, the universal sign of a welcoming, warm person. You give a firm handshake—don't give the limp noodle, which grosses out the other person—and don't give the death grip like you're trying to show how much you can bench.

When you hear the other person's name, you remember it. The name is the most important thing you possess, the hallmark of your identity. Wouldn't you feel belittled if this person didn't go through the trouble of remembering your name? If you forget it, even within a couple of minutes, be honest and ask again that person's name again. That's your one-time bailout move, because if you do it again, you are now officially a jackass.

If you claim that "I'm terrible with faces" or "I can never remember names"...I call bullshit. That's about the lamest copout excuse there is. Because if a gorgeous man walked through that door and started flirting with you, or if a blindingly successful woman had the means to offer you a life-changing job, or if a vagrant said his name and then slapped you across the face, you damn sure that person's name will be seared into the neurons of your brain. (Same for emails or texts. "I didn't respond because oh my God you don't know how busy I've been and so incredibly stressed and I think I may be having a—" Come on, man. It takes five seconds to write something that conveys this sentiment and not make the other person feel like a total loser.) Willpower. Shun Fujimoto.

My father admired the politesse of British royalty so much that when I was young, he actually wanted me to address him as "sir" on occasion. I can say it now. This is stupid. The thought of a child addressing a parent by "sir" or "ma'am" is liable to make me cry. That being said, especially with work elders or even contemporaries, it's never a bad thing to use those terms. With familiarity and in the right situation, you shouldn't hesitate to throw in "dude" and "man" and "chief" and "sister." Words of bonhomie can sound contrived, but when you do it sincerely and appropriately, it makes a huge difference. Come on, who doesn't want to be called "boss" by the NYC deli guy when he's taking your bacon egg and cheese sandwich order? You say that to someone else, that's an instant connection right there.

An easy way to sound older than you are: talk more slowly. I remember reading this from a Bob Costas profile, when the preternaturally youthful announcer wanted to sound more distinguished and with more gravitas. It's certainly easier said than done; it takes some time and is borne of the natural confidence you gain as you age. When you're young, you're not as confident and you tend to want to fill silences with anything, even if they are your rambling, stream-of-consciousness thoughts. Remember, it's helpful solely in the work context; if you start taking Howard Cosell-like pauses between words when talking to your friends, you're going to be punched in the face.

Cursing. I still remember when you, Sofia, came up to me as a first grader and announced that you now knew what the "S word" was. I inhaled sharply and asked nonchalantly, "Oh yeah? What is it?"

"Stupid."

The exhale was much louder than the inhale.

"Yes, it is, Sofia. Yes, it is."

When you're young, there should be close to no cursing. I still remember breaking out in a sweat when my father asked me to repeat what I had just said at the dinner table, just to make sure that he hadn't misheard me. "I better get my ass in gear." I was a junior in high school. And I was referring to the amount of studying I needed to do.

I can understand what my father was thinking. When you're not familiar with someone and you hear him curse, it instantly conjures up an image—uncouth, brusque, oafish. You meet someone and if she immediately starts dropping f-bombs and doing an Andrew Dice Clay routine, it's natural to view that person as classless. It lowers you on the societal totem pole and makes others think that you weren't raised properly. And the problem is that similar to annoying verbal expressions such as "like," "know what I mean," and "you know," once you start cussing, it's awfully hard to stop. It can become this crutch you use to seem funnier or tougher. Why do you think litigators swear all the time? Sure, it could be the soul-sucking existence of fighting every day for a living. But part of it is just bravado, the necessity of talking the language before combat. A New York litigator who doesn't curse is either brilliant or a doormat.

When you get older, though, you start to realize that the well-timed, appropriate expletive can be a Swiss Army knife. It imparts a familiarity to a nascent relationship. It signals to others that you're one of the guys. It gives the type of urgency that can be even more effective than shouting. The more of an academic or an intellectual you are, cursing has the opposite effect, because it makes one seem more human. Kind of a signal that this person is all right. Not an uptight fuckstick, amirite?

For me, table manners reign paramount. I have spent about two full years of my waking life telling you two to keep your mouths closed while you eat. I have gotten into hellacious fights with your mother and grandmother about letting you have gum because I feel that it will make you more susceptible to chomping loudly at the dinner table (and I am completely right on this). And all of this is well worth it, because when you open your mouth while you eat, or when you slurp soup, or when you cut your steak holding your knife and fork like sawing equipment, you reveal everything about yourself. Table manners—and really, any manners—are a surefire indicator of where you are in life, or at the very least, where you aspire to be.

You may be thinking how all of these rules seem elitist and judgmental, which would appear to run contrary to my pleas for you to be humble and kind. They are not inapposite. One set of rules is a non-negotiable guideline, while the other set is for dealing with the practical realities of the real world.

Another question may nag.

"Why does this mean so much to you?"

The immigrant experience.

Your grandfather and your grandmother grew up in two of the most populous countries in the world. They left their comfort zones and came to the United States because this was the place where they could have the best opportunity to succeed, the one country that values effort and a will to learn than over a caste system. They wanted to distinguish themselves from the millions of other Asians who immigrated here, all scratching, clawing, desperate to survive. They learned a foreign language. They integrated into American society, even if the customs were strange and people were unwilling to let them in. To be even able to claim that they were upper-middle class was a tremendous achievement in and of itself, and I was the vessel to further that ambition. They taught me the value of etiquette and how to conduct myself in social circles where I was forced to punch above my weight class. All the while, I labored. I am that third category of New Yorker, the one who was born somewhere else and came to a city for a quest. I put in the hours and made sacrifices—fundamental ones that impact personal enjoyment—for a semblance of a respectable job and a comfortable life.

Don't you dare undo it.

Because as unfair as it may seem for me to impose these strict rules regarding the way you project yourself, you will find that you yourselves will be subject to that very same unfairness. You will undoubtedly be future victims of racism and sexism.

I do not like having to be the trumpeter of doom and detail all of the ways in which you will encounter the darkness of strangers' hearts just because of your gender or race. Even trying to shoehorn this discussion into the tail end of a chapter is woefully inadequate. It is the subject of an exceedingly soberer and—really, depressing as hell—tome. But pretending that it doesn't exist is far worse. I guarantee that the person who wails, "Why does everything have to be about race?" has had the luxury of not having to think about race as a fundamental part of his or her identity and being penalized for it.

You may start by asking, "If I'm half Western and half Asian, how come I'm considered to be a member of a minority?" The lengthy and convoluted answer involves the history, socioeconomic origins, and racist legacy of the "one drop rule," where if there was even a trace of a sub-Saharan African ancestry, one was considered to be black. The simpler answer is that as long as you look "different" based on your fundamental appearance, there will be enough hate and epithets and social exclusion to go around. Guess what—you won't miss out on it.

Having grown up in New York, you will take for granted the diversity all around you. And as much as it seems that race relations are more roiled than ever, there is much to be thankful for. The overt racism definitely ain't what it used to be. Sure, even by the time that you're grown, there may be many places where you may be called a chink or a jap or a nigger like I was (the last slur more puzzling than hurtful). Hopefully, society will be moving toward a more tolerant space. Or at the very least, society will be intolerant of those who openly use those slurs and think those thoughts. Which leads to the more insidious and pervasive problem.

It will be latent. Maybe the racism and sexism will be so imperceptible as to be unconscious biases, tougher to pin down and root out, and it will be the type of prejudice inextricably linked with work. It may start with assumptions on how you got there. There may be preconceptions of what you're capable of before you've even started an assignment. Any misstep or weakness may be pounced upon and more readily used as a black mark against you personally. If that happens to you, know that I have gone through some variation of it as well. People have been quick to categorize me as meek and unassertive, which dovetails with a general stereotype of Asians. (There are Asian males of a certain age who have a deep well of untapped rage as a result of their desire to conform to parental expectations and yet break stereotypes.)

Sometimes the perpetrators are unexpected. I hate to say this, but some of the worst supervisors of women are other women. I won't even try to back this up with statistics or empirical evidence, but your mother and I have seen it enough times to know that it's not imagination or a coincidence. Jealousy or insecurity fuels this kind of behavior, and you do not contribute to this cycle.

I hope that by the time you've grown, the social biases will have abated. Maybe you will not wonder about whether a person hates Asians or is simply an asshole after you smile and say a hearty hello and get an icy glare in return. Maybe you will not experience the feeling, as I often did, of being acutely aware that I was the only Asian in the room. (This was a distinctly different feeling from when I was in Italy years ago and spoke the language; people would stare at me as if a dog got on its hind legs, carefully put on a tutu, and started juggling marshmallows.) Maybe you won't grasp that you will need to work twice as hard to prove that you belong. Maybe you will not wonder about whether your race is a factor as to why you haven't cracked the inner circle of your firm. Maybe when you hear Chris Rock's Oscars monologue definition of "sorority racist" ("We like you, Rhonda...but you're not a Kappa"), you won't really get it. Maybe those last bastions of prejudice will have been stormed and overtaken. But I would not rely on it.

"How am I supposed to deal with this?"

Balance. There's the world that we wish we live in and the world that we actually live in, and navigating the latter requires that you strike the proper balance between the two.

You concentrate on you. You outwork everyone else. You give it your best damn shot. Don't give those dipshits any excuses to denigrate you. And if you find yourself to the subject of trumped-up bias, you fight back.

FUCK THOSE FUCKERS, you hear?

You assume that everyone you meet has an open heart and is not judging you based on your skin or your gender, and the moment you realize that it's not the case, you punt that fuckwad into the next county. I damn sure know it's better than the alternative, where you're making your own assumptions and imagining demons and fashioning excuses. That's when the racism claims you. You do not surrender to your conditions and provide more ammunition for your enemies. You be you, doing what you do, standing on your principles, confounding expectations, going against stereotypes, blazing your trail. Dr. Z and the Round Mound of Rebound would approve.

11

ADVICE ON HOW TO SUCCESSFULLY NAVIGATE SOCIAL WATERS FROM SOMEONE WHO WAS NEVER VOTED PROM KING OR WON ANY SENIOR SUPERLATIVES

At the annual firm summer outing many years ago, I began talking to a partner's wife about our kids and about my and your mother's childhoods as only children. And the woman, an only child herself, leaned over and said, almost conspiratorially, "Well, you know, only children never want to have just one child."

It was the type of observation that rang true. It explained why, as ecstatic as we were to have one child, we felt that impulse for a second one.

An only child's existence is unique. She can be the sole focus of her parents, shouldering alone their fears and dreams, or he can be an afterthought, unable to break through the primary relationship between the mother and the father. In any event, it is a lonely trek. For two people who grew up as only children and moved frequently to one unfamiliar locale after another, your mother and I developed into two spectacularly different social creatures.

If the difference between an extrovert and an introvert is whether the person relaxes during spare time by being social or by being alone, then your mother is definitely the former. Your mother has a knack for keeping her friends and acquaintances close. True to her Italian roots, she will be the one suggesting to have a random group of people over for dinner. She reaches out to people she hasn't heard from in a while, any reservations about face-saving be damned. She makes that effort. Maybe if you're keeping score of who is contacting whom more and who is going out of her way more and who is "reaching," she comes out on the short end. But her mind doesn't work in petty ways like mine, and she doesn't see how it hurts to do it.

Our friends and acquaintances are surprised to hear that at heart, I am an introvert. They never got to see my younger self, who saw large social gatherings and instantly relived the insecurities of being the new face at school; who felt more comfortable eating in a restaurant solo or going on long vacations by himself; who was more likely not to say hello to someone on the street, a self-defense mechanism in case he was not recalled immediately. Sure, when the situation called for it, I could be social and entertaining for an evening. But like a hockey player coming off the ice after a monster six-minute shift, afterward I would need to retreat and have some alone time.

Now, years later, your mother and I have gradually converged to a happy medium, and it's because of you two. After an exhausting day of work, your mother no longer wanted to fill up empty evenings with social events. She wanted to be with you. And when you two entered school, I started to meet lots of other parents who weren't asshole lawyers or boring lawyers or even normal lawyers. Socializing became more fun.

There are more studies concluding that being more social and interactive with other people leads to greater happiness. Whether or not the initial emotion is forced, I really believe that you do feel happier with a stronger sense of community. My world has certainly gotten bigger. Yeah, it was kind of nice to be in my little world, but it was damn lonely sometimes, you know?

As someone who has gradually evolved to become a more gregarious being, here are my tips for you to be able to get along well with others and just be more likeable.

RENAISSANCE PERSON

A balanced person is well-rounded, with varied interests, and informed in many fields.

The first name people think of as a Renaissance man is Leonardo da Vinci, whose expertise stretched across a staggering number of disciplines, such as painting, drawing, sculpture, anatomy, architecture, engineering, math, music, cartography, astronomy, literature, and fantasy football (but not fantasy baseball, which was too much of a time commitment). He is one for whom "genius" is an apt moniker, but it would not have been fully realized without his unquenchable curiosity, his desire to seek answers to how this world works.

You need to have this curiosity, not just of the world, but of your fellow human. The easiest way in which you connect with others is by asking questions. I see this particularly in you, Alessandra, and it fills me with joy. You ask what are taxes and what's homework like in third grade and who's the best soccer player for Roma (and I respond "CHE CI FREGA DEL PIERO NOI C'ABBIAMO TOTTI GOL. TOTTI GOL...TOTTI GOL..."). There is something, however trivial, that you can learn from just about anyone. If you're humble, you shouldn't feel shy or embarrassed about not knowing anything—you have this opportunity to talk to someone about their chosen field, so you take it. Be curious about this world and the people who inhabit it and draw that information out. If you find yourself next to a person who drives a taxi or majored in 18th-century French literature or creates anime or interprets umbrella insurance policies or plays water polo, or likes to read 18th-century French anime depicting water polo and drives a cab on the side...dammit, make it your mission to find out more. Have that inquisitive mind.

By the time you've grown up, the aspiration to be a polymath may seem quaint. In your world, people may be more focused on surviving financially, so they feel the need to find a specialty earlier and earlier, to carve out a niche. The temptation may be to not care for knowledge that does not directly impact a chosen profession, expertise, and earning potential. And to a certain extent, it does appear to be justifiable. If you're a budding cardiologist, does reading *Othello* help at all in that pursuit? Recognizing a Degas? Knowing Southeast Asian history? But this craving for money and financial security should only go so far, and should never become the unyielding driving force in your lives.

No matter how important it is to choose a profession, there's still a world beyond those confines. If you decide to go into the sciences, you must not neglect the arts and culture, which are usually the first casualties of such a practical approach. If you go into the arts, you have to force yourselves to understand the sciences. They will benefit you equally and immensely.

When I was around eight, I started to read some astronomy books that piqued my interest, stoking the general little-kid fascination with space and celestial bodies. After I told my father that it would be interesting to be an astronomer, he responded, "That's the dumbest thing I've heard. Don't be ridiculous. People looking through telescopes to look at stars that are millions and millions of light years away?"

Well, that comment pretty much squelched any further ambition of mine to look through a telescope. As harsh as it was, many, many, many years later, I can see my father's point. We should arguably try to be engaged in the world we are living in, surrounded by seven billion other human beings, instead of looking at things that are seven billion miles away.

Thus a knowledge of world affairs is a must. You need to be an informed citizen without being drawn into depression about all of the shitty things happening in the world and feeling the urge to climb into bed with the covers over your head. But when you take a reserve from the real world, then the things that take place into your substitute world—work, friends, leisure activities—take on an outsized and disproportional importance.

In time, having accumulated this varied knowledge, you will be able to talk to just about anyone. If you can make conversation with anybody, on topics that you have no particular interests in—Formula One racing, coolest movie poster one sheets, Patagonia travel, U.N. policy in Central America, artificial intelligence—you can make better connections to people. Not necessarily as a way to schmooze your way to the top of society, but you will become a richer person for it. Life will seem much fuller when you have a varied palette to work from. It's the human experience.

SENSE OF HUMOR

Judd Apatow observed that in a presidential election, the funnier candidate wins: "Reagan was funny. Bill Clinton was funny. Bush was funnier than Gore. Obama was funnier than probably anybody who's ever run for office." What probably was meant to be a joke has, in this age of media, hardened into fact. And with the presidential election of 2016, that streak continued, although there must have been people who regretted choosing the better insult comic as the leader of the free world.

We enter this world with laughter and joy and we rarely leave in the same way. The average baby smiles anywhere from

200–400 times a day. The average adult male smiles only about 10 times a day—and one of them is false. We don't need to go into the reasons for this decline, but researchers are beginning to find out the power of the smile. The mere act of smiling is contagious, as evidenced by people who are around babies. Even in New York, it's hard to be an asshole when you're looking right into a smiling face (unless the smiling face is really an "asshole smile," in which case you're justified in punching his lights out). There are few things as satisfying as a good laugh. If you can laugh in the face of suffering, as Garry Shandling said, then you've taken one step in neutralizing your troubles.

Making someone laugh is hard. It's criminally underrated—you never see a comedy on the list of Best Picture nominees. And even then, there's a huge disparity in opinions as to what actually is funny. If you looked at the American Film Institute's list of the 100 funniest movies until 2000, it's a bunch of black and white films that are guaranteed not to split any of your sides—more likely, one would tilt his head slightly backward, do a *sotto voce* "ho ho ho" and then adjust his monocle. In other words, NOT FACKIN' FUNNY AT ALL.

You don't need to go out of your way to be funny—in fact, the harder you try, the less funny you are. Conan O'Brien's observation in a Howard Stern interview comes to mind: "I always think the class clown, the guy who gets up and sets the clock ahead 20 minutes, that guy always dies in a motel shootout." You don't need to be that guy.

Context. You know when talking about balance, I referred to how some hot guy can be perceived as being extreeeeeeemely kind just by acting like a normal human being, just because people are overly impressed with a man who has reaped the benefits of being good-looking and yet not turned into a complete dickwad? Same concept. If you go into any academic or professional career, but show flashes of humor here and there, you'll get way more credit for being funnier than you are. You climb that mountain, and the people you meet further up are increasingly bereft of the ability to be funny, like the thin air is depriving them of the ability to see the humor in life.

But aren't you just born with a sense of humor—you either have it or you don't? Again, I have to believe that the answer is not absolute or preordained. I'm not talking about making a living from making others laugh—there seems to be an innate quality that lends itself to that path. While you may be born with a certain appreciation of laughter, you can also easily acquire a sense of humor from watching good comedy. In that sense, comedy seems to be no different than any other craft: you watch the classics over and over again, and you'll absorb that comedic sensibility into your personality.

Here is my completely biased list of what you can watch, listen to, and read in order to have a good sense of humor. There are few things as insufferable as a non-professional attempting to dissect hilarious material and explain why it's funny, so I won't do that. And sure, it's not definitive—there are about a million lists of what are the all-time funniest movies or TV shows. But if anything, this will give insight into what made your old man laugh his ass off:

• David Letterman: Just thinking about the *Late Night with Letterman* show on NBC brings me back to a familiar place—being at college, staying up past 12:30 in the morning, pining for New York, laughing in a way that I had not before instead of going out and trying to meet women. Good times! I saw the Letterman/Leno ratings battles as a fight for the soul of comedy, which meant I needed to get a life. When I finally moved to the City, I was probably less excited about living two blocks from Central Park than being four blocks from the Ed Sullivan Theater and *The Late Show.*

• *Cheers:* Through the magic of syndication and the lack of any female companionship, there was a time when I could watch the first two or three minutes of any episode and tell you the exact joke or exchange that ended the show. Exactly zero women were turned on by this feat.

• Seasons two through seven of *The Simpsons*: I own the DVD box sets for all of these seasons and spent the early 2000s rewatching every episode many multiples of times instead of going out and dating.

• *Saturday Night Live*: Lorne Michaels once said that he could tell the general time frame when people went to high school based on their favorite SNL era. It may explain why I revered the grandiose and self-aware style of Phil Hartman. Almost 20 years after it last aired on SNL, I went as Unfrozen Caveman Lawyer one Halloween. You're not going to believe it, but out of the millions of New Yorkers on the streets that night, there was absolutely no one who got it and my costume did not get me laid.

• Conan O'Brien and any skit involving Triumph the Insult

Comic Dog: One of the most inspiring speeches ever—alongside Churchill's speech to the House of Commons after France fell to the Nazis, the Gettysburg Address, Martin Luther King's "I Have a Dream," and the Inches monologue by Al Pacino in *Any Given Sunday*—is Conan's Harvard commencement address from 2000. I transcribed the speech, hoping that I could become as brilliantly funny and resilient simply by osmosis. Honestly, I would excerpt that entire speech here, except I'm fairly sure I'd be violating copyright law and worse yet, you'd wish Conan had written this book of fatherly advice.

• *30 Rock* and *Parks and Recreation:* The main casualty of having kids has been my lack of TV knowledge. But I think Tina Fey and Amy Poehler are gods and if they told me to take a crap in my pants for their amusement, I'd do it.

• Howard Stern: The first time I ever saw him was his old Channel 9 TV show, when I was absolutely horrified by some of the most vile, abominable, hateful, contemptible sketches to hit my eyes. Then I read *Private Parts*, and then *Miss America*, and then started listening to his radio show once in a while, which became pretty much every day, and then I would set my alarm with his radio show and I'd inevitably fall back asleep while it was blaring away, which led to some of the trippiest dreams ever. Listening to him now—a wiser, humbler, more introspective person who has developed into a sensational interviewer with no loss on his comedic fastball—makes me happy for him.

• When we got our first VCR in the late 80s (we were way behind the times) and I rented my first video, my parents were crushed by my selection: *Tootsie*, which I had seen back in Rome. This is what

Asian parents do—make their 15-year-old kid feel inadequate for not making his inaugural video rental *Hamlet* or *All Quiet on the Western Front*. I watched *Tootsie* over and over within those three days. This qualifies as rebellion for the Asian child.

• I've pretty much committed to memory the best Farrelly brothers movies (my personal favorites, in order: *Kingpin*, *There's Something About Mary*, *Dumb and Dumber*, *Stuck on You*) and the first three Zucker/Abrahams productions of *Kentucky Fried Movie*, *Airplane!* and *Top Secret!*. When I watch these movies now, it's like reading a letter from a long-lost friend involving the most juvenile and tasteless humor possible. If you want to seem slightly more sophisticated, you'll say that *Blazing Saddles* and *Young Frankenstein* are your favorite Mel Brooks movies, and the best Woody Allen movie is *Manhattan*, not *Annie Hall*, in spite of everyone automatically mentioning the Oscar winner.

• In an era when Soviet Politburo members were funnier than most "humorous" newspaper columnists, Dave Barry and Tony Kornheiser would make me laugh out loud. *The Onion* has taken that mantle now.

• You know how you'll go to a comedy club and laugh your ass off and still not remember a single bit afterward? No such problems for me with routines by Chris Rock, Jerry Seinfeld, Louis CK, and David Chappelle—I'll listen to them over and over and commit them to memory.

• People who could have me howling without saying a single word: Bill Murray, Martin Short, Steve Martin.

Looking at this list, it's not terribly diverse, right? I'd add more but then it simply smacks of tokenism. Be grateful that you are living in more enlightened times for women and minorities to be blazing those trails. You watch and read and listen to enough of this, you should be good.

Parents delight in emphasizing how funny their child is, when their kid's behavior is really no different than 99 percent of others. The other day, when you two were roughhousing, I explained the concept of using a "safe word" to signal when the playing went too far and one of you was really getting hurt (my subsequent research revealed that maybe it was too early for me to be introducing a term almost used exclusively in S&M).

A couple of days later, amid the noise in your bedroom, I could hear an increasingly urgent cry from one of you.

"COMBUSTION ENGINE! COMBUSTION ENGINE!"

You girls may already be comedic geniuses.

TELEPORTATION

Listen up. This is probably the most important quality to navigate successfully in society. You must have the ability to go outside of yourself and go into the shoes of another person. When you can do that, and imagine another person's emotions, motivations, and expectations, you have an advantage over others that is hard to quantify but nonetheless incredibly substantial. An overwhelming percentage of the human race will call this the ability to empathize. I'll call it to "teleport"— to dematerialize at some point and assemble within another person—because it sounds way cooler.

A significant part of teleportation is simply genetic. I won't set forth a reasonable justification for that statement, but it seems like some people simply don't have the genetic predisposition to be able to empathize. But I firmly believe that there is an environmental/learned aspect as well. If you want to understand, if you make that effort, you will. Shun Fujimoto.

Isn't being punctual the ultimate sign of teleporting? When you're late for a dinner with friends, class, or a work meeting, it's rude as hell. By keeping the other person waiting, you're essentially saying, "My time is more valuable than yours." If you can visualize and feel the toe-tapping impatience and inconvenience that you are causing to others, it shouldn't be hard for you start making more of an effort to be on time.

I live in fear of your teenage years and when you start giving us some attitude. As your bodies are going through seismic changes as you make the transition from girls to women, it's easy to imagine the resulting psychological transformation and your need to focus your anger and anxiety toward something, anything. You two will be dual Godzillas running rampant through the streets of a metropolis, and if I were to pass before my time, the only difference is that there would be one fewer Asian running and yelling poorly dubbed things. May God have mercy on your mother.

Supposing that I'm still around, I feel that how your mother and I will react to your fits of attitude will be critical. I certainly have no frame of reference: my parents never had to deal with me rolling my eyes, because I never did it, because I was petrified of being smacked into the next time zone. My impulse would be to do whatever my parents would have done, which would be to go ballistic and excoriate you for disrespecting your parents. But if I try to put myself in your shoes and try to imagine the growing pains you're experiencing, your attempt to assert your independence, or see that your nonchalance is really an attempt to preserve your pride...that eye roll is placed in a different context. It's still not acceptable and we would need to emphasize that, but my response would certainly be more measured and hopefully more well-received by you.

Omoiyari is a Japanese word whose roots are "omoi," to think or feel, and "yari," to do or undertake. *Omoiyari* is normally translated as thoughtfulness or consideration for others, but has a much deeper significance, one that can be said to define Japanese society altogether.

In the words of Japanese anthropologist Sugiyama Lebra, *omoiyari* is "the ability and willingness to feel what others are feeling, to vicariously experience the pleasure or pain that they are undergoing, and to help them satisfy their wishes...without being told verbally." It manifests itself when you see a cool Steelers shirt online and get it for an acquaintance from Pittsburgh for no particular reason. It shows when you're walking the city with your friend and suggest a coffee break because you've noticed that she could use a rest. It drives your making of a sandwich for your mother when she's about to go on a bus trip home (and not taking offense when you are told that your sandwiches are barely edible).

In time, it becomes a type of radar in which you're in tune

with other people's feelings and their wants. *Omoiyari* explains why the Japanese are excellent at anticipating what others want and are the master of the little gesture that gives joy to one another. It can even go too far. *Omoiyari* can become a stifling burden because you're so mindful of others that your own needs are constantly made a lower priority. Taken to an extreme, one cannot really be true to himself or herself and simply do what he or she wants, which is an inalienable and fundamental part of the American way of life.

But when teleporting is dosed properly, something interesting happens. Your ability to become judgmental is diminished significantly. When you understand someone's background, his upbringing and what that person has been through, then it gets a lot easier to see why that person reacts in a certain way. It doesn't completely absolve the person's poor behavior, but at least you can see "where he's coming from." You are forced to be humbler and it cuts down on high-minded hypocrisy. It's harder to pass judgment once you have more information or even presume to have that information. It is exactly the sentiment expressed when Pope Francis said, "If a person is gay and searches for God with good will, who am I to judge him?" As groundbreaking as that statement seemed to be, it's kind of ridiculous that the head of the church who believes in a compassionate and merciful God would need to say it, no?

In your increasingly data-driven world where metrics can dictate the best plan and the most efficient way to execute it, the last frontier will be the human mind and its inner workings. And perhaps one day we'll all have sensors that measure the physiological levels of contentment and unhappiness and longing and resentment and jealousy and lust and the whole range of human emotions. And perhaps they'll be accessible only to your closest friends, maybe at the mere touch of a button (or more likely, the mere mental thought of touching a button). But until then, the best you can do is be good at being able to teleport and feel what your target is feeling. As Atticus told Scout in *To Kill A Mockingbird*, you can't really understand a person until you consider things from his point of view, "until you climb into his skin and walk around in it."

Who cares that it won a Pulitzer Prize and is universally regarded as a modern classic of American literature—that phrase totally creeps me out. Teleport! Teleport! Teleport! If I say the term enough times, I'm sure it'll catch on.

12

A CUBICLE MONKEY'S
VIEW OF THE WORLD

A parent's worrying never ends. It's short-sighted to think that it ceases when your kid learns to walk in a straight line without bashing his head against the corner of a table, or when she starts to excel in school, or finds a woman that he can trust, or when she's financially independent. No matter how old he or she becomes—I'm talking 88 years old and putting in teeth before having breakfast—that person will always be that baby whom the parent doted on.

Of all of the things that I could worry about for you, I think that your chosen profession occupies an inordinate amount. Part of this is projecting. I look at myself and your mother and the difficulties we currently face as middle-aged workers. But I can't be the only who sees this world as becoming more stratified in terms of available jobs, compensation, or a work-life balance.

I will not be able to provide a comprehensive piece on the

intersection of the historical, sociological, and technological changes affecting the work force since the mid-20th century, but it doesn't take a genius to understand that people then competed in a vastly smaller pool. For all of the benefits of globalization and technology, now you will not be in competition just with the kids living on your same street, or in your hamlet, or in your county. It is on, against anyone with a computer and with an internet connection. And between the kid living in a plush Manhattan apartment and with the conveniences of a New York City life and a kid in India who's tenacious and intelligent and has no choice but to struggle to survive, guess what— I'm putting my money on the poor kid. In my mind, for you guys, finding a spiritually satisfying job that will sustain you in financial comfort will alone be a tremendous achievement.

I went to law school because, well, my father told me to. Believe me, that's not an easy sentence to write. It seems incredibly weak-willed, even if I was a son who did as he was told by his father and wanted to please him. He said that all I had to do was go to law school and then I could go into whatever profession I wanted. Of course, when I agreed, it didn't occur to me that once I graduated, I would be in six-figure debt and probably the first job I would be looking for would be as a lawyer, and it would become increasingly difficult to extricate myself from the legal profession as I got older. Talk about not looking at the fine print.

Looking back, my poor performance in law school might just have been a subconscious attempt to rebel. Sure, I studied hard, but there were many nights when I watched the CBS investigative TV show *48 Hours* and imagined myself as a hard-charging reporter, or *Later with Bob Costas*, with me bantering with Martin Scorsese. And I harbored a dream. I would work in the law for five years, after which I would make my foray into journalism. That would have worked out fantastically. You probably would be reading this by candlelight in your very own refrigerator box under a bridge.

Let's preface this, as we must, with a dose of perspective. I have no doubt taken my career in law for granted. My life is not in danger every single day, or any day. My body does not ache after many hours at the job. It is not absolutely necessary for me to get a second job to pay the bills. I take as a given that every day I go into the office, I am most likely going to be mentally engaged and have a challenge awaiting. There are interesting problems to be solved or obstacles to overcome, which a hell of a lot of other jobs do not have. So it makes me seem like a complete douchenozzle to complain about a job that gives me a comfortable salary when there are so many more physically demanding, underpaying, and underappreciated jobs out there.

All right, all that being said...the regret of the untried is very deep. It kills me that I never got to truly try my hand at journalism or TV or writing. I write this book as a wannabe writer, someone who looks at these words, wishes that they are more eloquent, and wonders "what if" had I dedicated more of myself to it. Is it too simplistic to say that the more personally fulfilling profession you pursue, the more financially strapped you will be? It sure seems like it. You need to balance those twin objectives with the hope that you attain both.

To be fair, that lack of fulfillment runs in every profession—

pro basketball players want to be rappers and rappers want to be ballers—no matter how famous or accomplished or rich that person becomes. Andre Agassi and J.R. Moehringer's *Open* is the best sports autobiography I've read because of the raw honesty detailing one man's journey to a place of peace. The relationship between Agassi and tennis—which was forced upon him by an overbearing and demanding father, propelling him to fame and fortune but at the cost of much personal happiness—is tortured and complicated and reminded me of my own struggles to find a profession that was personally gratifying.

And of all of the stories that were widely reported after the publication of his book—Agassi's repeated statements that he hated tennis, his relationship with his father, his drug use, and his marriage to Brooke Shields—one of the first things I remember is on page 317. Agassi had admired fellow player Steffi Graf from afar for many years, and after many fits and starts, he finally meets her for an impromptu beach date in San Diego.

This exchange was emblazoned in my mind and it took me over an hour to find it in the book, flipping back and forth and re-reading sections over and over. I had imagined it to be this long, detailed setup and conversation. And instead, this was it:

> We talk for the first time about tennis. When I tell her that I hate it, she turns to me with a look that says, "Of course. Doesn't everybody?"

These couple of lines blew my mind. Because if Steffi Graf and Andre Agassi—two of the most talented tennis players of their generation, who've won a combined 30 Grand Slam singles titles between them, whose exploits have elevated them to a rarified level of fame and fortune—are talking about their profession like a couple of disgruntled Bill Braskys at the bar after the end of another ball-busting day, then maybe it's all right not to be completely happy with your job.

Unlike my father, I will not urge on you a particular profession. But I can give you a blueprint of how to attain what most of us want: control.

In general, control—over our social schedule, our working conditions, our financial independence, our ability to attract others—makes us happy. And essential to the evolution of your career is a recognition of how much control you have. These perspectives are from the view of an office drone, a glorified cubicle monkey, so much of the advice in this chapter is suitable for the "traditional" work path, but it can really apply to any professional endeavor you choose.

HARD WORK

Allow me to go into cranky old man mode. There is no substitute for hard work. None. It's so important, I'll repeat it. There is no substitute for hard work. It doesn't mean that you have to work hard to be successful. It doesn't even mean that hard work will automatically lead to success. But if you work hard, you undoubtedly will be in a better position as a result.

It's noteworthy that someone who tries massively hard at the office and gives his or her all is the opposite of someone who is skilled socially, who manages to not appear to give a rat's ass about anything and can make everything seem easy. If you give your very best effort to be friendly and cool and social, chances are that you'll just end up looking like a total try-hard. So it's uncommon to have someone who's an incredibly hard worker and also easy around other people.

Simple hard work is the great equalizer, which can make up for your deficiencies in social class, intelligence, education, looks, or hell, even as a person. And even faced with seemingly insurmountable problems/assignments, you can do most damn anything if you put your mind to it. Shun Fujimoto.

The value of a strong and genuine work ethic is most pronounced when you begin your career. You don't need to trumpet how hard you're working and tell others when you come in and leave. People will eventually notice, and when people know that you work hard, you get respect, which leads to better things. (In fact, the original draft of Oliver Stone's *Scarface* screenplay had Tony Montana saying, "In this country, you gotta work hard. You gotta put in the hours. Then get good employee reviews. Climb the corporate ladder, get five percent annual raises. Then when you get the money, you get the power. Then when you get the power, you get the women." True story.)

When you're willing to bust your ass at your job, you also get the benefit of a doubt. Believe me, you can be of mediocre intelligence, but if you're working hard, the co-worker/boss/ underling will be much more permissive of your shortcomings.

The thing is that you always have to maintain that work ethic. You may think that once you ascend to a leadership position, you don't have to work as hard. WRONG. You will have to work even harder. You want to be a good leader, so it actually becomes more critical that you do. When Larry Bird and Michael Jordan and Tom Brady and Kevin Garnett are the hardest workers on your team, everyone around them feeds off it, is inspired, or even shamed into being the best that they can be. That's one way you can lead without raising your voice.

A true work ethic is not flashy, because it's the repeated attempt of splitting the rock every single day with absolutely no promise of a reward. There is no instant gratification, which seems almost contrary to a more efficient society.

Back in the late 80s and early 90s, Weiden and Kennedy made ad campaigns for Nike that were so inspiring that I—having parents who would consider it justifiable homicide to kill their only child if he got his skin inked—actually considered a tattoo of the Nike swoosh. Out of the many magazine Nike ads that I still keep, my favorite one doesn't have any famous athlete. It's a two-pager of a football play, with anonymous red- and white-jerseyed players diving and falling in multiple directions. And the copy reads in this jagged format:

No one knows the day.

Time.

Or place.

Only that it will happen.

You will get an opportunity.

The question is, will you be ready?

Or caught off guard?

Developing your game?

Or talking a good one?

Hitting the books?

Or the bottle?

Using your head?

Or a gun?

Conditioning yourself?

Or succumbing to your conditions?

Now, it won't be easy.

You'll get some bad calls.

And the ball will take

some funny bounces.

But just relax.

Keep playing your game.

You might be shut down for one,

two quarters.

But eventually—

you'll get an opening.

Just do it.

I'm ready to run through a brick wall now.

You have to keep faith in this truism, which should sustain you during the dark periods when it seems that your hard work is not paying off and you're going nowhere.

Much like all good things, there is a cost to an unyielding work ethic, and it's to your personal life. As busy as I've been at times, I have managed not to go completely AWOL from my circle of friends for months, haven't felt the resentment from my parents for missing holidays with them, and haven't much suffered from the repeated loneliness working on Friday and Saturday nights. When you start working, you probably won't be in survival mode because you'll be thinking your mother and I will probably bail you out and it's no guarantee your efforts will ever come to fruition anyway...well, you may think that you don't want to go through that door and make these sacrifices.

You must go through that door. At least when you're young. You can always decide at a later time that you want to scale down and not be as unrelenting, which presents its own set of challenges. But you want to have that choice, that control. When you're 25 and it suddenly hits you that hard work can open a lot of doors, you'll also realize that your road is all uphill, and that it's a hell of a lot tougher when you're not conditioned for it. And by then, it may simply be too late.

SELECTIVE MEMORY

Being armed with an exceptional work ethic means that you are correspondingly conscientious. When you start gaining experience, you begin to realize that there is so much that you don't know—and if this doesn't dawn on you, then you're either mind-blowingly brilliant or obliviously dumb, with really not much of an in-between. When you don't know anything, then you start to make mistakes, which is completely natural, but in the wrong environment, can be debilitating. Every error you make, whether excusable or not, will cause you to second-guess yourself, never mind your superiors' judgment.

But when it appears like you're wrong repeatedly, and as a result, can no longer trust your instincts...what then?

Having a selective memory—to take lessons from past mistakes but not be paralyzed by past wrong choices—becomes paramount. Think independently. You will be surprised to discover that the answers to problems are not necessarily fixed in stone. When you're confronted with a problem to which you don't really have an idea how to solve, your natural inclination is to just go to your boss and find out what you're supposed to do without giving any thought as to what could be done. And that, my children, is acting like sheep. You are not being paid to act like sheep. Your employers could pick up any jabroni from the street if they needed someone to follow orders. You are not that person.

My revelatory moment arrived when I was still in law school and doing an internship at the SEC. If you needed someone to put cases into proper format and make sure there were no typos in a document, I was your guy. Otherwise, when it came to the Investment Company Act of 1940 and the Investment Advisor Act, I didn't know my ass from my elbow. And one day I was trying to formulate an answer to an inquiry by a company and went to my boss, Ms. Doberman, who was EXACTLY how you picture someone named Doberman, just as long as you add horn-rimmed glasses.

I was asking her all these questions as we were walking down the hall, like I was a dogged reporter following a politician. "Who are the players in this scheme? Where does the money lead to? Does this conspiracy lead all the way...TO THE VERY TOP?!?" And she was saying some things absent-mindedly, and then she came to a halt, and in complete exasperation, she said:

"COME ON. THINK LIKE A LAWYER!"

Even though I wished at that very moment that I had never been born, it was the best thing that could have happened to me.

I had to think independently, to use my best judgment and fire away. If it was wrong, so be it, but presumably I would have provided a basis for my reasoning. And now that I've been managing people for a number of years, I can completely appreciate this principle. One of the worst things you can do is to go to your boss and say, "What should I do here?" At the very least, if you really aren't sure and want to save time, you go to her and say, "Here's the problem. I see three solutions, A, B, and C. I'm inclined to go with B because X, Y, and Z. What do you think?"

Related to this, when you're trying to get to the next level of excellence, remember that the difference between good and great is...volume.

Let's assume that you had enough of a skill set to write, or paint, or create music. If I asked you to create a new piece that would knock my socks off, I'm sure you could do it. If you dedicated your time, you could come up with something that is quite beautiful and exquisite.

The catch is that it would take a ton of time. In fact, you could keep holding onto the task of creating this opus, forever tinkering and adjusting it, that the mantra of "it's not done yet" would hold you hostage to its expected perfection. Maybe this will take the form of a never-ending book project dedicated to your children that will never be perfect, because your idea of perfection will constantly change as you yourself change. The great ones are able to forge a piece without being shackled by doubt. They recognize perfection is unattainable and see each work as something to be worked on and done with. You do your best job in the time that you have and go onto the next. Sheer repetition will guarantee improvement and confidence.

My favorite team while growing up in the 70s was the Pittsburgh Steelers, a completely fabricated allegiance given that I had no ties to the city. It didn't mean that my adulation for that team wasn't real—I continually read the Steelers' media guides, memorized team records, and collected anything team-related (my Terry Bradshaw peanut butter jar was a particularly prized item). Following the passing of Chuck Noll, the coach during that dynasty, *Sports Illustrated* had this story from Rocky Bleier, who fought in the Vietnam War, earned a Purple Heart and then was a Steelers running back:

> I recall a week in 1978, after we had lost one game and snuck by in the next. Things just weren't clicking, and we needed a jolt from Chuck—a boot up the ass. So he pulled us together after practice and said, "Let me tell you a story about two monks who are on a journey. Sometime during their journey they stop at a clearing, and in the clearing is a stream. On one side of the stream is a fair maiden trying to cross. And the first monk, without any hesitation, picks up the fair maiden and carries her across and sets her down.
>
> The two monks carry on in silence. Sometime later on their journey they stop at another clearing. The second monk says to the first monk, 'You picked up that maiden. Do you know

it's against our beliefs and our religion to touch a person of the opposite sex?'

The first says, 'I set her down back there, but you carried her all the way here.'

I'll see you guys tomorrow at 10 a.m."

When you get completely bummed out about a work thing, and you're rolling it around in your head, wondering what you did wrong and how stupid you were and what you should have done instead and how you completely blew it, remember the Chuck Noll story and your father's obsession with a team with which he had no geographical connection.

SET BOUNDARIES

Now once you have the work ethic and the ability to, in the words of Churchill, bounce from failure to failure with the same enthusiasm, then that means you're getting older. And the older you get, and the more employment and familial responsibilities you have, it's advisable to compartmentalize and create boundaries.

Creating boundaries means that you have enough capital to build them. Coming in on your first day of work and announcing that you won't work weekends will probably lead to one of the fastest and most hilarious firings on record. This third principle assumes that you have established enough of a reputation at the office where people respect the work that you do and value your presence.

The first boundary has to be within your office, which is

tricky. But assuming the above, it's wise to create a bit of separation between you and your bosses and your clients—whoever has the power to dictate the terms of your employment.

It's no secret that with the advent of email and other forms of instantaneous communication, the expectations for an immediate response, an opinion, a detailed analysis, have grown exponentially. Instead, you should always take a moment to think before you act and respond. First of all, unless you're a genius, your instant reaction, especially when you're young, is not brilliant. I can't tell you how many times I had to stifle my impulse to fire off an email, only to realize that I had just avoided looking like the biggest moron in the world. You need to think about it, roll it around in your head, let it marinate.

You need to retain a little air of mystery in how you function and your responsiveness, to hit the sweet spot between promptness and seeming like you're blowing it off. Once you respond immediately to an email, especially a superior, it starts to create a certain expectation in that person, and in the wrong hands, it can create hell. Because I'll tell you about the supervisor who said, "She's not responding as quickly as she used to...but hey, I'll give her a pass." THAT SUPERVISOR DOESN'T EXIST.

An essential part of the boundary is vacation. Take it. All of it.

This is a particularly European notion and not a Japanese or American one. And again, this is really dependent upon one thing—when you're in the office, you work your ass off. When you go on vacation, you really go on vacation, because you've earned that vacation.

It starts with the notice. Stake out that time, let others know, find coverage, and set up the autoreply on the email. Then be strategic about its length. You've been too young to notice, but nearly every family vacation we've taken has started a couple of extra days around a three-day weekend, because those weeks after Memorial Day/July 4/Labor Day tend to be slow anyway. Once you've accumulated enough goodwill and a favorable reputation, it's time for a week-long one, but NEVER take it from Monday to Friday. That's for amateurs. Be an iconoclast and take off on a Wednesday or Thursday and come back on a Wednesday or Thursday (or maybe an extra day—no one will care). You'll have two half-weeks to ease out and into work. And then repeat with a two-week vacation. And go somewhere foreign and awesome.

There will be a temptation to say, "No one else can do my particular work. I am so incredibly vital to the team that my not being there at a moment's notice will cause this entire project to collapse." It's now time to be introduced to another Churchill quote:

"The graveyards are full of indispensable men."

There may be someone who raises a stink about your egregiously long vacations. This is usually the work bully.

Over the course of your work career, you will have to deal with one. Let's first make sure that he or she is properly identified. NOT someone who is simply demanding or seemingly never satisfied. NOT someone who raises his or her voice once in a while. NOT someone who couldn't give two shits if you dropped off the face of the earth tomorrow. Those people are merely run-of-the-mill superiors.

No, the work bully takes a particular glee in your suffering. There is no method to the madness, the berating, the further attempts to denigrate you, the public humiliations. Over time, this person will be in your head. You, with the overactive imagination, will actually start to imagine exchanges with the bully and her cutting comments, then your responses, then her snarky replies. Despair will seem to be the only option. And maybe you will need to put up with it for a certain period. But if the shit you're getting is completely undeserved, and it's gone on too long, and you really want it to stop, you need to do the following, which is what you do with any bully.

Fight back.

You fucking punch the bully in the fucking face. I wish it were literal, but it's not. You make it clear that the behavior is unacceptable. You tell the bully personally. If that doesn't work, you go to your boss's boss. Or you make it clear that you won't do it. Or you ignore it, until you get that incendiary confrontation that lets your boss know that you are not a pushover, that you're not some shy and respectful Asian girl who lets other people walk over her. From personal experience, I know that bullies do not stop as a result of some internal attack of compassion. Only a cataclysmic event can reverse the bully's course, and you are that event.

And if standing up and justifiably asserting your rights gets you fired...well, good thing the job doesn't define who you are, right?

Because there should also be a boundary standing between your profession and your identity.

By the time you're of middle age, your job should not define you. Someone whose identity is inextricably intertwined with his work—and the sign of a boring conversationalist—is how quickly he asks you what you do for a living. You should resist that label of your job. You should have friends and a social life and have hobbies and a higher purpose that does not involve how you make a living. Otherwise, that is an unbalanced life. In other words, you damn right you should be playing the lottery once in a while.

When the job does not define you, then it's theoretically easier to establish the most important boundary—that between your work and your home. Employers will have no conscience about wringing the very last bit of your availability and your energy for their purposes. I've noticed that compared to their married counterparts, a single man or woman will get tapped again and again for mountainous assignments, to the point where the single status was threatening to become a lifelong, self-fulfilling prophecy. You always have to keep in mind the limits that you're willing to approach.

If you do end up having a family and if you want any semblance of a happy home, you have to leave the stresses of the office behind. Believe me, I know how simplistic that sounds. But the alternative of everyone else in your household vicariously living out your work stress and being the collateral damage of your occupation is completely unacceptable. I know a lot of people would silently disagree. They would point to the benefits or create justifications. The material comforts. "We're locked into this lifestyle." The fear of reversing course. But nothing that happens at work is worth destroying the home.

• •

I've spent the entire chapter talking about putting yourself in a better place to succeed at work. But you will always need to remember that in the end, it is exceedingly rare that any employer or boss really cares about your personal life. They simply do not care about whether your relationship with your wife or husband is deteriorating because you have no more free time. They won't have to deal with the resentment of two children whom you never saw because you were too busy. Your employers are just concerned about the bottom line, which is your performance at the office. No matter how important your job is and how all-consuming it may be, you have to be concerned about what happens in the home. In the end, it's up to you to find a better place to be. You're worth it. Your family is worth it. That is your North Star.

13

HEARTBREAK AND THE MAGICAL HEALING POWERS OF MAHALIA

At some point in your lives, you will be prancing around the fields of love, in super slow-mo, with swelling music, and blissful thoughts overwhelming your mind. And take a complete pratfall.

The moment will arrive when that person says that he's no longer in love with you. Or you will have this sinking pit in your stomach telling you that this relationship isn't going to work out. Or there's a burning sensation in the base of your brain saying that it's not going to happen, because you're actually watching your man playing tonsil hockey with this other trollop. This heartbreak can come in the form of a bad breakup, unrequited love, or a decision by only one side. It's exceedingly rare that both of you are equally committed to splitting up—

one of you won't want it as much, and you will be left wanting.

It doesn't matter at what point it happens in your life. It doesn't matter in retrospect how frivolous and doomed the relationship was. If you were truly in love and had your heart broken...you will feel like ass. It will hurt, in a very physical way, and it will hurt like hell.

And yet heartbreak is a necessary component of the human condition. To fully experience life, you have to have had your heart broken at least once. The person who has never been hurt by a breakup because he or she hasn't ever committed to someone is not engaging in life. And the one who's never been dumped because he's so gorgeous and keeps on breaking up with other people—well, screw that guy, right? (Please, not literally.)

I realize that the above means little to you when you are sobbing into your pillow or catatonic in front of the TV or mowing your way through pints of ice cream in the middle of the night. You'll do this while thinking how the promise felt so ironclad and now nothing seems so sure. The constant flashbacks to better times and the stabbing sensation you feel in your chest are normal. And even darker moments when you wonder what your ex is feeling and the near-certainty that it's not close to as bad as what you're going through. I've felt all of that, and really, so has much of the human race.

The worst thing that you could do is withdraw and resolve that no one will ever hurt you again and give up on love. You don't get prideful over that. The benefits of being bonkers, irrationally, walk-on-your-knees in love with someone are too great to miss out on.

Oh, but when you fall from those heights.

My previous relationship before your mother was with someone 10 years my junior, which sounds relatively tame, except that we started dating when I was 29 (I'll spare you the math lesson). I remember getting the eyebrow-raised, "This most likely isn't gonna work out but enjoy it" nod of approval from other guys even as I tried to point out that the age difference was nine years depending on the month it was. She studied and lived in Milan while I was in New York. It was one of those relationships where you don't necessarily think it is doomed to failure—and by God, if you're in one of those, please get the hell out of it ASAP—but you kind of know that there will have to be boulder-sized obstacles moved for it to survive. But at the same time, even if you see these challenges, you believe, right? You need to. Then why even bother, dammit?

A couple of years after we started dating, on a fall night in Milan, she was in the middle back seat of a car and wasn't belted in—I guess this is as good of a time as any to tell you that you should always, always, always have your seat belt on—and the car was slammed from behind. She pitched head-first into the dash, resulting in a fractured skull. That led to a couple of transatlantic trips where I helped monitor her recovery. During these visits, I was oblivious to what she was probably feeling: that if she ever was in a life-threatening situation, she wanted to be in her native land and surrounded by her family, and that a speculative, long-distance relationship wasn't the answer.

The end came in rapidly disintegrating fashion, with her telling me on a Monday in December that she didn't think this relationship would work out. It wasn't an official breakup call, but the relationship was on life support and the priest was coming in about five minutes to give it last rites. In the overwrought and anguished language of the lovelorn, I did say on that call that in spite of everything, I did still believe in love and it was a very powerful thing. I'll readily admit to crying like a sorority girl at the drop of a hat, but I had kept it together and stayed oddly stoic during this conversation and other follow-up calls to family and friends, even when I thought my heart was literally going to make a piercing cracking sound. Plus, seriously, I just got dumped by someone 10 years my junior (or nine years from April to November). Dear Jesus, I needed to keep my dignity intact.

In the ensuing wreckage of that call, later that day, I realized that I had already booked a ticket for her to come to New York during Christmas. That afternoon I called Expedia.

A customer service rep answered the phone. An African American for sure, and with her Southern drawl, I imagined her as matronly, maybe named Mahalia. I'm sure she imagined me as horribly racist.

I explained that I needed to cancel this trip and to know my refund options. Mahalia said that I could get 50 percent of my money back, or the soon-to-be-ex-girlfriend could get the full credit of the booked flight. Well, I may have been a broken-hearted dumbass, but I certainly wasn't a doormat. But then again, 50 percent did seem completely harsh and I didn't like the idea of just throwing money away. I hemmed and hawed for a good 15 to 20 seconds, and when I say I hemmed and hawed, I actually made indecipherable noises while Mahalia waited on the other line.

Finally, the internal monologue ended with me thinking some sort of a variation of "Fuck it," and so I said to Mahalia, "All right, go ahead and cancel it." And I just stewed.

And stewed. And stewed. Until basically I realized that the line had been silent for a good 15 to 20 seconds again.

"Ma'am, are you there?"

Her response was instant. "Did you not want to cancel?" Completely unexpected. Who asks that?

And then I hemmed and hawed again for another five seconds. I felt so weak and indecisive. Mainly because I was so weak and indecisive. I made the decision to break the wall and go right to the point.

"Well, the thing is, earlier this morning my girlfriend and I broke up, and I'm not sure what to do here."

"Yeah, I knew something was wrong."

Another pause. Something was bothering me about the previous long pause and her instant comment afterward, so I asked, "How come you were so silent just now? Did you cancel anything?"

"No...you seemed so angry."

What I didn't realize at the time was that when reservations are cancelled, they're gone forever, and she wanted to make absolutely sure that I wanted to release this one into the wild. Already, Mahalia was by far the most compassionate customer service representative I had ever encountered in my life. And while tears were beginning to pool in my eyes and I was making a pouting pucker face in my shitty junior one-bedroom apartment, she said, "Just give it a little more time. You never know what might happen."

And ladies, that's when my voice cracked and each successive word hiccupped out of me and climbed another octave:

"I...don't...think so. She said...it wasn't...going to...work out—"

"You just never know. You never know."

And that's when I completely lost my shit and started bawl-
ing while on the phone, not with my parents or my friends, but
with a customer service representative who was telling me that
everything was going to be all right.

Viewed in the rearview mirror of history, this is a pretty
entertaining story, right? Certainly something that would be
imprinted into my consciousness for many, many years, no
matter how much time has passed and even after I moved on
to new and better relationships?

The God's honest truth is that several years later, I only remembered this anecdote because I read it in my journal. It didn't
take long for me to recall—you tend to remember the time when
you started crying while talking to an Expedia customer service
representative—but it didn't sear into my brain and soul permanently. The relationship and the breakup and the detritus loom
large in the immediate aftermath, but with time, that all recedes
into the background. After you get your heart stomped on, as
long as you remain a good person with an open and loving soul,
there will be another person for you. There has to be, because
there are seven billion fucking people on this planet.

Our perception of time varies greatly depending on our enjoyment or our pain. Time does not necessarily heal all wounds,
but it gives you the perspective by which you can deal with the
pain. This is not just about heartbreak, but about any momen-

tous event. Memories can be notoriously short. I've worked on cases every single day for a couple of months, inspiring panic at odd hours where I ultimately thought, "Yep, that's it. This case will definitely end in disaster and lead to me getting fired and ruining my life." And being absolutely flabbergasted several years later when for the life of me, I just can't remember the name of that case. I remember in the aftermath of September 11, people actually wrote think pieces wondering whether it was the death of irony. People are incredibly resilient. The human spirt can be incredibly resilient. There will be a scar for sure, but that's preferable to the open wound. What will seem like the most excruciating heartbreak in the history of mankind will fade into footnote 28 in the 11th chapter of your life.

To this day, I can't remember how that conversation with Mahalia and me ended, or what I decided to do on that call. But I remember, clear as day, that Expedia gave me a full refund. Thank you, Mahalia.

14

THE GENTLEMAN IN YOUR LIFE

Y ou do not seek love because society expects you to, or because your friends are doing it, or you're trying to make someone else happy. You do it because you are fulfilling an innate urge, an urge to be connected with someone. And at some point, like I did with your Uncle Dave in Basel, you are likely to feel helpless and believe that the only way you'll find true love is through a series of cosmic, random events. But there are still things—actually, many things—that are within your control.

I've been through the torment and the sleepless nights and the pining because of the opposite sex. However, the purpose of this chapter is not to make sure that you never go through these same emotions. If I'm not around to give this advice to you in person, then at least it can serve as a bit of insight into the male mind. So this advice is limited. As I have never really sought love other than in New York and I have never been a lesbian, this advice only works if you are heterosexual and looking for a guy and you are living in a place where there is a large supply of eligible men and women. The caveats:

1. What I say doesn't apply to all guys, and
2. What I say doesn't apply to what I think, and
3. I am not completely telling the truth as to 1 and 2.

Let's begin!

YOU GLANCE HIS WAY

We'll start with the moment when you glide into the Metropolitan Museum of Art for an event to raise funds for an environmental charity. You lock eyes with a gentleman (please indulge my use of this term). What is he thinking as he looks at you for the first time?

When it comes to women, guys are superficial assholes. If you have this baseline expectation, then really, then there's nowhere to go but up.

Guys really and only care about the following:

Face.

Breasts.

Rear end. (Fact: the last time a guy said "rear end" was the late 19th century.)

Wait, that's it? Nothing else? Well, of course there are a million other considerations. But they are all secondary and operate as factors on a sliding scale.

Right now I'm visualizing Tina Fey and Amy Poehler shooting laser beams of disapproval at me and shaking their heads. And it's heinous and a sad fact of the male condition that he is driven primarily by his libido and horribly embarrassing to even put these thoughts to paper, but dammit, even Tina and Amy know it's true. Right, ladies?!? Can we, uh, have a threesome? (This is, uh, what the asshole guy would say.)

Suppose a normal-looking chap had a choice between 1) a woman with supermodel looks and body who has rocks in her head and uses her hands to eat steak and is prone to insane fits of jealousy and 2) a woman who is just above average in all physical and intellectual and emotional qualities. Whom would he choose? If you are actually re-reading the above sentence and thinking about how the average guy would approach this decision, you're COMPLETELY out of touch with how guys think. That dude is whistling a jaunty tune as he boards the Crazy Train, carefully buckling himself in double tight and deluding himself into the idea that this can somehow work out between two crazy, star-crossed kids, one of whom is a supermodel.

When women talk about "chemistry," it's invariably in reference to whether she and a guy share that sense of humor, that extra kick of attraction, that certain *je ne sais quoi* that dooms budding relationships and elevates others to another level. For guys, chemistry is simply code for "not attractive enough."

Guys have different speeds, certainly much more than women. We're not consistently acting a certain way around the ladies no matter what. You drop a guy into a party with women he finds unattractive, he can still manage to act like a respectable human being. But I guarantee that if Jennifer Lawrence or Cate Blanchett walked into a room, this guy could be wearing the exact same clothes and yet you wouldn't be able to recognize him—his personality and charm would be in another dimension.

The paradox of choice in a metropolis compounds the superficiality when there's a single guy hanging out with this wolf pack of other guys. When none of them is dating anyone with regularity, there tends to be this peer pressure that builds up among them. In a vacuum, a guy will have his own standards of attractiveness and personality and social standing and employment he seeks in his life mate. But when he's hanging around this crew of other single guys, he ends up having to fulfill his friends' expectations as well, and he starts second-guessing himself. "I can't tell whether this girl is good-looking. I wonder what my friends think?" "Too immature?" "Good enough body?" "Good sense of style?" "Or too much?" "She have a good job?" Notice that none of these questions have anything to do with the connection between the two in question. But this peer pressure will actually cause the kids in this social circle to be less hesitant in admitting their true wants. The first guy within this group who commits to a girlfriend is kind of like the first one who shows his hand at a poker table.

You may have two reactions to this, the first being, "This is ludicrous. How stupid are men?" And the appropriate answer is, "Very," with a neatly-drawn arrow pointing to the line about two pages ago: "Guys really and only care about the following."

The second possible reaction is, "This is absolutely, positively not true." This is very dangerous, because now you're not living in a world with gravity and the rule of law and money as a payment for goods and services. Because should any guy maintain that there is no iota of truth to this, he's essentially saying that he's impervious to any outside pressures, which is an admirable and aspirational sentiment, but a crock of horse-shit. On some level, all humans have some level of craving for approval and validation; those who claim that they don't care are in denial or damaged. If it's not your friends you're trying to impress, you're seeking approval from your parents or an authority figure or the rest of the populace. It's usually a lot later when you kind of realize that this peer pressure is real-ly stupid, because you should be doing what you want to do, unencumbered by the expectations and standards of others.

And this occurs among women as well: if they're in hus-band-hunting mode, they will have a list of deal-breakers, or they'll want their soul mate to come in a neat, socially accept-able package. Don't follow that crowd. You have to have an open mind when you meet someone. Yes, the bald guy or the one who's been divorced or has kids or doesn't have the greatest body or who could use a little work in the style area or—heav-ens to Betsy—not white. It's not the worst thing in the world to broaden those horizons and go outside those lines.

Well at least, I was completely immune to all of these pres-sures and temptations to succumb to superficiality when I met your mother, right?

Um.

I'm not looking forward to revealing this, which is so un-flattering that I only told this to your mother when I decided

I would write about this...more than nine years after we met.

In the weeks after our encounter at the Emergency charity event, there was one burning question I had about her, the one thing that gave me any sense of real pause. Her age.

This is a perfect synopsis of the quandary and idiocy of dating in a big city and the paradox of choice. You start saying and thinking things like, "I really think this person is THE ONE, the one that I have a real connection with, someone with whom I can share the rest of my life...I just kind of wish she were seven years younger so we could have some time before we have kids." You want the relationship to fit your construct of a perfect relationship, however distorted it may be. I was fairly sensitive to any age difference to begin with, especially when my previous relationship was with that woman nine years my junior during seven months of the year. By the time I met your mother, I was nearing 35 years old.

The problem was that in our first few dates, it just wasn't apparent how old this woman was. She grew up abroad, so I couldn't just name-check George Harrison's "Got My Mind Set on You" and have her say, "Junior year of high school!" to which I'd think, "Okay, got it." If she was younger than me, great—the pressure on the relationship wouldn't be so acute and we could let it breathe and bide our time. If she was as old as me, that was obviously still fine. But maybe if she were a couple of years older, then it made this dynamic a bit more complicated. And then I'd look at her olive skin and speculate some more, too scared to ask and find out the truth.

Finally, four weeks after we first met, during a quiet moment at the Whitney Museum, I tried to be as casual as possible in asking how old she was. And when she said she was five years older than I, my eyes may have bulged ever so imperceptibly. But it was telling that afterward, I didn't race back to my friends and get their take on the merits of dating someone who would be 40 in several months. The resolve never wavered. When you know, you know. The relationship would have to progress as though we had the life spans of a couple of fruit flies.

YOU DANCE AND BOB AND WEAVE

Back to the gentleman at your charity event, for whom you are borderline filled with contempt for being such a superficial jerk even though all he's done is make eye contact.

Now, not all hope is lost. First, maybe this guy isn't delusional enough to think that he should only be going out with supermodels and finds that your attractiveness meets a certain threshold. Second, even though I believe you girls are the two of the most exquisitely beautiful creatures to ever walk the earth, if it so happens that this man does not share this opinion, I mentioned a sliding scale.

A deficit in the looks department can be overcome with other factors and considerations. A beautiful and generous heart, always seeking to do good for others. A blazing wit that can elicit belly laughs. A preternatural sense of calm, no matter what the stakes are. A book and/or street-learned intelligence that finds solutions to problems. A strong ethical streak that acts as a lighthouse. A shared love of certain interests. An alchemy of all of the above. Even for the superficial male, there is definitely a tipping point where these qualities will unequivocally overcome that initial assessment of a woman's looks.

People can be divided into those who love dating and those who do not. If you love it, that's great—have a grand old time. If you think it's a gut-wrenching experience and you hate the uncertainty, the pining, the overthinking, then you may be gladdened to know that I have been well familiar with all of it.

In the mid-1990s a book called *The Rules: Time-Tested Secrets for Capturing the Heart of Mr. Right* came out. This was a self-help book that was about...well, you know. The basic premise of the book was that women shouldn't be aggressors in seeking out men, but rather get the men to pursue them. The way this was done was by playing the coquette, creating an air of mystery and not completely being available for the man until he finally broke down and presented a 50-carat ring on the hills of Positano while the London Philharmonic played "This Will Be An Everlasting Love," at which point she would presumably say that she had to think about it.

When I initially heard about this, I went ballistic. I was the upstanding guy who took pride in not presenting myself as anything more than who I was, who believed in complete transparency, and who was tired of the bullshit flooding the city. If you weren't going to be honest with your future mate, then with whom exactly were you planning on being completely honest? If you had to play games in order to land the guy of your dreams, then what happens when you run out of the sporting equipment? The last couple of sentences sound like what Carrie Bradshaw would write on *Sex and the City*, and don't get me started on the old bats on that show.

You want to hear the kicker? In time, I began to agree with that book's general concept. Not in a sense of playing games—I couldn't get past the seeming manipulation. But I think the principle is correct: it doesn't matter how hot he or she is, someone who is stifling and overbearing will lose appeal. At the very beginning of the relationship, no matter how excited you feel about a guy, there's a need to cultivate that mystique, that distance. Balance.

(In other words, that time when I freaked out in my office and called your mother in the middle of the day to ask whether she wanted to have kids is not what you should be doing. But I GUARANTEE you, I DOUBLE GUARANTEE YOU, that if she had responded, "Yes. I want babies. Lots of babies. I've already picked out several names for our half-Asian, half-Italian babies. They will honor our bond, one unparalleled in recorded history," I would have spent that night in a bar with my friends going, "Yeah that bitch crazy.")

By the way, *When Harry Met Sally...* is pretty spot on. A straight and unattached guy will not seek to be your platonic friend without seeing some potential for a romantic relationship. It's not all nefarious—the dude may not completely driven by his libido and may actually, you know, like hanging out with you. But you can always expect guys to have an ulterior motive.

It never ceases to amaze me how women will be completely blind to the underlying motives of a single male friend or otherwise downplay it with the following remarks:

"Oh, we're just friends."

"I already told him I have a boyfriend."

"He knows I'm not interested."

"He's already seen that he's completely not my type."

"I've said to his face that I don't find him attractive."

"I wrote him a five-page letter that set forth the conditions where I would consider dating him—basically, that we had to be the last two people on this planet and the future of the human race depends on us getting together."

The guy who hears the above is saying the following to his friends:

"Dude, I got a fucking shot, I'm telling you."

Not every guy is going to be a complete horndog and persist repeatedly in storming the walls. I'm not saying that the platonic straight male friend doesn't have genuine feelings for you. And once the guy is married, the odds of him still trying to get some goes down—somewhat. But believe me, there are plenty of dudes who will keep an eye on your situation, ready to nonchalantly slide in at the appropriate moment. Always keep it in mind.

A turning point in my dating life came when Uncle Dave and I were talking about some girl I had just met. I had called her and she didn't return my call or something, and I said I was going to call her again under some stupid pretense. I won't lie (basically it's extremely clear from the previous two sentences): I was acting like a desperate bitch.

Dave looked at me and said, "You're a good person. You

don't need to try so hard to show her that."

This was a revelation, the power of self-assurance. You need to keep in mind that your true self always comes through. You don't need to exert so much effort in showing who you are—your style, humor, intelligence, manners, kindness. Parts of it should emerge, without you forcing it, within 30 minutes of someone meeting you. It definitely should shine through if you meet someone on a recurring basis. If you're not attractive to him after that, great. He can go fly a goddam kite.

YOU HANG OUT AND WONDER

So now the gentleman you're having a relationship with is not a turd. What should you be looking for? Is this the one?

There are an exceedingly high number of positive qualities to seek in your lifelong partner and they are obvious. There also will be the seemingly trivial but incredibly instructive give-aways—like the way he talks to his mother, treats those less fortunate, whether he is wasteful, or whether he holds the door for others—that will tell the tale. You should find someone who has those qualities I've written about in the pages up to this point: humble, honorable, nice, well-rounded, inquisitive, hard-working, conscientious, funny. Your equal.

Ultimately a relationship is the emotional connection be-tween you two, but it should not be confused with being insep-arable. You need someone who can give you space and doesn't feel like you have to go out as an indivisible unit at all times. There's a notion that to be truly close, you should do everything together, but that's a load of romantic bullshit. You should feel secure in yourself where you don't need to keep 24/7 tabs on your partner, because in the end that's an impossible task. Usually the urge to be so controlling stems from insecurity and jealousy, and if you start to notice this streak in a guy, it's a huge red flag. In my experience, it doesn't matter whether your relationship becomes exclusive or whether he proposes to you or whether you get married or whether you have kids. That possessive streak does not abate.

The overall point of *He's Just Not That Into You* is completely on the mark: if you have a good bit of hesitation about whether a guy is really as into you as you are into him, I'm fairly sure he's not into you. You can tell. Put it this way—when a guy likes you, you'll know. When you're agonizing over what this guy is thinking, whether he really likes you in that way, or whether he wants to be serious, that's a bad sign. Not insurmountable, but do you really want to go through all that bullshit?

A corollary of the above is that if it's early in the relationship and it's not easy, you're in trouble. The beginning of the relationship should be incredibly blissful, when you feel like twirling around in a field and breaking into, "The hilllllllllls are alive with the soooouuuuuund of muuuuuuusic..." If you're spending that time arguing about what bar to go to or which TV show you want to watch or whose feelings got hurt more, you guys are probably in trouble. Spoiler alert: there will be larger things you're going to fight about. If at that time the regular sex isn't completely eclipsing any reservations you're having, then it never will.

I'll leave the birds and bees talk to your mother, but I'm in favor of giving that talk to you as soon as practicable. For Asians, my parents were unusually open about sex; when I was in college, my father bought a box of condoms from Japan ("They're the best in the world!") and urged me to use them, always and without exception.

I actually managed to find an even better contraceptive: abstinence imposed on me by the entire female student body at Johns Hopkins. A year later Uncle Matt came to visit my dorm and explained that I needed to at least break open the plastic wrapping around the box of condoms to give the impression that I was using them regularly. After I went through high school and college and law school without even a hint of a regular relationship, my parents suggested that I should, you know, get out a little more, and should the right moment arise, they could leave their home so my hypothetical girlfriend and I could share an intimate night together. Good Lord, God bless my parents.

I will say that you need to envision a relationship with your man without sex. If the sex is a predominant part of why you're together, then it's cause for concern. Because in time, and in spite of every resolve not to succumb to cliché, the sex will diminish. There is simply too much else to do in your life. It should still be pretty great when it does happen, but if you're doing it like rabbits when you're still in your 60s and 70s, it may be possible that you are getting paid to do it, and in that event, please excuse me while I go into the next room and light myself on fire.

You want to be with someone who sees you as an equal and a teammate. You divide the household responsibilities, you work together to solve problems, you encourage and exhort when the other is discouraged and you rebuke when the other acts wrongly. You provide balance for each other. But it takes time to even reach a certain level of maturity, which it means that

YOU MARRY

only after you turn about 30 years old.

This sounds extremely practical and unromantic. But it is best to be a more fully formed person when you meet your life mate. You should be more secure in your career, and hopefully you've managed to get to a point where you can make the choice to scale down your commitment to work. You should be more secure in the type of person you want and the qualities you find most attractive. And you need to be secure in yourself and to have that confidence to know that you deserve the right person. There should be no rush at all to get married.

"Like you and mom, right?"

Um.

I would not recommend having only 14 months between the day you first meet and the day of your wedding. I think that you need to see your partner during the worst of times—when you have money troubles, when he loses a parent, when you make that joint trip to IKEA—before you commit to spending the rest of your life with him or her. When each of you sees your partner's ugly side, and when you talk about it and come to some sort of resolution, then it should give you reassurance for the future, and a year normally isn't enough to view all aspects of your future partner's side. (I would subtract the last two months before the marriage because by then the fear of cancelling wedding plans can overwhelm all rational thought.)

All marriages are a leap of faith, but ours seemed like a larger one. Only years later did I realize that your mother is incapable of having a meal without a proper setting—table mats, silverware and glassware laid out, with leftovers to be eaten only in case of emergency. I also discovered later that she dislikes being rushed and having the dangling scythe of a deadline, whereas that's what energizes me. (On the other hand, she hates me wearing ball caps. Otherwise I'm perfect.) In this respect, I'll tell you that the fact that we married—did the ceremony, registered at City Hall, became legally bound in a church—meant a great deal to me. Because it can become tempting to give up and walk away from things when they get difficult.

The more heartbreak you go through, the surer you feel when you do meet someone different. I've said this—you have to experience the lows to truly appreciate the highs. You need to meet the boyfriend who isn't right for you or the one for whom there's unrequited love or the one with whom there are no sparks to be grateful for the one you have. When you have less of that drama—hell, when you are tired of it and demand something better—then meeting that person feels effortless. It's kind of like when you swing a golf club and the timing is perfect and the ball rockets off the face and you have perfect balance when you follow through and the club feels as light as a wand.

Oh fucking hell I miss playing golf since we had you two.

YOU MAINTAIN

And now, the hard part.

Several years back, I went to Miami for an asbestos medicine conference and ended up at LIV in the Fontainebleau. Nothing, and I mean nothing, can kill a vibe at a cool club than 30+ lawyers all wearing dark sport coats and baggy, tan khakis while holding beer bottles and trying to bob their heads to the beat.

A baseball star and his entourage were shuttled into the prime seating area; it was right after he led his team to World Series triumph. I watched this guy all night. He did not go a full minute without a gorgeous woman—a hard nine or 10—approaching him to chat. It didn't matter that he was reportedly in a high-profile dalliance with a Hollywood star. Those women kept coming at him like fembots on an assembly line, all perfect-looking and yet kind of generic, undoubtedly seeking his thoughts on incorrect assumptions in supply-side economics. Once I was able to get the overwhelming taste of bile out of my mouth, I thought of Chris Rock's best and most piercing observation:

"A man is basically as faithful as his options."

Horribly spirit-deflating and against all notions of romantic love. And pretty much right on the mark.

Unless you are committing false imprisonment, there is no way you can be absolutely sure as to whether your spouse is straying. This is not to say that it's inevitable or even probable in every marriage. But it's a reminder to you that even many years after you first locked eyes with your future husband, the most important flame to foster and keep alive is your appreciation for each other. I continually remind you two to be appreciative of the things that your mother and I do and to thank us, because over time, we take things that are constant and reliable for granted. It is no different between two who are married. You should still be seeking your partner's approval and you should be giving it liberally. You should be asking whether your spouse would continue to say that he's proud to be standing next to you—physically, professionally, and emotionally—and whether you would say the same.

With expectant parents, one of the two pieces of advice I give is that after the baby arrives, you still have to carve out alone time with your spouse. This is more difficult than it sounds. You've just experienced this mind-blowing event of creating new life and you want to dote over it and make sure nothing happens to it and there's absolutely no way that you can ever let anyone—not a caregiver with years of experience, not your mother because the last time she did this was 30 years ago and she doesn't know the latest techniques in bottle-feeding, and definitely not your father who's more interested in the football game—watch over your little jewel. You have to get over it. Force yourselves to get someone you trust, and if you cannot find someone you trust, force yourselves to trust, because there is someone worthy of it. The principle of gradual entrainment can apply to you guys too. First, it may be for a couple of hours while you two get away, then an actual meal, then God forbid, a meal without obsessively texting your sitter, and then a meal where you both don't spend 75 percent talking about the baby.

Because in the end the relationship with your spouse should not be secondary to the relationship with your child. This is not PC to say, because any person on this planet should immediately think of Whitney Houston crooning, "I believe the children are our future." The very idea of your kids being not the primary driving force in your life seems heretical. But if the relationship with your spouse deteriorates, doesn't it negatively affect your children as well? My belief is that if you maintain a great relationship with your husband or wife, your kids will not suffer because they will be the beneficiaries of your love. If you truly love your spouse, you'll automatically treat the byproduct of that love accordingly. The only exception to this rule may be the couple who is head-over-heels in love with each other but whose mutual crack habits have made them completely oblivious to their kids.

• •

Romance is always much messier than what we see in the movies or on television. We see these two insanely gorgeous people mashing face on a hammock on the deck of an overwater bungalow on the Pacific with the sun setting and a table in the back overflowing with medium-rare fillet mignon and lobster and ice-cold Bud Lights and think, dammit, that's what I want: the best of everything. But as wonderful as it is, that shouldn't be the goal. Your goal should not be to find the most gorgeous, or most talented, or most grounded, or most charismatic, or most charitable, or most ambitious, or most family-oriented, or any other "most" coupled with a genuinely wonderful superlative. In the end, it's about fit. (This is where you should be saying, "Because there are seven billion other people on this planet.")

For you to find love, you will need to do your best to channel *Ferris Bueller* Charlie Sheen. Concentrate what inspires and attracts you and only you—not the expectations and chatter from others. When you know you have the one, and when you commit, then you emulate Personal Life Charlie Sheen in that you dial the energy to 11, devote everything you have to this person, expect the very best from your partner, tearing through life with abandon and leaving others dazzled with your partnership.

(Please, please, PLEASE make sure you don't confuse the order of the two Charlie Sheens here.)

15

"I BELIEVE THE CHILDREN ARE OUR FUTURE"

When I was about 13 years old, I read this column by Ann Landers. Back in your father's day, when someone had real urgent personal problems, he or she did not consult family or trusted friends. No, no. A person was more apt to describe them in a handwritten letter, send it via regular mail to a columnist for a newspaper (I'll wait until you google it) and pass the time until a stranger responded with advice.

The gist of this letter went like this:

All our lives, we have done the right thing with our son. We have showered this child with nothing but affection and he has had no lack of love.

Instead, he has turned into a nightmare. He's gotten into drugs. He's with the wrong type of crowd. He fights with us constantly.

What did we do wrong?

I remember this letter fairly well because, frankly, it scared the shit out of me. The idea of taking on this enormous responsibility with love and best intentions, only to have it become this miserable struggle causing intolerable amounts of pain was close enough to deter me from becoming a parent. Who would want to willingly subject themselves to Russian roulette?

I was never the type to dote on other people's babies, even as I progressed into my 20s. They were nice, I guess, but not a goal worth in and of itself. But sometime after I turned 30, thoughts of purpose and mortality and legacy began to dominate my mind. I certainly wasn't ready—anyone who says that he or she is completely ready to become a parent is probably appallingly ill-informed as to what's in store—but I knew the experience of being a father would define me.

But if life consists of a series of your attempts to get more control over what you do, then having a child is taking a huge leap backward. You sacrifice.

It begins first with sacrificing your identity. Just after Sofia was born, my assistant Linda told me, "You know that from now on, your name is no longer Mark, right? It's going to be 'Sofia's Dad.'" Working on three hours of sleep, I was completely overwhelmed and exhausted for that statement to register, but that's a pretty seismic shift in and of itself. Then you start to sacrifice the ability to talk about anything other than Your Precious Baby, which annoys the crap out of your friends who don't have kids, or even those who've already had kids and gone through that phase before. Then there's the sacrifice of the most important thing you have, your time. You can't dick around and watch the exact same episode of SportsCenter three times in succession from 7–10 a.m. You can't regularly go out until 4 a.m. and get blasted and become a vegetable the next day. And of course, having a child means that you need to set a good example. Swearing every couple of minutes in front of your kid? FUCK NO, DIPSHIT. Yes, a bag of a Cheetos on the couch can technically serve as your dinner while you watch HBO, but probably not a good idea to do it in front of your kids. And let's not forget cleaning up someone else's poop. Oh geez, how your mother and I wrung our hands over that.

This chapter is no blueprint for raising model kids, which is a flawed notion to begin with. I've come up with rules that will keep your kids under control until a certain point, probably just before or around puberty, when they start to realize that they can do a lot more than they initially thought, akin to the moment the machines became self-aware in *Terminator 2* or when the velociraptors started to open doors in *Jurassic Park*. After that, you're on your own and may God have mercy on you.

FIRST RULE: HAVE GIRLS INSTEAD OF BOYS.

All the stereotypes are true. It cannot be understated how different boys and girls are during this early development. Girls tend to learn quicker, be less disruptive, potty-train easier, listen better, concentrate longer, be more sensitive to others' feelings, and obey their parents more. Boys are the exact opposite. Sure, the tables will be turned when puberty hits, but until then, have girls instead of boys.

SECOND RULE: KIDS WILL ABSORB
EVERYTHING FROM YOU.

One of the most important and eye-popping lessons I learned was when you, Sofia, started to say quite frequently that you were tired. You weren't even three years old. Taking naps regularly. The most stressful thing in your life was deciding whether you felt like pooping in the training potty chair or in your diaper. It was easy to point the finger at the culprit. YOU, ALESSANDRA, THE 15-MONTH-OLD SISTER. No, it was your mother and father, repeatedly complaining about work and how difficult it was and how little restful sleep we were getting and our backs were aching again and I know we need to be grateful for all of our blessings but why does it seem like we're not getting ahead in life and wouldn't it be great to get out of this rat race in New York City? It is astounding how closely and how soon children will start to mimic their parents.

When you two were about three and two years old and began bickering and fighting over dumb things, we asked your pediatrician what we could do to prevent it. And he said that the fighting and any crying was simply a method to get our attention, and it was a function of our indulgence. If at the sign of a couple of raised voices, one of us started rushing to the source of the dispute, that in and of itself satisfied your urges to get our attention, which would then become a regular, reliable dog whistle. According to your pediatrician, the solution was to not get involved, because it signaled that we would not get drawn into your game.

(That maybe lasted about a week, because just the sound of you two fighting was too much to bear for two only children who had never known the fights and disagreements common to siblings. I also found that I actually kind of enjoyed being involved. At work I always was at the mercy of a judge; now I was the Solomonic arbiter, carefully listening to both of you plead your cases, and then issuing punishment that best of all, left zero avenues for appeal.)

But the point was that the doctor's advice made me more aware of your behavior. Even when you were but a year old, when you started acting out, it wasn't really just because you were "having a bad day" or "my kid is just difficult" or "just because." There was usually a reason for it—not enough sleep, hunger, a denied wish, an ailing body part, teething, something.

Cause and effect and logic can still matter, even with regard to beings as seemingly mercurial and unpredictable as babies and toddlers. It's imperative to keep this in mind, especially when trying to create an appropriate environment for your child.

My other piece of advice for expectant parents is to get out of the apartment/house and to not be a shut-in after the birth of their child. It's tough, I know. After you, Sofia, were born, your mother and I would take you out in that stroller and I was gripped with this doomed sensation that some psycho was going to attack you. Little did I know that the odds of that happening in New York were merely 25 to 30 percent. But you have to get out there. Those first several months should be a time for you to go places with your kid, when the baby is sleeping a lot, even through the most chaotic environment.

You can go overboard. Soon after you were born, Sofia, your mother and I went out for a sushi dinner with you in tow. Afterward, we just needed to make the point that dammit, even though we were now parents, we actually could do whatever we wanted and were not lame, and so we went for a drink in Koreatown. This led to us being in this super-sceney club with all these twenty-somethings staring at the dowdy couple having a beer in the corner and gently rocking a Graco stroller back and forth. In the moment, we were verrrrry pleased with ourselves, unmindful to the fact that it marked another milestone: the sacrifice of whatever coolness we had.

I know what a pain in the ass it is to go out with a newborn. You've got to get the diaper bag ready, with multiple diapers and plenty of wipes, and a change of clothes in case there's a mega-poop debacle. Then you have to get the powdered formula ready in that plastic measuring container, and then you have to get enough water for the bottle, maybe several, and you need maybe a couple of pacifiers to try to keep the infant occupied. When they're a bit older, then you need some baby food with the spoons, which means you always should bring a food bib, and then if it's winter, you need to make sure the baby is bundled up, which means another blanket, and then you have to navigate the streets weighed down like a Himalayas Sherpa as you gird yourself to defend your child against the psycho who wants to attack her. I get it.

Big deal. Just do it. Stop making excuses, force yourselves to go that extra effort and make the experience happen. You'll end up having memories, like when your mother and I tried to change your diapers in a restaurant's one-toilet bathroom, with me paralyzed by the gigantic cockroach scaling the wall. You'll remember going to Paris and discovering that this city is so charming because it is not built for strollers of any kind, which led to your mother and I carrying these insanely heavy carriages with you strapped in them, up and down the Metro steps. You'll see in a more favorable light the time you took a flight to Tokyo and were so despondent by your ten-month-old's incessant crying that you were swigging wine directly from the mini-bottle, looking at your watch and thinking, "THERE ARE EIGHT MORE FUCKING HOURS LEFT ON THIS FUCKING FLIGHT." It'll be worth it in the long run, promise.

Have the baby adapt to the environment. Do not cater to the baby's every whim. I think going out frequently actually makes the child less high-maintenance, because these types of outings force him or her to adapt to a variety of surroundings and the baby won't be as fussy. (This has been backed up by zero verifiable evidence.) Sure, there will be meltdowns at inopportune times, but that just means that you need to improvise and find a way to not destroy other people's enjoyment (but any glare of disapproval from a crusty octogenarian should be met with, "Oh, you were never an infant, assface?"). Having kids is not "the end of having a life," and if that thought is overwhelming all other thoughts you have, then maybe it's not the right time to have them.

It is a sacrifice, to be sure, and so much more than we expect. New parents will readily give up their schedules and routines for the sake of their kids. When the baby is born, parents will do everything to make sure whatever is physically put into that little body is organic and not pumped full of hormones and made of the finest natural ingredients. But I find that those same parents—and yes, I put myself in that category—don't really think about changing their own attitudes in front of their kids. We fight with our spouses, act rudely toward strangers, bitch about the boss, swear at the injustices of life, and we think that it's fine as long as we're not talking directly to our babies or toddlers. We just simply assume that they're too young to understand us or that they know that the behavior is not directed toward them.

I have never worn a tie-dye shirt in my life and have only recently overcome my suspicion of anyone wearing Birkenstocks, but I will insist until my very last breath that the energy you emit will be absorbed by your children, no matter how young they are. Let's put it this way: you can spend a morning or an afternoon with someone, not say a single word or interact at all with that person, and that person can sense what kind of mood you're in—whether you're feeling lazy and unmotivated, anxious and worried, or seething with rage. The conventional wisdom would be that the baby can't process these acts or emotions, but given the research at this point, who can say? It's foolish to automatically discount the effect of your mood on your baby or kid just because she can't properly express herself. All I know is that whenever your mother and I have been stressed or cranky, you two inevitably started to mirror that behavior. What results is this spiraling dust devil of negativity, where my stress leads to your mother feeling anxious to you acting out which leads to us getting more worked up until a massive blowup occurs. And then the mood is definitely ruined.

Sure, it's unfair, because you're sacrificing true emotions, caught in the unenviable position of pretending to be calm when you in fact are not. But if you have to freak out, do it in the sanctity of your own room or away from the kids. Find a solution. Walk. A bath. Meditate. A treat. Work out. Whatever you need to do to relieve yourself. It might not seem right to deny your true feelings in front of your children. But don't we do that anyway? We don't explain to a three-year-old what war is or go into worrisome detail as to why we need to go through airport security or the odds of surviving stage IV cancer. Sometimes you just have to shield your children from that which is sad or troublesome or evil.

The flip side of the above is that you need to envelop your child with physical signs of affection. It starts with you smiling nonstop at your infant in the hopes that he or she will "mirror" your face. You shower that baby and toddler with physical affection, with innumerable and random hugs and kisses and pats on the back. I did not grow up in a house big on hugs and "I love yous" because my parents did not grow up in that type of environment, and that's completely fine. (At least that's what I say as I cry myself to sleep every night.) But I will not repeat that cycle with you. I will continue the Italian culture where kissing and touching and hugging is as essential as air. You, Sofia, are always at risk of a random hug or tickle from me. I will always perform my terrible drum solos on your back in an effort to wake you up, Alessandra. I want there to be no doubt that you have my unconditional love. And just to make sure you have no doubt that I love you with every molecule of my being, I say to you all the time, "No matter how angry I get, I love you."

You will need to do the same for your child. You smile and you laugh and you do whatever you can to provoke this child into a similar state, regardless of how you're feeling personally. It should not be difficult by any stretch of the imagination. In fact, if you have problems not being transformed by the joy, innocence and potential of your toddler, then maybe it's time to step back and recalibrate yourself.

THIRD RULE: KIDS DON'T KNOW ANY BETTER.

If we're giving credence to the thought that toddlers are more emotionally developed than we give them credit for, then it seems contradictory to say that their intelligence isn't very developed. But it's true. It is amazing how much a child (or really, a full-grown adult) will accept as normal just by virtue of growing up that way. I never thought it was unusual that I had a father who always seemed to be at home, never went to an office, never talked about work, and would happen to have people over for dinner who never came again. You naturally trust your parental figures so much that it just becomes part of your reality and you don't question it.

The adaptability is not limited just to the children. You will think that you cannot possibly fit a baby into your schedule, because your work, social, and/or biological programs will simply not permit it. I used to be a night person, getting all my writing done in the hours between 11 p.m. to 3 a.m. Well, guess what—that changed. Your mother used to moan that she didn't feel human unless she had eight hours of sleep. And now when she doesn't sleep eight hours...well, she still bitches like Barbra Streisand on a camping trip, but she goes without. Physically, you can get used to just about anything. And so will your child.

Because despite everything that you've seen and read and been warned about, you need to keep something in mind. You are still in control.

It may not seem like it while you're taking the fastest showers in the world so that your infant is not left unattended. Or when you bolt out of bed at three in the morning when your kid starts crying. Or when you're listening to a nine-month-old scream her head off because she doesn't want to go to bed. But believe it or not, you are still in control. You can decide to modify your reaction to what your kid does, or you can elect to start to set your own rules.

You are in control when it comes to spoiling your child. The temptation is certainly understandable. When your child is small, the amount of happiness that you can give to him is disproportionate to the cost. You see how a $5 toy can light up your child's eyes and create a smile beyond your expectations. When you're desperate to reverse the tide of a tantrum—hell, even just to stem it—letting your kid have what she wants is awfully tempting.

Let me be the wet blanket and say that you have to resist this urge as best as you can. Of course, you need not be so draconian in instituting the rules, and there is room for leeway. But whatever you decide, be warned that you should hold out as long as possible to indulge your kid, and whatever you do, you should really try to dose it out as gradually as possible. I'm not trying to be flip here, but I really think that certain things like TV, video games, and sugar are like drugs. When a kid gets that first hit, he wants more, and if it becomes a regular occurrence, the habit becomes extremely hard to break. You can't cater to your kid's every whim, because then it will become the norm, and will grow to satisfying bigger and more unreasonable wishes.

I want to avoid sounding sanctimonious. We all have sliding scales of what a good kid is and the dreams that we hold in store. But it is my fervent belief that yes, if you really set your mind to it, you can mold your child so that he or she does as you want: to go to sleep at a certain hour, to remain at the dinner table, to not need a screen every 10 minutes, to say "please" and "thank you," to greet your parents properly when they arrive home, not eat candy continually, to make eye contact when talking, to get in the habit of reading, to not interrupt when you're talking to someone else, to be physically active. All it takes is repetition and discipline, and eventually, the child will adapt to any rule, any ritual, anything. Willpower. Shun Fujimoto.

We tend to think that kids just have immutable likes and dislikes. "My kid won't eat vegetables." Well, that's not necessarily true. You're enabling your kid to not eat vegetables by creating excuses. You'll gladly substitute fries for those vegetables just because you want this child to eat anything and you don't want him to starve before your eyes, but then what? This kid might still be pooping his pants, but he isn't that stupid—

he recognizes this concession and will refuse to eat vegetables the next time. Regardless of your insistence that your child has a particularly sensitive palate, if you withheld all food except vegetables, your kid will eventually eat them (whether he'll really enjoy them is another matter).

If you take the attitude of, "Well, I would like to let my child develop without rules," that's commendable and it certainly makes things a lot easier for you. But then you forfeit the right to complain, "She's seven going on 13 years old," or "Why did she just say that she hates me?" or "I can't believe he just tried to set fire to our house." I actually admire the parents who let their kids roam free and with abandon...from a distance, like when I'm watching Joe Schmo play blackjack at $1,000 a hand. Hope it works out for him, but too rich for my blood. I'd rather be strict first, then loosen the reins gradually.

There are a couple of important caveats when trying to impose a mode of behavior.

First, you have to start early. The longer you wait to impose the rule, the tougher it will be to reverse the trend.

Sometime before you, Sofia, turned two and when you were born, Alessandra, I found myself getting into more fights with your mother and I remember at one point saying, "I feel like I'm fighting for Sofia's soul," which goes to show you that extreme sleep deprivation and stress will make you say the most melodramatic things. (I may have been on my knees and clenching my fists as I bellowed it.) But there is something about those first couple of years. It's not just setting rules, but more of a tone. You want to set rules for the house, and coincidentally enough, this is about the time when toddlers are beginning to enter a phase where they want to test their boundaries.

I swear, during that time, I would be gone for several days for work and when I got back, you would act differently after being coddled by your mother and grandmother. I know every child is going to go through a rebellious phase, but if you want to, you can nip some of that in the bud. Any attitude—a rolling of the eyes, the "I know that" tone, a sharp response—should be met with one of those record-screeching-to-a-halt moments, where you drop whatever the hell you're doing and let that child know that it is simply not acceptable to talk in that way to your mother or father. Because when you think to yourself, "Well, that's just part of growing up," or "It's just a phase," you're setting yourself up for the next act of rebellion, which will be just a little worse, and then for the next, and before you know it, your own flesh and blood will be telling you to fuck off in front of her friends and then heading off to do some meth in the parking lot of the local 7-Eleven.

There is a cost to making rules and it's having to deal with the crying and the tantrums. Bedtime is always a source of endless fights, with lots of yelling and arguing and tears. One night, when you, Sofia, were about two and a half, we got around to putting you to bed, and it was hell. Put you into the crib and you started screaming and crying like a banshee.

When your child is crying in a crib, I would like you to have the presence of mind to conduct an experiment. Note the time when the crying starts. Then check it when you think 10 minutes has elapsed. You will be astounded as to how vastly you

will overestimate the amount of time your child has been crying. It will often be a mere five or six minutes instead of ten. On
more than one occasion you will be off by more than 10 minutes, which will defy all notions of the time-space continuum.

Anyway, on this evening, both your mother and your grandmother were at home. After five minutes of nonstop screaming,
which really felt like 10, they insisted that I bring you back out
of the crib—calm you down, sing a lullaby, maybe bake some
cupcakes and feed them to you—because you were crying and
it just wasn't right to be so cruel to you. I declined.

Another five minutes passed, which felt even longer than
the first five minutes. Your mother and your grandmother
begged to go inside the bedroom. Veto.

At the 15th minute...you were still screaming like you had been
shot. Both mother and grandmother were starting to grumble under their breaths. I sat on the sofa, pretending to read a magazine.

The 20th minute...still going pretty strong, actually. I was
now the grizzled sea captain, the ship lurching from side to
side, blasted by torrents of rain, while the faint of heart next to
me pleaded, "It's too dangerous! YOU'RE GOING RIGHT INTO
THE TEETH OF THE STORM!"

The 25th minute. By now, your mother and grandmother
were getting openly mutinous and attacking my general un-
fitness as a parent. We were now fighting among ourselves.

By the 30th minute—which, without exaggeration, really
felt like a solid hour—you had fallen soundly asleep in your
crib. The one positive aspect of a toddler screaming and crying
at an insane level is that it really saps the kid's energy.

The next evening, Sofia, you did not forget to wail at bedtime. As all three of us were girding ourselves for another wretched 30 minutes, the crying stopped. It had been only five minutes.

The evening after that, you went down without a peep.

To this day, neither your mother nor your grandmother has apologized to me.

The second consideration to keep in mind when trying to mold your child's behavior is that your partner in raising the child must be on board; there cannot be any undermining of authority and you two need to present a united front. Even if the other parent doesn't say anything, kids are perceptive enough to see when one parent is the asskicker disciplinarian and the other seems to be dragged along reluctantly. And there is no doubt that your child will exploit it with the cold-bloodedness of a hacker with way too much time on his hands until both parents are screaming at each other and insisting whose method was right.

Shortly after you, Sofia, was born, we started to think about a nanny, because we knew that your mother would have to eventually go back to work. We met 10 to 15 candidates and subjected them to the kind of scrutiny reserved for people who would have access to the bowels of the Pentagon. And why shouldn't we have? Normally, you could say that this type of decision wasn't permanent or could be overcome, but in this case, not really.

It came down to two women. One was a Greek woman, a bit on the older side, who was sweet and projected a calm, grandmother-like aura. We imagined you becoming fluent in Greek by your fourth birthday. Then there was a woman from St. Vincent and the Grenadines, whose wild and frizzy hair seemed to reflect her ebullient, unbridled energy. We imagined you at four years old being the most hyper kid on the playground.

We simply could not make up our minds. Maybe it shouldn't have been surprising. It's easier to compare two similar types, but with two polar opposites, the frame of reference is skewed. Your mother decided that she would try out each woman for an afternoon and see how they worked. I thought it was a waste of time and money. It wouldn't be helpful, according to my brilliant mind, to have a half-day tryout, because each of them would be on her best behavior.

The Greek woman showed up late. We also discovered that she didn't have a cell phone. The idea of an emergency arising and us having to resort to the most dysfunctional and increasingly profane game of telephone suddenly made this a very easy choice. And that's how Desree came to be the third-most important adult in your early life.

Through the years—when she got married and had her own child—she has loved you like one of her own. Her total commute from the outer reaches of Brooklyn is close to three hours, and yet I can count on one hand the number of times that I've seen her in a bad mood. And when I see both of your girls' good energy, the happiness you radiate, the way you're eager to smile and do new things, I think that it's in no small part due to Desree's influence, because she's exactly like that.

But beyond that, the most fortuitous part of Desree coming into our lives is that her morals and sense of right and wrong dovetail with ours. It's not the kind of thing that you can figure out in a 30-minute interview or even a half day spent together.

But she has a keen sense of ethics, no doubt informed by her faith, which is a powerful force in her life. When I first called Desree to let her know that she got the job, she exclaimed that her prayers had been answered, which reassured me that we had made the right choice. The very first songs you learned were gospel, complete with the rhythmic clapping. (This caught the attention of many passing shoppers at the supermarket, the two Asian toddlers singing gospel songs at the top of their lungs.)

During the week, the amount of waking time that you spent with her has dwarfed ours, and Des was the one who helped reinforce our principles of what's right and wrong, to tell the truth, to not cut corners. When you've strayed, she's told us immediately and more important, we've never second-guessed her and undercut her authority. She has been part of our united front in our discipline and our love for you.

Like most children/caregiver relationships, it will come to an end. With you becoming older, there will no longer a need for her to be present. She may want to go elsewhere. And with the passage of time, she may become a faded memory. But you should never forget her and her impact on who you've become.

•••••••••••••••••••••••••••••••••

These three tidy rules, one of which is God-mandated, all come with a caveat. When we get the occasional compliment about how well-behaved you two are, I feel a tinge of guilt. It's because in addition to the above, I know what's kept you in check. My temper.

When people who have just met us mention that I seem like

such a mellow and chill person, your mother's eyes roll so hard into the back of her head it seems like she's having a mini-seizure. She has seen me stress out over inane things, has seen me stew over slights real and imagined, and has seen the moment when the dam of frustration bursts and I go completely apeshit.

Unless you have a truly extraordinary child who has the ability at less than two years of age to regulate his behavior in accordance with the norms of civilized society—and before you start mentally arguing that he can, it is not yours—you will need to cajole and reason with your child to behave in a certain way. I know that in your mind, you will gently tell your child that no, honey, it's not right to put your sister's head in the toilet, or dear, we're going to be late for school for the third straight day if you persist on having a tantrum about what clothes to wear, and your progeny will then listen to your measured tone and will listen. I wish I could tell you that. But raising children is no fairy tale world. There will need to be a moment when you have to put the fear of God in them. My personal feeling is that without some sort of fear of the parent—fear of punishment, of scolding, of disapproval—the child will go unfettered. When I say unfettered, that child will walk all over your soul.

Your discipline of your child will invariably be reflected in the way you've been disciplined yourself because that is all that you know. When I lied—really, the worst thing that I could possibly do—then I got the whip, and that was because my father got the whip as well. I will never, ever do the same to you, and so this cycle will be broken, but I have given you swift spankings. In my mind, that constitutes a much more reasonable mode of punishment, but in time, I'm not sure that that it will be viewed as correct either. I know the temptation among other parents (and certainly myself) is to say, "Well, I was raised this way, and I turned out fine." Well, about a hundred years ago, it was perfectly defensible to have children work in factories. A couple of generations ago it was accepted for kids to get the switch if they acted badly. A couple of decades ago it would have been no big deal to let your kids have a sleepover where you barely knew the parents of the other kids. The point is that times change. There are research and studies coming forth every month on how to talk to your kids, how to discipline them, how to encourage them, how to let their creativity flow. That's your responsibility to keep up with that—not necessarily to automatically adopt a study's conclusions, but to really read up on and subject to your personal scrutiny. But sticking to what you know only because you grew up with it and "turned out fine" is not right.

In my mind, it's permissible to discipline your child harshly as long as it's coming from a place of love. And it's easy to figure out in your heart of hearts whether you're yelling at your kids because they're truly being bad and they need to know that their behavior is unacceptable or whether it's because you had a shitty day. The truth is that even though I experienced tough discipline, I never resented my parents and could tell that despite some of their human fallibility, they loved me. As harsh as I may have been, I pray you feel similarly.

Whenever you feel "My parents don't understand me," or "My father was too strict," or "My mother could have done better," please remember that we were never parents before you two came along. Please remember the sacrifices. Not just the melding of an identity. Not just the midnight feedings or middle-of-the-night ailments, which can drain your soul. Not just the phase where we stalked you when you were one year old as you wobbled your way throughout our friend's un-child-proofed house, trying to make sure that you didn't tumble backward and smash your head. Not just changing your diapers when you were a newborn. No, please remember the continual vigilance of a different sort—being attuned to your development, trying to find that balance between letting you grow and steering you toward the right direction, setting rules but not curbing your personality. These sacrifices need to be remembered, as does this.

They were all worth it.

16

WHEN YOU BELIEVE

My favorite moment in *The Simpsons Movie* is a throw-away joke when it appears that the end of the world is at hand. The people in church and the regulars at Moe's Bar come out into the street and see the darkening sky. Then the churchgoers rush into the bar while the drunks make a beeline into the church.

I am from the latter group.

Studies have shown that new generations become less religious in tandem with economic development. In general, religious commitment is lower in countries with higher education, higher GDP, and greater income inequality. I can see this in a city like New York, and I can't help but believe that compared to days long past, we live in a more deeply cynical world, one where people demand proof to overcome their rigorous skepticism. Clearly, Jesus Himself would not be able to survive today, because after every article reporting His latest miracle, there would be thousands of asshole commenters typing "FAKE" and "PHOTOSHOPPED LULZ."

If there were a debate between two super-intellectuals, one a fervent believer of Catholicism or Protestantism or Islam or Judaism or any organized religion, and the other a nonbeliever, the nonbeliever would win, hands down. The nonbeliever could easily pick apart organized religion as the inconsistent bundle of principles that it can be, especially when it comes to non-adherents. If you're fundamentally a good person, but not a believer, can you get into heaven? On the Day of Judgment, does God really let the terrorist believers into paradise and tell the virtuous nonbeliever to take a hike? And forget about getting into the details of historical religious events. Anyone with basic cross-examination skills could eviscerate the believer to the point where the only defense is to point to the Bible or Torah or Quran.

One could take this debate even further as to whether there is a God or Supreme Being, and the agnostic super-intellectual still wins handily. Forget about super-intellectuals—these are common sense questions that even you girls could come up with. Where is the concrete evidence of This Being? Why are there so many senseless tragedies—tragedies that by all objective measures cannot be said to have resulted in silver linings—in this world? If your God is a vengeful or impassive Being, then what does that say about the way we should live our lives morally? The demand of proof of God butts up against the believer's faith, and hard evidence will always seem more persuasive than simply, "I believe."

You girls are too young to know this yet, but religion can

also lay bare the worst hypocritical tendencies in man. If every religion begins with a just and kind God with a directive that its followers believe in teachings based on love and goodwill, then you can see ample evidence of exactly the opposite. It can be as petty as when someone cuts in line to get ashes at St. Patrick's on Lent—to which I can personally attest is every damn year— or when people use an ancient document from unenlightened times to suppress others. When I went to a wedding between two gay people and saw them laugh and dance and tremble with tears and experience the purest of joys, it made me ask myself, "Really, would God want to deny them this pursuit of happiness?" The hypocrisy is amplified when religious leaders commit or conspire to cover up heinous crimes and others fail to speak up. And of course, over human history people have killed and will continue to kill in the furtherance of what is essentially, "My interpretation of God is more right than yours."

Thus it is tempting to dismiss religion as a wedge that separates rather than unites, and it's enough to make you give up on the idea of any faith at all.

Which I've come to realize is wrong.

One night Uncle Dave pointed out to me that you need to distinguish between the message and the messenger. Whatever religion you believe in, it presumably has overriding mandates of goodwill and peace and tolerance. Well, human beings are the propagators and vessels for this message, but we are decidedly imperfect. Yeah, there are always going to be religious nutsos who invoke God to promote their own agendas, but that shouldn't be a reason to discard all of the God-fearing people who perform beautiful deeds, both routine and extraordinary, because of their faith. Uncle Dave's words really resonated with me, because I remembered them long after we had all those drinks in that Irish bar on 55th Street.

Being religious, he told me several months later while we were drinking in Mexico, doesn't necessarily make you a better person. What it should make you is more conscious and accepting of other people's flaws. That consciousness and ability to see why others may act the way they do—which countless people, beginning with Jesus Himself, have called "teleporting"—has to be part of you. You need to have that moral base. And that is why I periodically bring you to church to pray for others and why we pray at night to give thanks.

Religion became a much stronger influence in my life after we moved to Rome when I was 11 years old. My parents started to befriend a number of Jesuits, especially Japanese priests. When he was in his early 20s, my father had alienated himself from the Catholic Church, but with the encouragement of our priest friends, he rediscovered his faith. As part of the process, my father confessed his sins for the first time in almost 30 years. His love for decadent times and unflinching honesty merged into a prolonged confession so graphic that after 30 minutes, the stricken priest actually said to him, "You really don't have to tell me every sin you've ever committed."

Several years later, on April Fools' Day, your grandfather started to feel bloated. There's a photo of him in front of the Vatican where his face is puffy, the skin looking unusually taut. He went to his doctor, who insisted that he had gas and that it wasn't serious. I remember all of us laughing with relief when we heard that diagnosis.

It was wrong. His kidneys were shutting down.

He was hospitalized, the Italian doctor was kicked aside, and the American doctors swooped in. He was diagnosed with nephrotic syndrome, a condition where the kidney filters fail to work properly and are leaking too much protein into the urine. Protein in the blood keeps fluid in the bloodstream, so when there's less of it, the fluid leaks out into the body's tissue, which was causing the edema in my father.

This was not your grandfather's first brush with mortality. He was wracked with numerous asthma attacks and once had a near-fatal allergic reaction to medication he was taking. He was an alcoholic and a chain smoker and in the 70s, suffered two separate bouts of pancreatitis, which he described as more excruciating than the gout attacks he had. He stopped the smoking and drinking before I had any memories of him doing either; to give you the kind of willpower that he had back then, he quit both at the drop of a dime without any relapses or reconsiderations about taking them up again. In fact, he lamented that the only times he really thought about drinking was when the CIA forced him to go to Alcoholics Anonymous meetings. So your grandfather had a sturdy constitution, as they say.

But this time, he was up against something more ominous. As with many diseases that end in "syndrome," there are many mysteries about nephrotic syndrome, not the least of which is the cure, especially in 1985. And my father, now bedridden, began to balloon with this excess water weight.

I confess that even at 13 years old, I did not exactly process what was happening and remember only snippets. Silent evenings at home. Visiting my father at the hospital, the giant windows open to bustling Roman streets. Staring wide-eyed at my mother as she broke down in hysterics—I had never seen her shed a tear until that point—when she discovered that he had clipped a lock of his hair for safekeeping. "He knows he's about to die."

By the time the Americans realized that there would need to be some sort of a larger intervention, it was getting too late, as my father would not have survived the flight back to the United States. Instead, he would have to be transported to a U.S. base in Germany. He was given three days to live.

Just before my father was about to be moved to Frankfurt, Father Giuseppe Pittau came to visit. He was born in Villacidro, a small town in Sardinia, and became a Jesuit. In his mid-20s, he arrived in Japan as a missionary and spent most of his academic life at Sophia University in Tokyo. He was the bridge between Japanese and Italian worlds, who eventually led the Society of Jesus and was named an archbishop. About 24 years later, he was the one who baptized you, Sofia, and then a few days later, presided over the Catholic wedding of your mother and me.

At the hospital, Father Pittau gave his rosary beads to my father. Then he said, "I want you to give these back to me when you return."

My father began to protest. "That's not fair. You are asking too much."

"I want you to give these back to me."

My father was transported to Germany. And when he got there, something happened.

Cells started to function the way they were supposed to and generated in the right way. The body stopped storing water and started to expel it.

Four weeks after he was airlifted to Germany, my father returned to Rome. He gave the rosary back to Father Pittau.

There was no medical explanation for what happened. It was simply, "He got better." When doctors—about the most inquisitive, cynical people around—are baffled, maybe there is something else at work here.

As much as we want answers and explanations and logic, we need to recognize that maybe there is something completely beyond our level of comprehension. It might not be logical that God is literally everywhere. It might not make sense for God to be invested in a high school football game. But we need to be humble and open ourselves to that possibility. For every person who is correct in claiming that there is no empirical proof that God exists, there is someone who is right in saying that there is no empirical proof that God does not exist.

Twenty years after my father's brush with death, in the summer of 2005, my mother and I went to our local bank and opened our safe deposit box. Among the items was a sealed envelope. And on it, in all caps and written with red marker, was the following:

PLEASE OPEN IF I SHOULD DIE
UNDER MYSTERIOUS CIRCUMSTANCES AND
INVESTIGATE THE PEOPLE IN THESE PHOTOS.

Inside were photos of my father's former associates.

I couldn't help but scoff.

The previous years had not been kind. My father had decided to retire at 52, an unusually early age, but one that was wholly necessary. The daily prospect of being uncovered, of risking his life and his family's life, had taken an immense toll. If you think that the office politics are bad at your workplace, just imagine what they're like at The Company. He expected that he could seamlessly transition into a second career in consulting. But it was a rocky journey, full of exciting possibilities that were soon dashed, populated with dangerous characters (explaining that envelope in the deposit box) and ultimately not sustainable.

Armed with his overt retirement, he had also written a book about his life as a spy under a pseudonym. It was translated and published in China, Taiwan, and Japan, which allowed him a degree of minor celebrity, but that also dissipated. (The two-inch-high manuscript sitting in a drawer of our apartment has gone unread by both my mother and me, which would provide a psychoanalyst with abundant hours of entertainment.) The family finances got even tighter. In retrospect, he said that he shouldn't have left the CIA so early; I don't doubt that it had an effect on the way that I've pursued stable jobs and how I've avoided taking bold steps in my career.

Physically, the cumulative effects of a life lived to the maximum and without heed for future consequences started to add up. The number of pills he took was staggering, treating a variety of ailments from gout to high blood pressure to bladder control to pancreatitis to Lord knows what else. They caused side effects that required more medication, neutralizing the potency of others, until he was taking north of 20 pills a day.

My father started to suffer from transient ischemic attacks, mini-strokes where a clot blocks blood flow to critical regions in the brain. They caused him to shuffle his feet, lose his balance and fall, dulled his senses, made him babble. Death by a thousand small blows, each one sapping the life from him. When you're a role player with ordinary capabilities, of which I readily include myself, the diminution of those skills is noticeable but not mourned. For someone who could speak six languages, was knowledgeable in literature and politics, and was an undercover spy during the Cold War, the indignities of getting old became devastating. He had transformed from an asset to a burden.

He had a tendency toward depression, which revealed itself during darker moments. "I just want to die," he said, and it was in line with his grandiose and dramatic personality. Self-pity was a weakness of his, and it manifested after fights with my mother. His mentality had changed. After enduring a profession in which he fought to remain concealed, fought against colleagues, fought simply to stay alive, and after battling the wants and subsequent reactions of his body, he was done fighting.

No matter what his personal foibles were, and no matter what his profession required him to do, my father always placed honor and code above all else. The particularly Japanese notion of this concept is *bushido*, the "way of the warrior," which was the unwritten moral code of principles followed by the samurai, based on honor, courage, duty, loyalty, and self-sacrifice. If a samurai was about to fall into enemy hands, the *bushido* necessitated him to perform *seppuku*, whereby he would follow a highly ritualized ceremony, complete with a last meal and cup of sake and dressed in special robes, before plunging a knife into his abdomen and drawing the blade from left to right. We often hear the term *harakiri* to describe this act, but my parents always pointed out that it is a casual, almost vulgar term and not appropriate as a metaphor for self-destruction. For something as portentous and honorable as an elaborate ritual suicide by disembowelment, one uses the more formal and correct term, please.

Seppuku was a means for samurai to exit this world with honor, on his own terms. It was more preferable than being captured by his enemies, to face punishment for his sins, or to continue to live in disgrace. It served as the deepest apology one could make.

Perhaps in another time, one where samurai walked the land, the manner of his death would have been more dignified. But alas, on a Sunday, six months after my 33rd birthday, my father turned a gun on himself in the bathroom.

Of all the random times, I found this out while on a date, which really bears emphasizing, happened with the regularity of Halley's Comet. This woman and I had met maybe a month earlier and had just been getting to know each other, and we made plans for walking around that Sunday afternoon. She had to take some work calls, finished them up, and as we rounded a corner onto Hudson Street—just a couple of blocks from where you go to school now—I noticed that I missed a couple of calls from your grandmother.

The date and I cabbed it back to my apartment, and then I packed for a train to Washington, D.C. And I remember saying to the woman that while I liked her and I wasn't sure whether this relationship was going to work out, I would be always be grateful that she happened to be with me when I got the news that my father had passed.

(Spoiler alert: the relationship did not work out.)

I can't decide whether the seven stages of grief—shock, denial, anger, bargaining, guilt, depression, and acceptance—is the most perceptive theory or merely the most obvious one, because every time I have experienced such loss, I can start checking off each one like a grocery list.

What people rarely tell you after the death of a close family member is that the first week, you are incredibly busy. Even if you're able to take the week off (and if you can't, you better find an employer or a boss that treats you better), you will be astounded at the number of things that you have to do. Calls to update relatives. Calls from friends to support you. Cremation or burial? Would dad want the really nice coffin or would he not care? Wake or memorial service? What readings will be at the memorial service? How is the distilled essence of your loved one reflected in each reading? Who will do them? Writing the eulogy and steeling myself so that people's lasting memory wouldn't be me mouthing a word every five seconds, breaking down, and eventually being carried off on a gurney. And what to say? I'll never forget being on the phone with a woman from the church who said that people tend to eulogize much too long and that it would be advisable for me to keep it short. That's lovely, thank you. Why don't I tell a few jokes at the beginning to get the crowd loosened up? Maybe fire up a couple of funny movie clips on the PowerPoint to grab their attention?

And this all assumes that you're even generally functional, because if you are, don't forget about fitting in the 30-minute crying jag as well. I began to understand why people make or send food after a death. Between the grieving, commiserating, organizing, and working (the last of which I vividly remember doing that week), it really didn't occur to me to eat. If an apple or bagel was there, I ate it, but purely as fuel.

It was not long before my thoughts turned to The Last Time I Spoke To My Father.

It had been earlier that Sunday morning, and I was mediating one of the frequent arguments between my parents. In replaying the exchange, I started to feel this dull and persistent ache of remorse, because he did not deserve the harshness of those last words. You want your last conversation with your father to be: "They say that anyone can be a father, but it takes a real man to be a dad...I would not be half of what I am today had it not been for your guidance and love. I have finalized the preparations for the Viking funeral as you prepare to make your journey into the great beyond. I love you." Not: "Mama is right. You're acting like a child."

I've read of many instances where that last conversation with a loved one who then passes suddenly or unexpectedly will haunt the survivor for years or cause that person to spiral downward into new depths. And of the many conversations I had the week after my father passed, the most important one was with the judge I used to work for in Las Vegas, Judge Leavitt. I told him about the guilt I felt and how maybe if I had been more patient or understanding, events would not have unfolded the way they did. And now my father was gone, forever.

My judge was emphatic in saying that I should not—in fact, could not—have any regrets. Because if you treated any interaction with a loved one like it was the last, then you could never level criticism from love, or never be able to express a true feeling. It's a fake world of thought and emotion. And just like that, many potential hours of tears and teeth-gnashing and sleepless nights were washed away.

Six days after I had one of the worst days of my life, on a blue-skied, wondrous morning, I had one of my best. The memorial service was a modest gathering of friends. This was before your mother and I met, so my circle of friends was vastly smaller, but I remember as clear as that day those who made the trip down to Bethesda to attend. I made it through the eulogy—which mentioned how he learned French and his pride when I got my first job and his renewed faith after recovering from his near-kidney failure—without dissolving into a puddle. No one complained that it was too long. Our friends cried and shared laughs. If the primary objective of every funeral is to shift the focus from mourning the loss of a life to celebrating the joy in it, then it was accomplished on that day.

The problem, of course, is that the funeral or memorial service lasts just one day. There is no proper way to grieve, and everyone is different, but I've found this pattern to hold fairly true.

If you are ever thrust into a situation where you are the comforter-to-be, I know that it's uncomfortable as hell. You have no idea what to say. If you haven't experienced that kind of loss, you don't want to be fake. The last thing you want to do is compound the person's pain by saying something stupid or inadvertently offensive. And then your instinct will be not to try at all, because it will be easier to not do anything and assume that others closer to this person will step in and provide the words and actions necessary for this person to begin the healing process.

You DO NOT do that.

This is not about you. However awkward it may seem, however futile, your primary purpose is to let this person know that you feel his or her pain. "I'm so sorry" is completely and absolutely fine. You say that you will be sending prayers and positive energy to him or her, and you make sure of it. If you are good friends with this person, then you say that you'll be there any time you are needed—if this person wants to just talk, to hang out and not talk, to watch TV, to sling playing cards into a hat, whatever. The simple act of letting this person know that you will be ready to step in at any moment will alone be of immense comfort. When you say that you care and you're thinking about someone, I guarantee that the person hearing this feels better. All it needs to be is heartfelt and true.

If you are the one who needs comfort, then the first three months after the death will be not good. The shock and the pain and the anger and the guilt and the depression will tumble together until it coalesces into this big ball of crap, rolling a putrid path of destruction. Every day will be a struggle, although hopefully, one that will sting incrementally less with each passing day.

But at the very least, you should have friends and family who will tolerate you, check in on you (like the nice random person who said he was very sorry for your loss), make sure that you're eating, going to work and being a functional human being. So actually...those three months aren't as bad as you think.

The three months after that? Ah. That is when things will really suck. As good as your friends and co-workers and family have been during those first three months, after that period, they will start to go about their own lives and return to normalcy, which they're absolutely entitled to do and is completely natural. The problem is that sometime around then, the finality of your loss is just beginning to sink in. What is your belief system? That crossing of paths—when one path leads to recovery and the other to further mourning—is fraught with turmoil. If you want to be a really good friend, you make a special effort to check in after the three-month mark and see how you can be supportive.

Externally, there were few manifestations following the death of my father. I accepted condolences with a smile, nodded back when the empathetic nods came my way, wrote the thank you notes, tiptoed around the circumstances of his passing, and continued to do my work.

Internally, I was an angry dude. The rage fanned out into numerous directions. It did not matter that my father had repeatedly said that he did not want to be a burden to the rest of the family; instead, I dwelled on the person who exhorted me to try my very best and then gave up, leaving others to clean up the mess. When I sensed that people close to me were not feeling my emotions or grief in tandem, I would snap them back to attention. The relationship with that woman, the one with me at the time of the call, inevitably disintegrated in the crucible of that moment. I was alone, burning slowly, while there was someone who curiously did not appear to have suffered any severe aftershocks. My mother.

Following that initial week—she said that she hardly heard the eulogy because of the blood pounding in her ears—she dove back into her routine. I felt she was too busy, cramming her schedule with church, volunteer work, lunches with friends and acquaintances. Activity for the sake of activity. I struggled with addressing the stigma of suicide, but she was open about it. She simply viewed my father's final act as someone, addled by all the medications, who was no longer himself. In fact, more than ever, she seemed more capable than ever of spotting those silver linings everywhere.

I did not begrudge her, of course, but blew a gasket when she asked why I couldn't be more like her. No, that wasn't the right question, it was the inverse: why couldn't she grieve like a well-adjusted crazy person like me? "She's going to come back to reality," I muttered to myself again and again, month after month, until it finally occurred to me that maybe she was able to suppress her grief, to summon all of her post-war Japanese and Catholic repression skills, tamp that down and bury it. Who was I to judge?

At around the six-month mark, on All Saints Day, I went to St. Patrick's Cathedral during my lunch hour for a little prayer. And while I was praying and thinking, a sense of calm washed over me. It felt very natural. You know how athletes are told not to force the action, to "let the game come to you?" After grasping for answers, I was now kneeling and asking for Divine Guidance, and the moment came to me. He did what he did partly because, in a sense, he saw where I was in life and felt like his work had been done. It was time to stop being angry, to forgive my father and move on.

We inevitably focus on the way a person exits this planet. It is the ultimate example of recency bias, the way humans tend to focus on something that happened most recently, as opposed to the totality of circumstances. But with the possible exception of autoerotic asphyxiation, the manner of death should not obscure the totality of a person's life. When it is a loved one, we need to remember how that person lived his or her life, how that person treated others, how that person taught us and loved us, and how that lifetime of memories and interactions will sustain us. You do not ever, ever, ever need to feel somehow embarrassed or ashamed by the manner of your grandfather's death. He lived his life with courage and integrity.

There are many, many times when I've imagined you two girls sitting on your grandfather's lap in his favorite chair. (I distinctly remember my father telling me that the cutest age of a child is in the two- to three-year-old range, and feeling aggrieved because I was then a pimply 13-year-old.) How his face would have lit up if you handed him a drawing for his birthday or a gift for Christmas. How his voice, at times so harsh and unforgiving toward me in my youth, would have turned several shades softer when addressing you. How he would have enjoyed answering your questions, like what he was reading or his favorite sweets or why he got into so many fights when he was a kid. How he would have doddered down a path as you two broke into a run, a uniquely childlike trait. How he would have patted your heads, his own tilted to the side, not saying a thing, just observing. The sentimental old man—the one who sobbed in the theater when Apollo Creed died in *Rocky IV*—would have been moved to tears every time you did something remotely cute. But ah, it was not to be.

About five years after my father's death, I started to get into these periodic hellacious fights with my mother. It takes two people to fight, of course, and I hardly absolve myself from blame. But I became alarmed by my mother's erratic behavior, this pattern of saying hurtful things and making irrational demands. You were three and one years old, and a lot of these disputes centered on how we were raising you. It is already written in stone that you will be arguing with your mother about the proper angle to tilt a milk bottle when feeding so as to reduce gas, but my mother and I were getting into it on a more fundamental level. When I was raising you, I inevitably flashed back to my own upbringing and every deficiency of my parents' parenting skills. Why didn't they do things that now seem so obvious and beneficial? Resentment pooled within me and was turning me into a martyr. When I resolved to do things differently for you, I'm sure my mother took this as a direct refutation of her as a parent on some level. (By the way, I am not looking forward to the phase when you do the same to us.)

Sometimes, I wasn't even sure what we were arguing about. These arguments weren't the neat, lawyerly ones that I was accustomed to: there were communication issues, as I simply can't speak Japanese as well; my points would go unanswered, and she would bring up grievances from eons ago; she would jump from one point to another, with no common thread. Any blunt questions about why she was feeling a certain way would be answered with denial, misdirection, counterattacks, or silence. I would hang up—seriously, I would slam that receiver into my office phone like I was auditioning for the Jimmy Conway role in *Goodfellas*—and start to shed tears of frustration.

She never said that she no longer wanted to live, but she kept on referring to the possibility, or more accurately, the comfort of "God taking her away." Aside from the disturbing parallel to my father's words, it was infuriating and perplexing to hear at this particular time because your simple presence should have seemed to be an ideal opportunity to reaffirm life. It just didn't seem productive for your grandmother to pine for the possibility to follow the footsteps of the Virgin Mary and ascend into heaven, Assumption-style. I started to be open to the possibility that maybe it was time for God to take her away. But during all of these arguments, I also knew that I needed to speak my mind and without regrets.

I spent many, many hours talking with my friends, your mother, your grandmother's friends. I retraced, back and forth, every conversation and argument between my mother and me, seeking any clues as to my mother's thoughts and a better understanding of her. And finally, it dawned on me that five years after my father's death, your grandmother had just started to grieve. Remember, she never asked for this.

She had lived all of her life in Japan until she met my father, got married, and was told by him that he was in fact a deep-cover CIA intelligence officer. On their honeymoon. Worst honeymoon ever.

The Japanese citizenship became an American one. The expectation of spending her life in the comfort zone of Tokyo was replaced with unfamiliar cities like New York, Washington, D.C., Boston, and Rome. As she struggled to pick up English and Italian, her Japanese got worse and worse. All friendships, old and new, were now built on a shakier foundation. During this time, she had to endure my father's alcoholism, his numerous health issues, his antiquated notions of marriage and parenthood. Only 17 years later, when my father retired, did I even start to see my mother's more natural personality, one of curiosity, exuberance, and gregariousness. When my father's hard-living habits began to catch up to him, my mother was the one who suffered just as much. She now had to take care of him, to be the caregiver and the nag. It was not fair.

There were other factors explaining her behavior. She was now approaching same age of the death of her husband and felt a sense of guilt outliving him. She perhaps saw how we were living, with friends coming in and out, and contrasted it with her previously secluded life. My father had an outsized influence on my development, and maybe she wanted to make her own similar imprint on you two children. But really at its core, my mother was acting like a lunatic—and I say that with immeasurable love and complete accuracy—because she was mourning. You can try to fight the process, to repress your emotions, but somehow, someway, at some time, those emotions will eventually manifest. And dammit, she was entitled to it.

When I initially brought this up to my mother, she vehemently denied it (I think this led to even more fighting). She was always dismissive of therapy, but as a result, didn't have that self-awareness, that ability to identify certain emotions that were percolating and that needed to be addressed and soothed.

The fighting subsided. Over time, she started listening to the voices, not just mine, but of people who said that it was futile to be asking for and wondering about the exact moment of deliverance from this earth. She saw you two grow into sentient beings, who began to recognize her, who started to kiss and hug her, who looked forward to her visits, who scrawled indecipherable birthday cards, who asked for her help and started to ask perceptive questions. The girls who love their *Obachama*, their grandmother.

Years later, I again brought up this period to your grandmother and reiterated my theory that she had experienced a belated period of grieving. This time, she didn't lash out. I asked why she didn't let her emotions run their course naturally, instead of suppressing them to the point where they exhibited themselves years later.

She had no alternative, she said. She wanted to protect me.

She was the one who argued with my father yet another day, then sat in a recliner. She was the one who heard the popping noise, almost like a cork, and heard the thump. She was the one who saw my father in the shower, almost like he was resting, so soon that the blood had not yet started to flow. She was the one who made the call to 911. She was the one who met with the detective and asked for all of the guns in the house to be taken away. She was the one who left me repeated messages, in a voice that I had never heard, never heard since and will never want to hear again.

To dwell upon it and succumb to the horror and fall into pieces and to have me bear witness to it—she could not risk that. Not all warriors have their names on a NOC list downloaded by Tom Cruise while he avoids triggering sound, heat, and motion sensors. She just went about it in a quiet and understated way. She always had a certain strength; it allowed her to persevere all those years by my father's side. But when he passed, she summoned an extra reserve that allowed her to survive, to see to it that both of us would not be consumed by the conflagration. She wanted to protect her boy. She needed to see to it that her boy would not be damaged permanently, that her boy would find someone and get married and have kids. And perhaps only then could she afford to let the emotions spill out of her.

One of the first people to arrive at our home following my father's passing was the priest from her church. He, along with Uncle Matt, initially righted her ship. She continued to go to church every day, to seek guidance, to pray for others, to search for meaning. Regardless of what the most intellectual atheist or agnostic would say, the power of this belief is undeniable. It sustained her during those darkest times. It defies logical explanation.

She was blessed with faith.

17

THE YEAR YOU WERE
FOUR AND THREE

S ofia, for your fourth birthday party, we had a Disney princess come to our apartment. Both of you girls and your
friends chose different princess dresses and basically
turned our living quarters upside down. It was a good time, because it was one of your last birthday parties where the adults
drank freely and mingled like the party was for them.

Meanwhile, my insides roiled.

By now, I had been at a reputable New York litigation firm
for almost 12 years, where I was Special Counsel. That's a title
for people who aren't good enough to be "partner material,"
which at a lot of firms means anything from the perception
that you're not smart enough, you don't have enough business,
you don't have the potential to generate business, or you don't
have the right people going to bat for you. The net result is
that the firm doesn't think you're worthy of owning a piece of

the firm. But Special Counsel is a sort of warped consolation prize, a sign that you're tolerable enough to still be around and generate money for the firm.

This arrangement was absolutely fine with me. I had no desire to be partner. I knew the toll it took on one's family and social life. Making partner was not even wholly merit-based; you had to make sure you were kissing the right ass. The thought of being focused on law for eight years, and not having any sort of guarantee of making partner, and in the event that I did, being a junior partner—where I would essentially become again the low person on the totem pole and subject to a whole new set of assholes barking orders—did not remotely appeal to me. And so I worked pretty hard, but not to an extreme, and it allowed me to have a life and travel when I wanted, to make and maintain good friends, and when I met your mother and had you, really enjoy you.

I was able to make this choice in great part due to the attorney I was working for, whom we'll call Charles. Whip smart, he had several qualities that made him stand out from your typical litigation partner. He tended to be a minimalist, which sounds easy to do but requires a certain confidence that what you're doing is completely on point. He wasn't a micromanager, which is a rare quality in someone pursuing that brass ring of partner. And in 12 years, I perhaps saw him lose his temper a handful of times; I never saw him in a foul mood, despite the usual shitstorms accompanying any litigation calling. He was the epitome of a good work friend, someone to go out to lunch with, get occasionally blitzed with after hours, go on business trips with and not feel like you were undergoing oral surgery. And when he made partner, I felt a vicarious sense of satisfaction, knowing full well that I would not be subjecting myself and my family to this process.

When he started to talk to me about moving firms, becoming a partner, and starting the New York office of this Atlanta-based firm that we both knew well, it was simultaneously frightening and electrifying. The nice little cocoon I had built for myself was now being disrupted, but that wasn't so bad of a thing either—after a number of years, I found myself restless and wondering whether I was going to die in the same office I had occupied for about 10 years. And flattering. Charles and I talked about grandiose plans to build our office with the backing of a 150-attorney firm, how the New York City office was going to be the crown jewel of this firm, how we could hire attorneys and staff and really have a say in determining the culture and ambience of the office, how we were going to bring over clients, develop business together, and generally crush life.

But through all of these conversations, a feeling did nag at me. Twelve years working together—through some of your major life events—will lend to a certain level of trust. But it wasn't complete trust. There were enough incidents when I caught him lying or shading the truth with others, and I wasn't naïve to think that I was never on the receiving end of that. But then again, I thought, wasn't complete trust unrealistic anyway? Seriously, how often are you able to completely and unconditionally trust a work colleague?

With these doubts reverberating in my head, there was only one rational thing to do. Your mother and I went to our really good friend Yelda with psychic abilities for my first-ever tarot card reading. A former lawyer herself, Yelda didn't know any of the specifics about my work situation other than I was contemplating a move. She first asked that I shuffle the pack of 72 cards while contemplating a question that I wanted answered. I divided the pack into three piles, then selected one for her. She said a little prayer and dealt these cards.

I don't have a strong belief in astrology, i.e., I'm not the type who hears that someone likes to brush his teeth and then reflexively say, "You're a Pisces!" But when these cards that you yourself have shuffled and cut are laid out, there is a weird sense of fatalism that envelops you, like your destiny has already been written and no amount of free will can change it. I ended up studying more of her reaction than the cards laid out in that tree-like formation. After some hmms and pursued lips and eyes that moved from card to card to card, Yelda wanted to know who would be accompanying me to the new firm.

Just one, the partner that I work with. You sure? Because I see two going with you to the new place, one older and one younger. Well, it was possible that the younger one would be a paralegal, but we haven't mentioned anything to him. All right, let's focus on the older one.

"What's his personal life like?"

Charles lived the white picket fence life in Westchester, with a wife he had known since college and been with for almost 20 years, and two preteen girls. He seemed to be ensconced in the upper-crust life—membership in the University Club, private school education for his daughters, luxurious family trips. But an odd question. Why?

"Well, this is the card that symbolizes him, and it's upside down. I see his personal life in upheaval, which means that there's more for you to do. You need to be okay with that."

Charles's enthusiasm for the impending move was infectious. In the gauzy morning after a night out with the new firm's attorneys, he proclaimed that we were going to make "boatloads of money." We were going in as a team, he set benchmarks for compensation for me within a couple of years, we were going to destroy. While money was not an overriding target, it felt important to make sure that the reward would be worth the risk.

Just before we got on a flight back to New York, as we were having another beer, he said, "After this move happens, I'm going to do something kind of dark."

A beat.

"I'm going to ask for a divorce."

No matter. The timing still felt right. The thrill of something new and different, of rebellion, the whole trite thing of embarking on a new challenge and establishing the legal equivalent of a startup company—that bell could not be unrung.

Of course, leaving the firm meant that I needed to give notice, and that meant envisioning the exact moment when I walked into the name partner's office at around eight in the morning and saying that after 12 years, I would be leaving. I felt like I was on good terms with him, one of the most intimidating people I had ever been around, but I prepared for the worst: the belittling of my skills, the "you never could cut it here anyway," or even more chilling, the blasé "oh, all right." This one-minute exchange-to-be dominated my mindset. I was constantly fatigued, and yet I would regularly wake up at four in the morning, visualize this very moment with the name partner, and my day would begin then, because there was no earthly way I could go back to sleep. That winter I slogged through a cold that lasted for nine weeks, one that seemed to be the physical equivalent of my prolonged and painful work situation.

On the day that I had decided to give notice, I woke with a start. I should have gone to the gym to get that excess tension out, but instead I found myself stalking the name partner's office at 7:45 until he arrived. And then I told him.

The day—stretching from 4:30 a.m. to 1:30 a.m. the next morning—was the most surreal of my life. After a number of meetings, conference calls, and consultations with others, I now had a competing offer from my current employer: a partner title. And a 40 percent raise. A lot of money. After being in private practice for 14 years and just doing my job and not caring about making partner, all of a sudden, I had two partnership offers on the same day.

This was not my intention. I certainly didn't think there would be a counteroffer, which the name partner sensed and appreciated. It didn't even cross my mind to go back to the new firm to negotiate a higher salary, which may have been wondrously naïve. I was a person of my word. And I wasn't completely comfortable being handed a partnership when it was clear that I had not been worthy before. I wasn't really sure whether I deserved it, which may have been further evidence of my incredible naïveté.

Over the next week I had a number of conversations with my colleagues that seemed to be unusually frank and deep.

Some of it was just plain seniority. The initial announcement of my departure seemed to trigger the type of "the firm won't be the same anymore" comments, along with the more ominous questions about the firm's health, the "you're getting out at the right time" ones. It served as a trigger for other attorneys who were unhappy or unsure about their career direction, which led to discussions consisting of advice/therapy. Other comments were less flattering. When I mentioned that I needed to shake things up, one said with a laugh, "Out of all of the people I know, you're the one who most needs to do that." Knowing that I had not sacrificed almost everything to get to this point, another partner said, "I know you. You don't like to work." And these were people who liked me! And then I was the one receiving advice. To be more vocal and be the equal of Charles, not simply his charge. And the statement from someone whom I didn't even know that well: "You're going to be successful," which was so assertive and matter-of-fact that it startled even me.

Interestingly, I noticed that when I talked to, for lack of a better term, the "rank and file"—my legal assistant, staff attorneys, and associates like myself—the prevailing question was, "Why weren't you made partner before?" They focused on the lack of respect, the perceived injustice of what hadn't been given to me earlier. They wanted me to get some sort of acknowledgement that I had been wronged, and that in this life or the next, I was entitled to get my vengeance. This was my moment to let my current firm twist in the wind a bit.

But when I talked to those higher up the totem pole, not just at the firm but at other companies, those in "upper management," the analysis became considerably less emotional and more pragmatic. The counteroffer was simply an attempt to solidify the relationship with the existing client. Sure, the fluctuating assessment of my value was disconcerting and meant that I was ultimately disposable. But then again, isn't everyone? What was important in the minds of these friends were more practical considerations: whether I would be able to retain my value, whether I could develop more business, whether I had a real future at the firm.

In *The Godfather*, a frail and raspy Don Vito Corleone tells Michael that the heads of rival families will seek to move against him. They'll set up a meeting through someone Michael absolutely trusts, at which point Michael will be assassinated. The Don then says, "I like to drink wine more than I used to."

At the Don's funeral, Michael is approached by Sal Tessio, a trusted capo in the Corleone family. Tessio relays a message that a rival family seeks to arrange for a peace summit on Tessio's territory, where the security will be his responsibility. On the day of the meeting, as Tessio is ready to escort Michael to Brooklyn, he is surrounded by several other men and told that Michael is going separately.

Tessio knows that this is the end for him. After a half-hearted plea for forgiveness, which is summarily rejected, he then says, "Tell Michael it was only business. I always liked him."

"It's only business." That's the line that everyone quotes and one of a million reasons why *The Godfather* is one of the greatest movies ever. But equally insightful is the consigliere Tom Hagen's answer. "He understands that." The higher up you go, the less personal you need to take things. We can decry the hurt to our feelings or we can focus upon the way the real world works and how you can fix problems.

There was a huge counterweight to all of the thrill of potential and setting off into uncharted territory, and it was the yawning gap in salary between the two firms. Upon hearing the new offer, my assistant, who had a daily three-hour commute from her home in rural New York, said, "Don't let the money corrupt you and take your soul. You can't become one of them." Despite my best efforts, I vacillated. I had talked to the managing partner of the new firm I was joining—let's call him Wally—and had verified the salary and bonus structure. In a face-to-face conversation with Wally, he asked me whether I had any questions. There were a ton, I said, but in the end, this was a leap of faith on my part, as much as it was a leap for them to take, and that it has to be built on trust. The money alone would not be enough. The next day, I informed the name partner at my old firm that I regretfully had to decline the counteroffer, and we hugged it out.

That weekend, it was your third birthday party, Alessandra, featuring the very same Disney princess theme we had for Sofia's fourth. Ariel sang some songs and fluttered about, with a bunch of girls and boys trailing after her. The party concluded with both of you and your friends once again destroying our apartment and the adults drinking until they forgot time. I reveled in my Jerry Maguire moment. I had gone against the grain, turning my back on conventional wisdom and deliberately choosing a path of less money for the promise of the unknown. All I had to do was get that lucrative extension for Rod Tidwell and I would end up with Renée Zellweger, right?

It is all great to take a stand for principle and turn down a lot of money, but in practice, it completely messes with your head. I would be working out at the gym and suddenly start doing a mental calculation of how much more money I could be making, and then envisioning all of the material things we could buy and the vacations we could take and the money pile up, conveniently glossing over details like whether it was guaranteed, when it would arrive, and most important, the hell I would have to go through to get there. Finances are one of the most common fights among couples, and soon after I started, your mother and I had our first big disagreements about them. Your mother had just begun her business as a design consultant and was no longer making a consistent salary. A vague sense of unfulfillment plagued her as well. Consulting allowed her to have a more flexible schedule, but it nagged at her that it was a variation of the same concept—her working her ass off to make other people's shoes successful, when she could be doing an even better job making them on her own.

When you change jobs, the first six months will be hell. Actually, they should be hell. You should do your best to fit in and be a little bland and work like a nut, because that will be the first impression of you, which will become increasingly harder for you to erase. But the client didn't move to the new firm as Charles had forecasted, which meant that during those first six weeks, I was unpacking office supplies and waiting for something, anything, to happen. I didn't even have the opportunity to work like a nut. And neither did our newly-hired paralegal, the third person who moved from our old firm.

Six weeks later, I was at the opposite end of the spectrum. Someone outside New York brought in a large client, and all of a sudden there were now hundreds of cases for me to physically receive, to look through, to attend depositions for, to update, report and summarize and ultimately start trial. Every day was another attempt to avoid malpractice. I had to answer to people in Atlanta who sure didn't act like your brash and in-your-face New York attorneys but seemed to have elbows and manners that were just as sharp. There was only me.

Because as our friend had foreseen, Charles was not working with the same urgency as I. He seemed to shrink away from work, even when I was clearly overwhelmed at times. The gears of his divorce had started churning; the drinking got worse. I couldn't help but catalogue all the times he showed up late to the office or had three-hour lunches or left early. Handling this client was an opportunity for me to show the Atlanta brass what I was capable of doing. But I was also accumulating a steady reservoir of resentment toward Charles.

In the midst of this, I monitored your development. I felt wistful when you, Sofia, first slept in your bed without a diaper, and elated after several tries that you woke up without wetting the sheets. My chest swelled when our preschool teacher informed us that you, Alessandra, were independent and socially adept. I saw you two at your ballet recital—a real one with music and sparkly costumes and pre-rehearsed movement, not like before, when a bunch of kids were playing grabass—and started to tear up. Your grandmother and your mother and I showered you with bouquets and praise afterward while we ate ice cream, and then I rushed to the office for the rest of that Sunday.

We also needed to get you in a school.

Several years earlier, when Sofia was in preschool, we needed to make what seemed like a monumental decision: whether we would send you two to private or public school. I understand how the hysteria can get out of control, but of all the things to freak out about, schooling for your kids is not a bad place to start. If you want to put your kids in an optimal situation, then hell yeah, you end up meeting with a "preschool consultant," the type of occupation that seems uniquely suited for New York City.

She told us that we would need to expect to spend about $800,000 in private school tuition. Per child. Before college. Thus the projected time to arrive at a consensus for this decision—one that would shape the rest of your and our lives, one that would require months of contemplation, debate, and financial projections—went from months and months to about 10 seconds. "Looks like public school!"

We did have enough resources to seek an apartment for sale in the city. The main factor in our search became the quality of the public school zoned for that address. The preschool consultant advised against this, because school zones could change or be overfilled, but we felt that we had no other alternative. We found a place in a great school district, literally at its edge; if we had lived across the street, you two would have been taught by dope fiends and vagrants. We took this apartment and renovated it, reveling in our good fortune that allowed us to live in a great neighborhood with such a great zoned school. All you had to do was become two years older.

That spring, we went to register Sofia for kindergarten in our first-choice zoned school. We didn't get in. We were on the wait list. Comprised of 132 kids. On that same day, I heard from your grandmother about her youngest brother and the spot on his lung.

Uncle Kazuo was an exceedingly rare breed, the Japanese bon vivant who ate well, drank, and gambled to excess and lived with the overriding objective of having fun. At my bachelor party in Las Vegas, there were seven of my close friends... and the 60-something-year-old Japanese salaryman. And if living to the maximum meant that he smoked a lot and didn't keep all the tabs on his health, then the result was a video chat in which I had to summon every bit of self-control to keep from bursting into tears.

The jolt of reality, when real life-and-death situations instantly recalibrate priorities, only seemed to provide the briefest of respite to me. I would desperately search for ways to put my dumb work problems into perspective. How could I be complaining about my job when others were struggling just to be employed? How lucky was I not to be dealing with natural disasters like the Oklahoma tornadoes? Why was I focusing on fleeting matters and overlooking more important things like the good health of my wife and kids? Each thought provided me maybe an hour or two of comfort, and then I would go back to tearing my hair out.

I was trying every stress-reducing trick possible. St. John's Wort. Some tiny pellets from the pharmacy that claimed to relieve stress and tasted suspiciously like sugar pills. Stress-relieving drinks. Trips to the steam room to loosen my neck muscles. Watching *Bridesmaids* on a loop. One of those neck pillows that you warm up in the microwave. Alcohol. Every trick I relied upon was like a silk scarf pulled out of a magician's hat, but only temporarily helpful, so that I was yanking a never-ending series of scarves out of that stupid hat. I broke my personal records for most lottery tickets bought in a three-month period and most tearful "I love yous" to you two. In May, I delivered a card to your mother that read, "My gift to you is to not have a nervous breakdown. Happy Mother's Day!"

Whenever I would feel stress at my earlier firm, I would go to my standard fallback thought: "What's the worst that could happen?" Before, that would have meant, "I lose this job, I get three months of severance, and I figure out an alternative life plan." But this was different. All of you were holding me accountable, and I knew that I couldn't use the convenient (and admittedly comforting) fallback of "oh, this is God's will" to explain my failure. Plus, there would have been something decidedly deflating about shaking myself out of a comfortable situation and embarking upon a new path, only to fail miserably—like *Jerry Maguire* ending with filthy, mentally ill Tom Cruise living under a bridge and lamenting, "Well, I could have done that differently."

My physical condition continued to reflect my mental state. The battle with the nine-week cold having just ended, I noticed that I was getting these sharp pains in my upper chest and tingling in my extremities whenever I tilted my head backward. The X-rays and MRIs pointed to spinal stenosis, but it wasn't too difficult to link stress to this. There is usually a cause and effect.

In time, I realized that this pressure was mostly self-inflicted. By being my own worst critic, I was compounding the pressure on myself, as though performing the task ahead of me would be more remarkable if I gave myself an even more difficult degree of difficulty. Instead, all I had to do was trust myself to be able to do a good job, like I had always done, and things would be all right. And they did. They got better, slowly, and the stress lessened, and I didn't have to say, "I love you" as some sort of soothing mantra.

There were breaks from the madness. You remember that we went to the Cayman Islands for Uncle Dave and Aunt Anita's wedding, where I was the best man. (After watching me walk down the aisle with the bridesmaid, Sofia, you remarked, "That was crazy when Daddy married Helena.") There were moments when New York felt very, very far away: when I watched you play in that gentle, clear water, with little fishies darting nearby; when we were caught in a rainstorm while still in the warm ocean, the cold raindrops hitting the surface like thousands of LED lights; when Uncle Dave, Uncle Matt, and I were knee-deep in the water around midnight, just the moon providing us light while we smoked Cubans and drank Johnnie Blue.

About a month later, I was at the beach again, without you two or your mother, this time in Hawaii. It was a family reunion for Uncle Kazuo, with 10 of us converging at this big house on Kailua beach. What Uncle Kazuo wanted was a "marvelous house," and it delivered, with a backyard overseeing full ocean views. If only Hawaii had a casino, Uncle Kazuo noted, it would be perfect. We ate wagyu beef smuggled through customs, took long walks on that white sand, avoided dwelling on his worsening condition, and drove our way around O'ahu. The prognosis was still cautiously optimistic though, and in true Japanese style, when we parted at the airport, it was with little fanfare. Just a nod and a hand wave. That was the last time I saw him; he passed less than three months later.

I couldn't take another week off for a vacation, so your mother made plans to go away with you two. I saw the week by myself as a godsend, in that I could marinate in my own tension and stress. And on the day you left I had an oyster that was so awful that as it was going down my esophagus, I thought, "Oh, this can't be good." After two days of excruciating abdominal pain, I was by myself at an emergency room, wondering when this bad stretch of luck was going to end. A couple of minutes later I was hooked up to a morphine drip and it felt absolutely faaaaaaaaaabulous and I forgot everything weighing on me. The pain was but temporary, and this too would pass.

The start of the school year approached. When we found out our number on the wait list—35, which felt like an encouraging sign, although there has yet to be a ticker tape parade thrown for anyone who's finished 35th—we resolved that we would employ every Italian tactic that came to mind. Which meant that we sought a meeting with the school parent-teacher coordinator, which led to us thanking this rude and standoffish woman profusely and sending her a gift. Which also meant that we applied for an exemption to the NYC Board of Education based on a hardship to our caregiver, seeing that she had to pick up one at elementary school and traverse to the other side of Manhattan to pick up the other at preschool within 10 minutes. Which also meant that we actually considered rejecting the school assigned to us because we thought it would give us a better chance of ultimately getting you where we wanted.

All this time, it didn't matter that our assigned school was very well-regarded, albeit less structured. We were convinced, no, we just knew that our first-choice school was the best possible option for you two, would set you two on the right path to a better life, and it couldn't go wrong, especially because we essentially bet our apartment based on it.

Following the Board of Education's summary rejection of our requests, on a hot summer day, we grudgingly went to register you, Sofia, at your new school, P.S. 3 at 490 Hudson Street in the West Village. You were a couple of months shy of five. You went into the registrar's office with us, where you picked out a plastic slinky as a welcome gift. Then we went upstairs to the playground on the roof, where there were a bunch of others yelling and having fun. And I watched you just stare at these kids, who must have been only a couple of years older but to you may as well have been college-aged. All you did was purse your lips and turn that little slinky in your hands, over and over. That night I asked you whether you felt scared about going to a new school. I told you not to worry and to let me know immediately if there was anything wrong. I would be there to protect you no matter what.

And on that first day at P.S. 3, your mother and I stood paralyzed as 800 screaming students swarmed through the front doors. We knew no other kids or parents, didn't know where classrooms were or what the procedures were. I had flashbacks to that familiar anxiety, that fear. That was when I started to understand why people move out to the suburbs, tired of struggling every day, fighting and scraping somewhere to a respectable place.

Now, several years later, when we take the both of you via the M8 crosstown bus to P.S. 3, I find it hard to believe how opposed we were to it initially and how we were so incredibly sure that this other school was best. The school is an oasis in the City—unpretentious, noncompetitive, nonelitist—and you have both thrived here, becoming socially aware, mindful, and kind children. The environment and the community transformed me into someone I never thought I would be: a super-involved PTA parent. Your mother and I squabble all the time about who gets to take you girls to school, because one of us wants to be hanging out on the sidewalk in front of P.S. 3 and socializing with the other parents, who come from all walks of life and are friendly, fun, and cool as hell. And it was once unthinkable to me that I would live in the Village and walk around there during the weekend and expect to run into someone I know, but it happens all the time, and it's because of you and P.S. 3.

You just never know everything.

By the fall, about six months after my move, the struggles at the office did not abate, but I had grown accustomed to them. I started to also push back. I was working with this partner from another office who seemed to revel in trying to keep me on my toes—emailing at odd hours of the night, always calling on my cell, giving me tasks that were clearly wild goose chases meant to fulfill his ego. It never reached a confrontational point, although I almost wished it did. Instead, I started to create that distance and dampen that expectation that every call to my phone would be picked up or that every email would get an immediate response. I had other items that merited priority, like the first clients that I had brought in on my own. I was, belatedly, learning more of the skill sets needed to build a book of business: pitching, assessing office space, hiring, cajoling. Running as though my very life depended on it.

The physical infirmities did not cease. A dull ache on the right side of my jaw had plagued me, and the dentist explained that the crown had broken off. Multiple visits—where the tooth was extracted, bone grafts were put in, a steel pole was jammed into my jawbone, and finally, a new molar—culminated in a peak of pain around my birthday, but by that time, I was more concerned by these persistent bites that both of you had.

A week later, it was confirmed. We had bedbugs.

Less than a month after that ordeal, around 11 or midnight on Christmas Eve, I found myself sitting on the couch in the living room. Everyone else had gone to bed. Even with the incredible commercialization of the holiday season, celebrated far in advance, Christmas had completely snuck up on me. I had no gifts for your mother and your grandmother staying with us. I didn't even put in the effort of thought to come up with any gift ideas.

It was not a great year for me. But it was an even worse year for the people living with me. I thought about all the fights that I started. Those that I continued instead of dropping. Those that people with cooler heads could have been easily diffused. Or maybe not even fights, but what could be charitably referred to as bouts of unpleasantness, when I snapped at your mother, my mother, you. Maybe they were worth getting worked up about, but certainly not enough to ruin a morning or an evening, that precious time we had together. But I couldn't help it, or at least I thought I couldn't help it—it was like slightly releasing a pressure valve and letting this toxicity out, but to the detriment of the people around me.

I took out a nice parchment paper. And, in a Mont Blanc fountain pen handed down to me by your grandfather, I wrote two letters, one addressed to your mother and one to my mother. They recounted all of the events of the year to date. And then in those letters, I apologized.

I apologized for being a deficient son, a deficient husband, and a deficient father. I resolved to be a more loving son, a more present, better husband, and a more patient father, no matter how stressful and awful the next year could become. No matter how trying the year was professionally, I could not justify my behavior in the name of "supporting my family." While I was writing the letters, I did not foresee that a week later I would check my bank account and see a deposit so small that I initially thought it was a rounding error. This was my bonus for the year—about 10 percent of the lowest range that Wally had mentioned. The last time I got this low of a bonus, I was a third-year associate.

Your grandmother really appreciated my letter. Your mother? Well, she liked it, but preferred there was a traditional "gift" as well. I couldn't blame her.

You are no doubt wondering why I have gone into so much detail about a bad year.

This chapter, first and foremost, serves as that Christmas Eve letter to you. You will most likely not have remembered any of what happened the year you were four and three, but it does not matter. I failed you. It did not matter that my intentions were good. It did not matter that it was a stressful year. It is not a question of whether I should have sacrificed. Don't you know that I would gladly endure many years of taxing and unfulfilling work if it were the only way to make you two happy? But I was not equipped then to handle the mental burdens, and you didn't deserve the noxious byproduct. There was only one year when you were four and three years old, and I needed to be more appreciative in the way you were growing and learning and living, and by the time I realized it, the year was gone. I am sorry.

More important, that year also serves as a reminder—if you don't get one weekly or daily—that not everything will go right, despite your best intentions or your best calculations. For me to say that I would have done everything exactly the same way that year is willfully ignorant and stupid; in fact, it would be easy to replay every scenario and agonize over what could have been done differently. Hell, I find it easy to wonder whether becoming a lawyer has been smart. But life is not meant to be a series of what ifs. There is a certain point where you say to yourself, this is who I am and here I am, armed with a unique set of experiences and skills and ready to meet my next challenge.

What I can remain proud of is how I didn't bend my principles for the mere short-term gain of a year. And out of that year, some clarity emerged.

After many years of agonizing over whether she was physically and psychologically capable, your mother decided that she would be starting her own direct-to-consumer shoe line under her name, SCLARANDIS (www.sclarandis.com, @sclarandis on Instagram, facebook.com/sclarandis, myspace page under construction). Following the 2008 financial crisis, shoe manufacturing in Italy virtually disappeared due to the high costs; she was determined to go back to her homeland and make shoes from the highest quality materials and craftsmanship, a line that reflects her aesthetic and better yet, is all her responsibility. Sometimes you need to set aside your mental blocks about all that could possibly go wrong and losing a ton of money and having your career go into freefall; instead, you shove that to the side and decide that you will not take regrets to your grave, that you will take that shot and give it everything you have.

For me, the silver lining in that year emerged from the dark moments when I began to realize that perhaps an alternate path was necessary if being a litigation attorney was too punishing on my soul and my family. During every moment of my free time, I would need to be Andy Dufresne, chipping at his escape tunnel from Shawshank State Prison—when I snapped awake at 3 or 4 a.m., long past midnight after a full day, weekend mornings or evenings before or after we had exhausted you, even while waiting for court appearances—and crawling through 500 yards of shit-smelling foulness to a different kind of freedom. I had written material before that I felt good about, but for one reason or another—a lack of polish, circumstance, or conviction—it had not come to be. This time, I would not be denied. It did not matter whether this writing project would be successful, or even published. My initial audience would only be two people. I had an idea.

18

HOW YOU WILL BE

Dear Alessandra and Sofia,

The very best reaction I could get from you after you finish this book would be an unemotional, been-there, done-that shrug.

Because that would mean that I was there. I was around to tell you all the lessons that I've learned. Maybe I would now be the doddering Don Corleone, drifting through senility, repeating his advice to Michael in the tomato garden. That actually sounds like a great scenario. I know that it beats the hell out of the one where my plane is going down and I'm furiously typing, "If you wish to project the sound of thine applause, 'tis best not to clap like a seal."

It would mean that you already heard all of these stories—with much less profanity and more florid detail with each retelling—again and again, until you were summoning every neuron in your body to resist rolling your eyes, because you knew how disrespectful and hurtful it would be to your mother and me.

It would mean that I spent vacations with you, seeing you speak Japanese with our relatives, watching you lay eyes on Venice for the first time, guiding you through the best parts of the museums of Paris, camping outside on a safari in Namibia, or seeing if a toilet in Australia really flushes counterclockwise.

It would mean that I came home and during that hour before we put you to bed, you made me laugh, the one bright spot in an otherwise lousy day. That around Wednesday morning, I daydreamed at the office and started to look forward to the weekend and the free time that I would spend with you.

It would mean that there was an additional guide to my behavior, the tuning instrument in my head. A reminder that when I want to give in to my worse impulses, you're watching and emulating. The notion, however saccharine it might seem, that if I act poorly, it will reflect poorly upon you.

It would mean that I've started to feel the pangs of hurt when you no longer want to hold my hand or when you think that hanging out with your parents is pretty much the lamest. That whole *Father of the Bride* crap that I never understood because I was never a father of a bride-to-be? I now would get it.

The simple fact is that an advice manual for life is about as wildly futile as it sounds. A book the length of three Bibles will not be able to prepare you for the vagaries of life. I can only show you the essential tools in a toolbox, tell you what they are for, and hope that you're equipped to use them when the right moment arises.

There is no substitute for a parent looking you in the eye and saying that you screwed up and that you better own up to your mistake. Nothing can replicate an arm around the shoulder when he won't call back. You'll forever remember the tone and urgency of encouragement, of exhortation, rather than the exact words, to use your every iota of effort to achieve the best. That will mean infinitely more to you than words on a page.

You too will be gone at some point, and it is probably not predestined to be in an airplane accident, which it should be noted, is less statistically likely than getting killed by a lightning strike or by a shark. If there is an ideal way to go, I would hope that you are surrounded by your loved ones, perhaps even your children, with the peace of mind that you have done your utmost for others, and that your children will take the best of you and avoid your worst.

And in the moments before you pass into the next world, as addled and foggy as your faculties may be, perhaps you will remember and find comfort in the following.

Our unabiding love. There should be no greater love than what a parent has for a child. There is no hate, no opposing force, that can possibly be as strong as our love for you. It should be your armor, protecting you when the arrows are flying all about. It should be the fuel that sustains you when you are flagging. It should be the cloud that lifts you above the pettiness. No matter how decrepit and infirm you become, and no matter how your memories of us will fade, our love for you will remain constant. There will be nothing as certain or as unyielding as it.

On a day during the fall as I was finishing this book, I took both of you to Washington Square Park. I wanted to avoid the crowds, so we got there early. We got bagels with cream cheese and sat on the benches around the fountain. We huddled together on that cold stone, trying to soak up the sunshine as much as we could.

I adjusted your helmet strap and helped put on your knee pads and elbow pads. When you got on the bicycle, I reminded you that when you start to pedal, you need to make sure that you weren't looking down, but looking ahead. There were some starts and stops, but you were not discouraged.

This time it felt right. Your legs started to move and the bike went forward. With one hand on the handlebar and one on the back of your seat, I was trying to make sure you did not veer wildly, and you kept your balance.

And then I released my grip, and you kept on pedaling. I was jogging after you, the rhythmic breaths falling in line with my heavy steps, and my pace slowed. You floated away, gaining speed, becoming steadier. I was laughing.

Love,
Your Father

ACKNOWLEDGMENTS

To Sofia and Alessandra, who spurred me to write this and left me no choice but to try to live what's written here. To Sarah, who saved me from a life of pining for alternate life paths. To my parents, who always wanted what was best for me—a life rich in experiences and comfort. No matter how we differed in our plans on how to get there, they loved me with everything they had.

At a time when I was writing only when I could set aside huge blocks of time and conditions were perfect, Yelda Moers gave me a writing plan and was a lighthouse throughout the entire process. Thank you.

The flip side of being a world-class grudgeholder is that I remember quite vividly every piece of encouragement I received after sending out drafts of this manuscript—from David Song, Gay Walley, Andrew Ketler, Craig Rubin, Kathy Koski, Matt Gaffney, Miriam Benor, Marc-Andre Franche, Ben Parrillo,

Holli Harms, Michael Signorelli, and Brad Hamilton.

Many others have been supportive of my writing—or actually, putting up with me talking about my writing—throughout the years: Nonna Silvana, Nonno Barry, Jens Nordvig, Greg Miranda, Middy Perkins (née Meredith Wolfarth), fellow PTA co-pres Nina Ritter, Ron Burman, Traute Worschech, Jen Cohn, Judge Leavitt, Cara Schaary, David Yu, Mike Rosenstein, Francisca Villegas, Esteban Sosnik, Nathalie Faubert, Jonathan Jacobs, Jisu Sanguinetti (I guess Diego Sanguinetti as well), Rocky Pan, Janie Monteleone, Bennet Dunkley, Lauren Malanga Casey, Gabriel Nussbaum, the Sclarandises, the Crnjars, the Dañinos, the Sugiyamas, and Joy Ferguson. No matter how casual the interest and encouragement, I remember it and I appreciate it.

P.S. 3, the best school and community a jaded New Yorker could ever hope for. Much love to the staff and teachers of this beautiful school. Way too many parents to mention, but whenever you need the emotional support and more substantive advice of friends, they will come to your aid. Rob Siegel thought of the subtitle; Adam Masry took photos; Josh Hill gave better legal counsel than I could ever think of; fellow PTA co-pres Rebecca Shine gave PR tips; and Ken Leung and Lee Berresford gave invaluable design advice.

If Al Lungen didn't have his monthly networking event, I would have never met Dan Gerstein. Thank you, Dan, for believing in this, and introducing me to Celia Blue Johnson. Celia really pinpointed exactly what the manuscript needed more of (more explosions, a cop on the edge) and I'll forever be grateful.

Mascot Books made it real, beginning with Naren Aryal,

whose conviction and enthusiasm is contagious and inspiring. Emily Temple has put up with more questions and demands than any production editor should; Erin Weston has no idea what's in store. Enormous thanks to Luisa Fuentes of the design team at Mascot, and to Carey Cecilia Shook, who copy edited this thing.

Finally, I would also like to acknowledge the following people: Larry Bird, David Letterman, Steve Martin, Bill Murray, the writers and cast of *The Simpsons*, Francesco Totti, Conan O'Brien, Howard Stern, Dr. Z, Cameron Crowe, Chris Rock, Tina Fey, Charles Barkley, David Grohl, Roger Ebert, Judd Apatow, Nelson Mandela, Jon Stewart, Pope Francis. I don't know any of these people and they have no idea I exist. I just would like to thank them.